Ari,

I wanted to thank you for all of your help and advice on this project, and in general, during my time at Davis. I hope you enjoy the finished product.

Adam C.

George Washington's Washington

Visions for the National Capital in the Early American Republic

ADAM COSTANZO

The University of Georgia Press

ATHENS

Most University of Georgia Press titles are available from popular e-book vendors.

Printed digitally

Library of Congress Cataloging-in-Publication Data

Names: Costanzo, Adam, author.
Title: George Washington's Washington : visions for the national capital in the early
    American republic / Adam Costanzo.
Description: Athens : The University of Georgia Press, 2018. | Includes bibliographical
    references and index.
Identifiers: LCCN 2017033390 | ISBN 9780820352855 (hardcover : alk. paper) | ISBN
    9780820352862 (e-book)
Subjects: LCSH: Washington (D.C.)—History—18th century. | United States—Capital
    and capitol—History—18th century. | City planning—Washington (D.C.)—History—
    18th century. | Washington (D.C.)—Politics and government—To 1878.
Classification: LCC F197 .C67 2018 | DDC 975.3/01—dc23 LC record available at https://
    lccn.loc.gov/2017033390

ISBN 9780820353890 (pbk. : alk. paper)

For Keren, without whom none of this would have been possible

Contents

Acknowledgments

This project began with a rather ill-formed and poorly articulated idea to study the local population of the District of Columbia, a population I referred to as "pioneers on the Potomac" in at least one clumsy draft of my dissertation prospectus. The project's evolution into a book that, I hope, will prove interesting to others is in large part a result of the assistance, guidance, and support that I've received from advisers, family, friends, and colleagues.

Since this book began as a dissertation, first priority of thanks goes to the faculty and staff at the University of California, Davis, and, in particular, my excellent dissertation committee. As my committee chair and primary adviser, Alan Taylor guided my intellectual growth as a historian and as a writer. As this project developed, Alan helped me to hone my ideas by persistently questioning my assertions and my conclusions. He reinforced those questions using the terrifying silence that filled his office as he awaited my responses with what can best be described as a caring but ruthless patience. Meanwhile, Ellen Hartigan-O'Connor pushed me to explore the implications of Washington's physical spaces and places. The themes and methods of inquiry she guided me toward eventually became central to the entire project. Rounding out the committee, Ari Kelman consistently offered high-quality advice on a wide range of topics. About my dissertation in particular, he stuck firmly to the invaluable advice that I should always "just do whatever Alan says."

And just as each of my committee members provided vital assistance at this project's inception, I also need to acknowledge the role played by my editor at the University of Georgia Press, Walter Biggins, as I brought the project to a conclusion. Walter, the staff at UGA Press, and the staff at the Early American Places Initiative have been very helpful navigators during my first trip through the complicated review and publication process.

Like all historical writing, this book would not have been possible without the assistance and expertise of countless librarians and archivists. In particular, I owe significant debts of gratitude to the staff and scholars at the National Archives and Records Administration in both Washington, D.C. and College Park, Maryland; the Manuscript Division of the Library of Congress; the Washingtoniana Collection of the District of Columbia Public Library; the Smithsonian Institution's Archives; the Massachusetts Historical Society; and the American Antiquarian Society. One archivist at the National Archives, William Davis, stands out in my memory as deserving of particular recognition. In 2009, in addition to offering advice on source material for my work, Mr. Davis was kind enough to escort me into the holding rooms behind the scenes of the Archives facility in Washington. Of course, his primary goal was to demonstrate to me that I had submitted a request for an absurd amount of material. But, for a young historian, that peek at the stacks containing the primary source history of the United States softened the news that I would have to submit a much more specific records request.

I need also to recognize the support of colleagues that I've worked with since joining the faculty at Texas A&M University–Corpus Christi. In particular, Eliza Martin, Jen Brown, Beth Robinson, and I have worked closely together to build a supportive community of new faculty, each of us having come on board at the same time. In addition, I received helpful feedback on this manuscript from a number of faculty who participated in the TAMU-CC Center for Faculty Excellence's "Dissertation to Book" workshop series. Members of that group not already mentioned above included Brad Shope, Claudia Rueda, Kathryn Vomero Santos, and Sherdeana Owens. Last, I offer special thanks to Robert Wooster, who bravely volunteered to read the full manuscript, offering line by line comments as well as broad suggestions for changes that might be requested by reviewers. I'm certain his insights helped smooth the book's passage through the peer review process.

Again, I want to thank my wife, Keren, to whom this book is dedicated, and also my parents, who were always supportive of my choices and goals.

Finally, my deepest appreciation goes out to Weezy, Miss Marple, Mrs. Fletcher, Mai, and all of the fosters who've briefly crossed our path over the years—even Latka, who bit me, twice. None of you helped one bit with the research or the writing. But you did continually insist that I strive for something resembling a work/life balance.

George Washington's Washington

Introduction

During the quarter century between the meeting of the First Continental Congress and the turn of the nineteenth century, nine cities and towns played host to the federal government of the rebellious colonies and the new United States. At that first Continental Congress in 1774, representatives from twelve of Britain's North American colonies gathered in Philadelphia to discuss a collective response to Parliament's passage of the Coercive Acts. Driven from place to place by British forces and sectional politics, the Second Continental Congress and the Congress established under the Articles of Confederation spent time in Philadelphia, Baltimore, Lancaster, York, Princeton, Annapolis, Trenton, and New York. And, finally, the government formed under the Constitution ratified in 1788 remained in New York for just over a year before moving to Philadelphia in 1790, where it spent the next decade before it departed for the new federal city of Washington in the District of Columbia.

In November 1800, when it removed to the shores of the Potomac River, the federal government took up residence for the first time in a newly built city, over which Congress had complete authority. Article 1, section 8, of the Constitution gave Congress the right "to exercise exclusive Legislation in all Cases whatsoever, over such District (not exceeding ten Miles square) as may, by Cession of particular States, and the acceptance of Congress, become the Seat of the Government of the United States." Congressional jurisdiction over this District made it unlike any other municipality in the nation.[1]

The desire to create a federal district separate from any state grew out of Congress's experiences during and after the Revolutionary War. Especially during their multiple stays in Philadelphia, delegates to the Continental and Confederation Congresses found that their presence in the Pennsylvania state capital created opportunities for political interference between state and federal authority. In June 1783, members of Congress found their security and, worse, their authority questioned by approximately 280 American soldiers, largely from the Continental Army's Pennsylvania Line. The soldiers had marched on the Pennsylvania State House to demand from the state's Executive Council a portion of the pay due to them for their service in the army. Although their service had been to the Continental Army and the Confederation Congress also met in the same building, the soldiers had not sought an audience with the representatives of the thirteen states. Well aware that Congress lacked cash on hand and the authority to compel payment from the states, the soldiers sought to bypass the national government by arriving on a Saturday when they knew that the council would be in session but the Congress would not.[2]

Worried about the dangerous precedent that would be set by allowing a state to answer debts owed by the federal government, a number of congressmen attempted to convene an emergency session at the State House. And although a quorum never materialized, those who did attend encouraged Pennsylvania's leaders to avoid undermining the authority of the federal government. That evening, the soldiers voluntarily dispersed after the council agreed to hold a meeting with their leaders and to review their petition. After the soldiers' departure, a quorum of delegates, representing seven states, met and unanimously agreed to remove the national government to either Trenton or Princeton. Those congressmen who advocated for a strong national government saw the move as a way to preserve the dignity of Congress, while those who supported a weaker central government welcomed the opportunity to separate it from the nation's largest and most politically and economically powerful city. This event also convinced many supporters of strong central authority that the federal government would require a territory of its own. And, not surprisingly, they included just such a district in the federal Constitution drafted in 1787.[3]

Like other controversial aspects of the new plan of government, the notion of a hundred-square-mile district controlled exclusively by Congress drew considerable attention during the ratification debate. Antifederalists argued against the strong central government proposed by the Constitution and worried that congressional control of such a large region would encourage degeneracy, venality, and unbridled corruption. Given their dislike of Philadelphia, a city with a settled area of under two square miles, it is easy to understand why one Antifederalist declared the enormous federal district "the most obnoxious part of the proposed plan." For the Federalists, on the other hand, exclusive congressional jurisdiction was the logical answer to the problems encountered in Philadelphia during the war. In one of his essays in what would come to be known collectively as the *Federalist Papers*, James Madison stated flatly that the "indispensible necessity" of complete federal authority over the District "carries its own evidence with it." If the government remained a guest of other states and municipalities, he warned, its "authority might be insulted and its proceedings interrupted with impunity." Finally, he added that dependence on a state government for protection would bring dishonor to the national government.[4]

In the end, the Federalists convinced Americans to adopt the new Constitution. And the decision of where to place the federal district fell to the First Congress. Even for that body, whose monumental achievements included passage of the Bill of Rights and creation of the federal judiciary, this task proved fraught with difficulty. Placing the federal district on the American landscape required bold legislative compromise. And in 1790, the First Congress settled this political and sectional dispute, which had raged since the Continental Congress first met in Philadelphia. In this compromise, Northern congressmen agreed to the placement of the national capital in the South along the Potomac River in exchange for federal assumption of state Revolutionary War debts, largely held by the Northern states.[5]

Although Congress held exclusive jurisdiction over the federal district, that body ceded responsibility for creating the city to President Washington. The Residence Act of 1790 moved the seat of government from New York to Philadelphia, where it would remain until 1800 when it would remove to a district along the Potomac River to be selected by Washington. After visiting and evaluating sites along the river, Washington settled on the southernmost point allowed by the act, the area at the confluence of the Potomac River and the Eastern Branch (now known as the Anacostia River). The president asked Congress to amend the act to include the area just south of the rivers' intersection, so that he could include within this district Alexandria, the city closest to his northern Virginia plantation. The act also gave Washington the authority to hire and supervise commissioners to oversee surveying of the District,

purchase of land, design of the city, and construction of the public buildings. In effect, Congress had delegated nearly all of its authority over the
District to the president. Eager to lay down the foundation for a federal
city that suited his vision of a powerful and rapidly expanding American empire, Washington put commissioners, surveyors, architects, and
craftsmen to work establishing a grand national capital.[6]

Washington's vision for the nation and the federal city differed considerably from the ideas held by many Americans, especially those who
supported a weak central government. In the fiercely partisan environment of the early republic period, the federal city became a symbolic
pawn in the contest between rival political groups. On one side stood
those who, like Washington, supported a large and powerful federal government. Their opponents, eventually led by Thomas Jefferson, hoped
to establish an agrarian American republic that drew strength not from
the power, wealth, or authority of the federal government but from the
relative equality of its landholding farmers.

Between 1790 and the 1840, the District of Columbia served as a
laboratory for the ideological experiments of politicians and federal
officials. Unlike the politically independent states or the far-flung and
only loosely governed territories, federal officials could use their exclusive jurisdiction over the District to create a model community for the
nation. This book compares the ideological visions for the nation put
forth by the parties in power to their practical answers to questions of
development and federal spending in the capital. In this analysis, the
design of the federal city, its physical, economic, and social development,
and, in particular, the buildings erected there, all reflect the impact of
federal policies regarding the District.

This analytical vantage point also exposes the practical limitations
encountered by federal officials who sought to shape the city according to their own ideological goals. In an era when the federal government had relatively few responsibilities, the construction, development,
and oversight of the federal city represented tangible intersections of
ideology and policy. During the Washington and Adams administrations, for example, Federalists lacked the funds, the political will, and
the administrative capacity to make their grand vision for the capital a
reality. Across much of the next three decades, Jeffersonian politicians
stifled the growth of the city by withholding funding and support for any
project not directly related to the workings of the government. Finally,
beginning in the late 1820s, Jacksonians set aside their preference for
small government and their distaste for internal improvements where

the capital city was concerned. Their actions ushered in a new era in which the federal government took responsibility for the District's development and began the much-delayed process of establishing a grand capital city on the Potomac. After decades of stagnation caused by rigid adherence to ideology on the part of government officials, only the more pragmatic approach begun in the Jacksonian era succeeded in fostering development in the District.

This book traces that history of the development, abandonment, and eventual revival of George Washington's original vision for a grand national capital. It concludes in the Jacksonian era when federal officials accepted responsibility for development and upkeep the city. Of course, the full story of the fulfillment of Washington's vision extends well beyond this period. The federal city experienced exponential growth in both size and national significance during the Civil War. And it blossomed during the twentieth century into a civic, educational, and cultural showplace visited by millions of Americans each year. However, to trace the initial acceptance rather than the eventual fulfillment of Washington's vision, we need not look beyond the early republic.[7]

By and large the residents of the District bought into the vision for a grand capital city articulated by Washington, especially the elites who wielded political, economic, and social authority there. Driven by a mixture of self-interest and national pride, these local leaders worked to make that vision a reality. Their efforts to create a large and dynamic national capital and to convince federal officials to accept their vision for the city mark the second major subject of analysis of this book. Whether they owned land in the District prior to the passage of the Residence Act or subsequently moved to the seat of government, these local elites served as stewards of Washington's vision for the city. Acutely aware of the dim view of the national capital held by many Americans but also of the District's role as a powerful symbol of the American nation, they embarked on social and economic development projects the scope and scale of which often suggested national rather than local ambitions. The three-way relationship between the local elites, federal officials, and the physical city lies at the heart of this volume. Understanding the development of the city and the idea of a grand national capital requires exploration of the ways that each of these actors influenced the others.[8]

Part 1 traces the origins of Washington's vision for the federal city. In particular, it shows how ideas provided by Washington, Jefferson, architect Peter Charles L'Enfant, and local boosters, found form in L'Enfant's plan for the city published in 1791. It also describes their inability to make that plan a reality during the 1790s. In particular, it examines how the unprecedented scope of the plan, reliance on the sale of city lots to fund construction of the city and the public buildings, the actions of unscrupulous land speculators, and the convoluted mixture of state, local, and federal authority in effect in the District all undermined Federalist hopes for creating a grand national capital.

Part 2 explores the impact on the city of the rise to power in 1801 of Thomas Jefferson's Democratic-Republican Party. While Jefferson had more influence on the capital than any federal official other than Washington, his desire to establish an agrarian republic with a comparatively small and weak federal government influenced the decisions he and his supporters in Congress made regarding the city. While in office, Jefferson supported only those projects that concerned the public buildings and the boulevard connecting them, Pennsylvania Avenue. He hoped to harness the powerful political symbolism of classical republican architecture at the White House and the Capitol while also preventing the city from growing into an urban behemoth of aristocracy and industry like the capital cities of Europe.

This part also examines the efforts of local residents to promote their competing vision for the city. Granted a congressional charter for a local government in 1802, elite Washingtonians laid down basic public services and, in an attempt to win respect from Northern critics, established a public school system, the first in the South. Locals also pooled their limited capital to form stock companies for infrastructure projects. And the District's wealthiest residents began to erect large and architecturally progressive homes, slowly filling the gaps in L'Enfant's spacious city plan and chipping away at the city's reputation as a backwater.

Part 3 concerns the aftermath of the British invasion of the federal city and the resulting destruction of the public buildings during the War of 1812. In September 1814, only weeks after the brief but disastrous British occupation of the city, the House of Representatives took up the question of whether to rebuild the public buildings in Washington or to abandon the Potomac capital entirely. A largely sectional debate ensued in which most Northern congressmen favored removal from the District of Columbia while Southerners supported reconstruction of the existing capital. And although Congress eventually chose to remain in Washington, the federal attitude toward development in the city changed little. By and large the government returned to the Democratic-Republican policy of funding federal structures in the city but leaving infrastructure and development to the locals. For their part, District residents worked hard to retain the government, even paying for the construction of the temporary Capitol building used by Congress from 1815 to 1819.

Buoyed by the sense of permanence that the government's decision to remain in Washington provided, local elites also stepped up their efforts to create an exemplary American city. In the years after the British attack, for example, Washingtonians established a local scientific society with decidedly national aspirations. And when the time came to erect a new city hall, the city government commissioned a large neoclassical structure that rivaled only the Capitol building in its scale and grandeur. During this period, Washingtonians also intensified their requests for federal assistance with the development and upkeep of the national capital.

Part 4 examines changes to the federal-local relationship that emerged in the 1830s during the administration of Andrew Jackson. After his election in 1828, Washingtonians expected that their relationship with the federal government would worsen because Jackson offered a reassertion of Jefferson's antiurban, agrarian republicanism. Fortunately for Washingtonians, their worst fears went unrealized. And, in time, the Jacksonians radically altered the federal government's relationship with the District and its residents. During the Jacksonian era, Congress came to accept local claims that it bore considerable responsibility for the federal district. As a result, it provided funding for local infrastructure projects and propped up the cash-strapped local municipalities. In addition, Jackson and his supporters in Congress embarked on a wave of new federal construction in the city, the likes of which had not been seen since 1790s. In particular, they began work on grand public buildings to house the Treasury, the Patent Office, and the Post Office. By erecting these large, neoclassical buildings, the federal government turned once again to the creation of an impressive American metropolis on the shores of the Potomac. Such a capital suited the continental empire rapidly growing westward in the 1830s and 1840s, as well as the new generation of politicians sent to Washington during the Jacksonian era. In addition, the capital had gained national stature and significance as debate over the institution of slavery heated up and both sides sought the symbolic victory of abolishing or preserving slavery in the District of Columbia. In the end, the Jacksonian federal city began to live up to the grand vision laid down by Washington and fostered by the local population for nearly a half century.

The District's peculiar status as a ward of the federal government and its role as a symbol for the United States as a whole have made it fertile ground for those interested in understanding the development of American democracy and the growth of the federal government. In the introduction to his study of Gilded Age Washington, D.C., Alan Lessoff noted that "great capital cities such as Washington deserve close scrutiny, because in them, through encounters with a series of concrete, observable problems, a government displays its personality." Likewise, Kirk Savage has described the monuments erected in Washington as an attempt by their creators to show the essential nature of the nation.[9] In the past few decades, a number of scholars have connected the social history of Washington with the workings of the government. In particular, recent work has explored the ways that the women of elite Washington society affected the practice of American government through their conveyance of political power and information, and by their very presence during congressional debates.[10] In many ways this project inverts the analytical framework offered by those scholars by seeking to determine the government's effect on the development of the city rather than the city's effect on the government. Focusing on these local issues also exposes the ways that broad party ideologies informed federal relations with the District.

To examine the capital as an urban space and to understand the meanings associated with the city's form and the buildings erected there, this book also draws on insights from urban and architectural history. The urban planning historian Anthony Sutcliffe once described capital cities as places where we witness "the conversion of authority and ambition into forms and spaces." Speaking specifically of Washington in his analysis of the city's regional identity, Carl Abbott called it a place where "the social and political construction of place has become a public process." This project builds on many previous explorations of architecture and city planning in Washington.[11] At the same time, however, it connects those efforts to national political ideologies and places both in conversation with the actions of the local population. By doing so, I follow the example set by scholars who have sought to unite traditional historical inquiry into political and socioeconomic structures with the physical and aesthetic explorations of urban and architectural historians. For instance, Dell Upton's work combines these historical methods to identify the factors shaping personhood and concepts of self in the early republic city. This history of Washington focuses more closely on ways that architecture reflected local and federal visions for the capital city and the nation. It places particular emphasis on examination of large public buildings but also considers the design of the city as well as its streetscapes, gardens, and private homes. By making the city both a subject of and a primary source for this historical inquiry, this project blends local and national affairs while revealing the deep connections between politics and aesthetics in early republic Washington.[12]

The eight other cities and towns that played host to the U.S. government prior to 1800 all had histories and identities separate from their role as a seat of government. As the ninth and final home for Congress, the city of Washington grew and developed right along with the nation it was built to serve, slowly growing to fit the grand design provided by Washington and L'Enfant. The chapters that follow tell the story of George Washington's Washington, not simply a history of the city during the first president's life, but a history of his vision for the national capital and of the local and national conflicts surrounding its acceptance and implementation.

PART I

Grand Visions and Financial Disasters

Early on a dreary Tuesday morning in late March 1791, George Washington set out from his lodgings at Suter's Tavern in Georgetown, Maryland, to examine the land between the Potomac River and the Eastern Branch. Two months earlier, on January 24, the president had declared that the national capital would be located within a ten-mile square, rotated 45 degrees to create a diamond, stretching north from the city of Alexandria in Virginia to encompass approximately sixty square miles of land in Maryland. This area included the city of Georgetown and 6,111 acres at the confluence of the two rivers that would soon become the federal city. On this early spring day, Washington rode out into a thick mist of rain alongside the three commissioners he had recently appointed to oversee construction of the city: Daniel Carroll, a former congressman and owner of land in nearby Montgomery County, Maryland; Thomas Johnson, chief justice of the Maryland General Court and holder of land along the North Branch of the Potomac in northwestern Maryland; and Dr. David Stuart, a landowner from neighboring Fairfax County, Virginia, and a close relative of Washington by marriage. Together they spent the day evaluating the different features of the landscape and considering the appropriate placement of the public buildings.[1]

Riding east out of Georgetown and crossing over Rock Creek, the four men would have quickly ascended to the top of a hill. On this spot today, the complex traffic patterns of Washington Circle frustrate visitors to the city and occasionally longtime residents as well. Drivers brave enough to divert their eyes from the fast-moving traffic can catch sight of a statue at the center of Washington Circle. It depicts General Washington, leader of the Continental Army, on horseback. As the president might well have done that morning, his copper likeness faces southeast, down Pennsylvania Avenue toward the White House. Of course no such road or building yet existed in March 1791. However, peering through the mist from this vantage point, Washington and his companions might have discerned the terrace of raised ground three quarters of a mile to the southeast on which the President's House would eventually stand.[2]

Over the course of the next decade, Washington, the city's commissioners, and its other promoters struggled to create a city suitable for hosting the U.S. government. Some of the difficulties they encountered stemmed from the grand design the president had approved. But this grand design anticipated a bustling metropolis rising up between the Potomac and the Eastern Branch—a metropolis that represented their vision for the nation as a whole. For them, a great city of broad avenues and riverfront vistas would aptly convey the authority of a powerful and dynamic American empire. Unfortunately, such an empire did not yet exist. And many of the problems faced by city officials during this tumultuous decade resulted from the weakness of the federal government. Inadequate federal funding forced city officials to rely on land speculation, professional speculators, and emergency loans to fund the public works. At the same time, the still poorly defined separations between state and federal authority stymied their efforts to control city development. Presented to the nation as an image of America's future strength, the federal city's first decade instead reflected some of the new republic's greatest weaknesses.

1 /   Dreams of Metropolis

Touring the area that damp morning in March 1791, Washington and his commissioners encountered a familiar landscape. This familiarity stemmed not merely from the fact that each of the men lived and owned property in the region but also because its hills, valleys, and creeks, its houses, barns, and slave shacks, and its fields of tobacco, wheat, and corn all typified the Chesapeake plantation society in which each of these men had lived much of their lives. In 1791, therefore, the federal district was not an uninhabited wilderness waiting for the details of a city plan to provide it with an identity. Amidst the forested hills were small plantations and private farmsteads typical of the region (fig. 1).[1]

Like the rest of the Potomac River basin, a network of creeks drained the land, moving rainwater downstream to the rivers. Modern myth holds that the landscape between the Potomac and the Eastern Branch was an unmanageable, disease-ridden swamp masquerading as solid ground. Well into the nineteenth century, low-lying areas at the confluence of creeks and rivers did flood with regularity. For example, water from Tiber Creek often inundated portions of the National Mall and Pennsylvania Avenue between the Capitol and the President's House. However, these lowlands were the exception rather than the rule. Steep bluffs once lined much of the area's shoreline, keeping the waters of the Potomac and the Eastern Branch safely out of the city. The city's swampy reputation traces back to unhappy visitors and locals alike who complained about these flooded areas and about unpaved streets that became impassable during wet weather.[2]

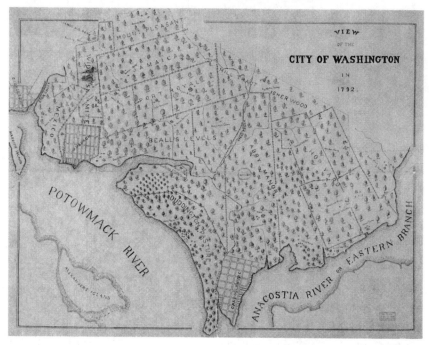

FIGURE 1. *View of the City of Washington,* 1792, showing the property lines of landowners along with several planned but never built towns. (Library of Congress, Geography and Map Division)

For his entire adult life, Washington had promoted the Potomac region. He suffered from what one historian has dubbed Potomac Fever, "a delusion-inducing obsession with the grandeur and commercial future of the Potomac River." Washington inherited this malady from his older brother, Lawrence. In the middle of the eighteenth century, the elder Washington founded the Ohio Company of Virginia with a group of other Virginia landowners. This company promoted the Potomac as a link to the Ohio territory, where both George and Lawrence Washington joined in land speculation schemes through which they claimed rights to tens of thousands of acres. Lawrence Washington also helped establish the port of Alexandria, Virginia, in 1749. Just ten miles upriver from Mount Vernon, the Potomac estate that George would inherit upon Lawrence's death in 1752, Alexandria served as a shipping port for plantation owners in the region.[3]

Since his earliest years exploring the region as a soldier and as a surveyor, Washington had come to know the Potomac River basin well and to believe it could support a magnificent urban metropolis. Although the president complained that the poor weather prevented him from deriving any "great satisfaction" from his tour with the commissioners that morning in March 1791, no amount of mist, or even a thick bank of fog, could have obscured his vision for a grand federal city on the shores of the Potomac. In May 1798, he predicted that by the turn of the next century the federal city would be, "though not as large as London, yet of a magnitude inferior to few others in Europe." And summing up the city's attributes, he declared it was in "a situation not excelled for commanding prospect, good water, salubrious air, and safe harbor, by any in the world." For Washington, the newborn federal city possessed nearly limitless potential. To tap into that potential, Washington wanted, as his brother had before him, to link the Potomac region to the Ohio Valley.[4]

Before the revolution, however, British policy stood in the way of the Washington brothers' dream. In 1763, after their victory over the French and their Native American allies in the Seven Years' War, the British had learned how difficult and costly it could be to govern the American interior. By changing the rules of the diplomatic and commercial traditions that had governed relations between the French and the Indians of the Ohio Valley and the Great Lakes regions, the British had antagonized their new neighbors. In response, Native Americans in the region attacked British forts and settlements. This uprising destabilized the western frontier of the British colonies and added to the already disastrously high cost of the empire's military activities in North America. Hoping to prevent an even costlier war between the Native groups and the colonists and also to contain the colonists securely within Britain's Atlantic empire, the British agreed to reestablish traditional diplomatic and economic relations with the Indians and to prevent colonial settlement on the western side of the Appalachian Mountains.[5]

Freed from this restriction in the aftermath of the Revolutionary War, Americans poured over the Appalachian Mountains into land once reserved by the British for Native Americans. Carving new farms, towns, cities, and, eventually, states out of this land, Americans used their victory over the British to establish their own rapidly expanding empire at the expense of the continent's Native inhabitants.

Keeping western settlers loyal to a union dominated by eastern states meant getting their surplus produce to Atlantic market towns and onto ships bound for Europe and the West Indies. Washington feared the influence of the British and Spanish Empires in these western territories. Still smarting from their defeat in the Revolutionary War, the British maintained a military presence in the Ohio Valley and in their own Canadian territory. And with control of both the Mississippi River and the port of New Orleans, the Spanish, in particular, threatened American interests in the region. Western farmers saved considerable time and expense shipping goods down the rivers of the Ohio and Mississippi Valleys to Spanish New Orleans. However, moving American goods down a Spanish river and through a Spanish port put the commerce of the United States at the mercy of a foreign power. At any time the Spanish could disrupt American shipping or, worse, entice American farmers to join the Spanish Empire. For Washington, the Potomac represented a potential solution to this difficult problem.[6]

To harness that potential, he used his considerable postwar influence to obtain charters and partial funding from the Maryland and Virginia legislatures for the Potomac Navigation Company in 1785. Under Washington's leadership, the company set out to improve navigability of the Potomac across the approximately 200 miles of river stretching from the port of Alexandria through the inland town of Cumberland, Maryland. The company removed rocks from the river, dug canals around the rapids at places like Great Falls and Shenandoah, and carved sluices into shallow portions of the riverbeds. They hoped to build a road from Cumberland connecting it to the Ohio River system. Such a link would enable western farmers to ship goods down the Potomac to Georgetown or Alexandria.[7]

Washington's desire to develop and secure the Potomac region, along with his considerable land investments in the area, also influenced the placement of the federal armory at Harper's Ferry, Virginia. In 1794, Congress appropriated funds and approved the establishment of as many as four armories and arsenals in the middle and southern states in order to complement the existing facility in Springfield, Massachusetts. Rather than build four small arsenals, Washington chose the small village of Harper's Ferry as the location for a single large arsenal. The president made this choice over objections raised by Secretary of War Henry Knox in 1794, and he stuck by the choice despite even more strenuous objections by Knox's successor, Timothy Pickering, in 1795. Positioned on the Potomac at what Washington viewed as the gateway to the West, Harper's Ferry represented an extension of American military authority and control into that region.[8]

Adding pressure to the efforts to develop the Potomac, promoters of other river systems hoped to make similar connections to the West. Both

Baltimore and Philadelphia boosters sought to link the Susquehanna River to the Ohio via the Allegheny. New Yorkers dreamed of linking the Hudson River with Lake Erie, and in 1825 they made that dream a reality with the opening of the Erie Canal. Closer to home, Washington's fellow Virginians proposed joining Richmond to the Ohio Valley via the James River and the Great Kanawha River (the latter of which is now known as the Kanawha and New Rivers). The promoters of each of these regions expected considerable economic and political benefits from a successful connection across the Appalachians. Local consumers, merchants, traders, and shippers would prosper as surplus farm goods flowed into eastern cities and manufactured goods and supplies made the return trip to the western settlers. At the same time, these close business connections would foster political and cultural unity between the East and the West.[9]

Promoters of the Potomac understood that reaping these benefits would improve the region's chances of being chosen as the location of the permanent seat of the federal government. Late in 1787, the future city commissioner, Samuel Johnson, spelled out this logic to Washington, asserting that the prospect of "5 or 600 miles of inland navigation" and the central location of the Potomac counted in the region's favor in the contest for the capital. Washington, of course, needed no lessons on the subject. His own promotion of the Potomac stemmed in no small part from his desire to prevent what he called the "great mischiefs" that would occur if the eastern and western regions were to remain separate. Washington knew that a connection would strengthen the fragile union that had only recently thrown off British rule. Part of his duty as the region's promoter in chief was to ensure that others understood the gravity of that situation.[10]

Following his tour with the commissioners, Washington met with some of the owners of land in the new federal district. He delivered a simple message: they must stop causing trouble. Many had been lobbying for the public buildings to be placed on or near their own parcels. Division arose between those who owned land near Georgetown and those who owned land nearer to the Eastern Branch. Washington viewed their petty bickering as a threat to the entire project. He assured the landowners that, whatever the layout of the city, everyone would prosper. And he warned that the two factions "were counteracting the public purposes & might prove injurious to its best interest." The capital's Potomac location had many enemies in Congress and throughout the nation. Washington knew it was unwise to allow divisions among the project's proponents to provide fodder for those who would challenge his placement of the city.

With forceful insistence that they follow his lead, Washington quieted the landowners' rumblings. During the next decade, the chore of navigating the divisions between the owners of land in the various sections of the city fell to the commissioners, complicating their already difficult task. However, many locals assisted the project by actively promoting the city.[11]

The most prolific and influential of these promoters was George Walker, a Scottish-born merchant living in Georgetown who wrote several articles boasting of the area's virtues. On January 23, 1789, two years before Washington's announcement of the federal city's location, Walker authored a promotional tract for the *Maryland Journal and Baltimore Advertiser* under the pen name, "A Citizen of the World." He asserted that the land between Rock Creek and the Eastern Branch was ideal for a national capital. Unlike Philadelphia, the area was centrally located. Also, it lay on a waterway that provided access to the sea yet remained defensible against foreign invasion. He predicted that the presence of the capital city would spur connection to the West and that the city would become a nexus for the nation, writing that in the city "a connexion and energy would be given to commerce and manufactures, the arts and sciences, civilization and elegant refinement, hitherto unknown in America."[12]

To fund the city, officials would distribute maps across North America and Europe detailing the city lots available for sale. The wealthy would purchase large lots close to the halls of government, while merchants and tradesmen could afford smaller lots in other areas of the city. Requiring landowners to build within a certain period of time would prevent rampant speculation from slowing city growth. By following this orderly and carefully planned system, the city would grow according to the government's desire while it simultaneously raised funds for the public buildings, which were "to be built in the highest style of modern magnificence and grandeur."[13]

In this and in his other promotional tracts, Walker wove together a bold vision with practical technical details. These efforts made him one of the most prolific and specific promoters of a Potomac capital, setting him apart from those who praised the region in general terms but lacked a formal plan for the city. The influence of his ideas reflects his effectiveness as a local promoter. Indeed, the city commissioners followed a system similar to Walker's: selling lots to raise money for public buildings. In addition, the French-born architect and engineer tapped by Washington to design the city in 1791, Peter Charles L'Enfant, included a number of Walker's suggestions in his plan. Walker may have sought out L'Enfant when he arrived in March 1791 to share his vision for the capital. And while it is impossible to determine Walker's exact influence on L'Enfant and his plan for the city, it remains clear that the Frenchman took local visions and desires into account. For instance, he placed the city between the Eastern Branch and Rock Creek and reserved large lots for the public buildings and smaller lots for civic structures as Walker had proposed. L'Enfant also spread the government buildings and other key facilities across the city in an effort to balance the competing local interests.[14]

For his part, L'Enfant had been contemplating the design for a national capital city since at least 1784. Writing to the Confederation Congress that year, L'Enfant advocated establishment of an army corps of engineers and suggested that such a corps should construct a federal city. In September 1789, as the first U.S. Congress took up the contentious issue of locating the seat of government, he requested that President Washington consider him for the project. Foreshadowing the scope of the plan he would later create, L'Enfant spoke to the profound implications of the government's decisions regarding the federal city.

> No nation had ever before the opportunity offered them of deliberately deciding upon the spot where their Capital City should be fixed, or of combining every necessary consideration in the choice of situation; and although the means now within the power of the Country are not such as to pursue the design to any great extent, it will be obvious that the plan should be drawn on such a scale as to leave room for that aggrandizement and embellishment which the increase of the wealth of the Nation will permit it to pursue to any period, however remote.[15]

Although the new republic lacked the resources and population to create a grand metropolis, L'Enfant allowed his faith in the American experiment to guide his vision for the capital.

Expressions of this faith were nothing new to L'Enfant. The son of a painter in the employ of King Louis XV, L'Enfant was born in Paris in 1754 and educated at the Royal Academy of Painting and Sculpture. In 1776, at the age of twenty-two, he cut short his studies and volunteered to serve in the American Revolutionary War. The American agent in Paris, Silas Dean, granted L'Enfant the rank of lieutenant in the Continental Army. L'Enfant crossed the Atlantic early in 1777 on a ship carrying weapons, uniforms, and supplies for the rebels. During his six years with the Continentals, he wintered with Washington's troops at Valley

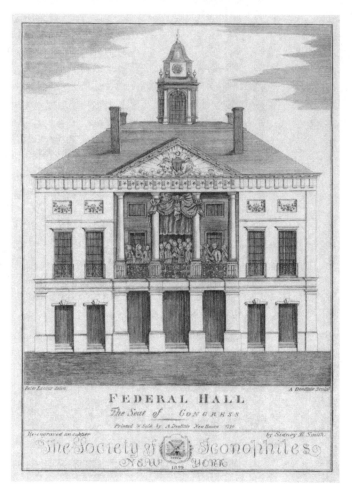

FIGURE 2. *Federal Hall, Seat of Congress*, 1790, copper
engraving by A. Doolittle, depicting Washington's April 30,
1789 inauguration and reflecting L'Enfant's redesign of the
building. Reengraved by Sidney L. Smith for the Society of
Iconophiles in 1899. (Library of Congress, Prints and Photographs Division)

Forge, was wounded at the Siege of Savannah, and was captured by the
British in Charleston. Following his release, he rejoined the Continental
Army and climbed to the rank of major. After the war, L'Enfant joined
the Society of the Cincinnati, an organization made up of soldiers and
naval officers dedicated to perpetuating the goals of the revolution. For

the society's members, he designed a medal in the shape of a bald eagle. In 1785, L'Enfant established himself in New York as an architect. He achieved fame with his redesign of the City Hall into Federal Hall, the first meeting place of the U.S. Congress in 1789. In this patriotic application of his skills as an artist and engineer, L'Enfant combined the classical revival architectural style with distinctly American elements, including placement of thirteen stars in the frieze atop the front facade and a relief of a bald eagle clutching thirteen arrows placed prominently in the centered gable (fig. 2).[16]

By using symbols like these, L'Enfant connected Federal Hall to a burgeoning tradition of uniquely American iconography. This tradition utilized images of indigenous fauna such as the bald eagle and the rattlesnake to signify American strength and images like the liberty tree, the chain of states, and even General Washington to evoke the political and ideological foundations of the nation. Americans began using these symbols during the colonial resistance to British taxation, and their prevalence in American culture grew significantly during and after the revolution. Americans also adopted classical imagery and architectural forms linking their experiment in republicanism with the Greek and Roman republics of antiquity. These symbols appeared on everything from wallpaper to punchbowls and adorned the flags, seals, emblems, coins, and medals of state and local governments as well as private institutions and societies. In 1780, for instance, the members of the newly established American Academy of Arts and Sciences developed a seal for the organization that featured an image of Minerva, Roman goddess of wisdom. On the seal, she stood amidst a field of American Indian corn surrounded by the instruments of both science and agriculture, representing America's ingenuity and its natural abundance (fig. 3). In the realm of architecture, a field that Thomas Jefferson once lauded as "an art that shews so much," use of classical forms and imagery would bind the new federal city to this emerging national symbolic tradition.[17]

In March 1791, Washington answered L'Enfant's long-held desire to create a federal city. Secretary of State Jefferson instructed him to proceed to Georgetown where Andrew Ellicott was already at work surveying and mapping the federal district. Jefferson asked that L'Enfant create "drawings of the particular grounds most likely to be approved for the site of the federal town and buildings." By the end of the month, Washington had instructed him to lay out the city on the land between Rock Creek and the Eastern Branch. While creating his plan for the city, L'Enfant received input and assistance from both Washington and Jefferson.[18]

FIGURE 3. Seal of the American Academy of Arts & Sciences as it appeared on the cover of the Academy's publication, *Memoirs*, in 1785. (Image courtesy of the American Academy of Arts & Sciences)

At the architect's request, Jefferson loaned him maps of a dozen European cities, including Amsterdam, Paris, Marseilles, Turin, and Milan. Via Washington, L'Enfant also received a sketch for the city drawn by Jefferson. This draft placed the government buildings in a simple grid of streets spanning the area between Rock Creek and the mouth of Tiber Creek. L'Enfant may have been influenced by Jefferson's linking of the President's House and the Capitol by a public walk. However, he did not incorporate the small scope of Jefferson's city or its simple grid of streets into the final plan. L'Enfant regarded rectangular street plans as "tiresome and insipid" and therefore unsuitable for the seat of government. And Washington wanted the city to cover as much ground as possible

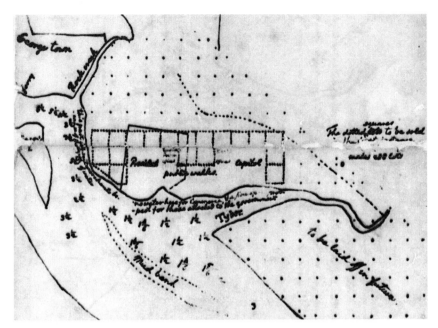

FIGURE 4. Central portion of *Jefferson's Plan of the Federal District*, included as a part of *George Washington, March 31, 1791, Proclamation of Federal District with Map*. (The Thomas Jefferson Papers at the Library of Congress, Library of Congress, Manuscript Division)

to increase the number of saleable lots. L'Enfant's plan also lacked distinguishing features found in the European city plans loaned to him by Jefferson. The primary outside influence for the Frenchman seems to have been Washington with whom he often met and corresponded while designing the city. Working rapidly, L'Enfant produced his now-famous plan for the city by late August 1791 (fig. 4).[19]

L'Enfant's training as an artist coincided with a broad transition in the arts away from the rationalism of the Enlightenment and toward the ideals of the picturesque and sublime that marked the Romantic period. His consideration for the local topography, for example, allowed the city to blend in with the existing landscape. By working with, rather than in spite of, the topography of the city, L'Enfant allowed the strict geometric details of his architectural features to contrast with the natural and fluid details of the surrounding natural landscape. As a result, views up and down the city's great avenues and down the central public walk (now the

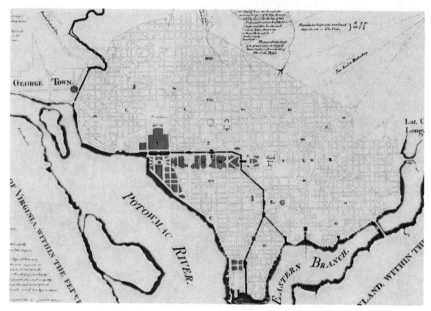

FIGURE 5. Detail of *Plan of the City Intended for the Permanent Seat of the Government of the United States*, 1791, by Peter Charles L'Enfant. (Library of Congress, Geography and Map Division)

National Mall) prominently showcased the surrounding rivers, hills, and farms (fig. 5).[20]

L'Enfant also took advantage of the city's topography when placing the primary public buildings: the President's House and the Congress House. Likely following the advice of Washington and Jefferson, L'Enfant chose elevated sites for both buildings. The Capitol rests on the south-western edge of a plateau stretching east to the Eastern Branch. Similarly, the President's House sits atop a hill about a mile and a half northwest of the Capitol. This position offered the president's residence a view of Tiber Creek and the broad expanse of the Potomac River to the south. Placement on high ground made both buildings focal points for the avenues that radiated out from them. Using the hills also allowed L'Enfant to separate the two branches of government, with each dominating a portion of the cityscape. Washington approved this separation for two reasons. First, he hoped the distance would free executive department clerks from the interruptions posed by congressional business. Second, he wanted to ensure that owners of land on both sides of the city would benefit equally. Of course, political symbolism in L'Enfant's city went well beyond separating the branches of government.[21]

The architect firmly believed that the capital city could unite and strengthen the new American nation. In particular, he hoped it would attract Northerners to come to live alongside their Southern counterparts. In April 1791, he suggested that such cohabitation "would deface that line of markation which will ever oppose the South against the East [then the common term for New England], for when objects are seen at a distance the idea we form of them is apt to mislead us . . . and we fancy monstrous that object which, from a nearer view, would charm us." L'Enfant proposed the assignment of fifteen city squares, many located at the intersections of the city's grand avenues, to the individual states. Each would then improve the square and provide symbolic republican ornamentation. These areas would welcome citizens of the infant republic and allow them to consider the lessons of the revolution reflected in the "Statues, Columns, [and] Obelisks" erected by the state and federal governments. L'Enfant hoped that once they had responsibility for a small portion of the city, the states would promote settlement around their squares. These evenly distributed settlements would grow and eventually connect.[22]

L'Enfant also planned avenues and canals to attract residents and spur economic success. The large diagonal avenues that crisscross the grid of streets in the city would connect its distant parts. On the plan, each such avenue was 160 feet wide. Ten feet of pavement bordered by thirty feet of graveled walkway planted with trees lined each side of the road and framed an eighty-foot-wide carriageway at its center. Providing "reciprocity of sight" from place to place in the city reduced the perceived distance between any two areas connected by the avenues. L'Enfant believed that this would "promote rapid settlement over the whole extent" of the city. The canals were designed to harness two of the city's existing creeks: Tiber Creek and St. James Creek. Joining just west of the Capitol, the two canals would connect the governmental heart of the city to the commercial areas expected to rise along the shores of the Potomac and Eastern Branch. These canals link L'Enfant's desire that the city become a commercial metropolis with the vision offered by Washington and other Potomac promoters. Whether bringing goods to market from the western frontier or distributing them across the city, canals represented the investment in public infrastructure required for the city to reach its full potential. The architect developed all of these ideas as well as a plan for construction, promotion, and development of the city within five months of receiving his assignment from the president.[23]

Unfortunately for L'Enfant, the passion that fired his creative genius got in the way of his efforts to execute his plan. As focus shifted from design to implementation, he proved incapable of productive collaboration with the project's other stakeholders. In September 1791, for instance, after disagreeing with the commissioners about their plans to begin immediate sales of city lots, L'Enfant failed to publish copies of the city plan in time for the first offerings. While L'Enfant expressed "great surprise and mortification" at the incompetence of the Philadelphia printer he had hired, the commissioners attributed L'Enfant's failure to a willful refusal to cooperate with them. Informed of the problem by the commissioners, the president observed how common it was that talented men "should invariably be under the influence of an untoward disposition . . . by which they plague all those with whom they are concerned." The lack of a published plan undermined these early sales because, as Washington would put it, investors were being asked to buy "a pig in a poke."[24]

Later that fall, L'Enfant ordered the destruction of a home owned by Daniel Carroll of Duddington, the largest landowner in the city. Because the building was located at what would eventually be the intersection of city avenues, the architect felt justified in having it pulled down. When pressed by the commissioners to explain why he had not consulted them prior to damaging relations with the local population in this way, L'Enfant simply asserted his independence from the board. He had, after all, issued written warnings to Carroll. And, thus, he argued, "It was him—then—if he thought himself wrongly used—who ought to have required the Interference of your board—but it was not my business to call your attention on the matter." L'Enfant's presumed independence from the board on this and all other matters drove a wedge between him and the Washington administration. L'Enfant rejected Washington's delegation of authority to the commissioners and subsequently refused to turn over his plans for the city to them. Washington and Jefferson hoped that L'Enfant might reconsider and remain with the project. But the architect was only willing to work for, and answer to, Washington directly.[25]

After L'Enfant's departure, the commissioners turned to the city surveyor, Andrew Ellicott, for production of the final plan. Ellicott had worked closely with L'Enfant since his arrival the previous spring and, thus, was qualified to reproduce the architect's design. Working without

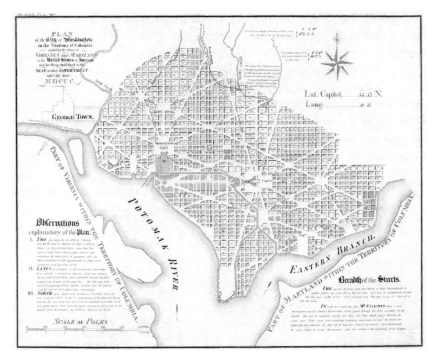

FIGURE 6. *Plan of the City of Washington in the Territory of Columbia*, 1792, by Andrew Ellicott, engraved by Samuel Hill, Boston. (Library of Congress, Geography and Map Division)

L'Enfant's original, Ellicott produced a plan for the city that was published and distributed around the nation and in Europe. Ellicott's design adhered largely to L'Enfant's vision. Notable alterations included the straightening of Massachusetts Avenue, the removal of five short diagonal avenues, and the elimination of a dozen civic spaces (fig. 6). Ellicott and the commissioners also did away with L'Enfant's plans for funding the city, erecting the public buildings, and establishing state responsibility for certain city squares. Notably, the published plan lacked any mention of its designer. It would be more than a century before Peter Charles L'Enfant, then widely referred to as Pierre, would gain renown for his design.[26]

By 1792, a vision for a national capital had been articulated through public debate and private discussion by men devoted to the establishment of an ambitious, grand federal city on the Potomac. L'Enfant folded the ideas of national leaders like Washington and Jefferson and local promoters like George Walker into his ambitious design. This plan for the city reflected the political and economic goals Washington held for the new nation. Commerce would flow down the Potomac and through the city's deepwater wharves. At the same time, the central location of the city, its linkage to the West, and state sponsorship of city squares would bind the nation together. This seat of government suited a strong American empire built on commerce and western expansion. L'Enfant referred to the city as "an undertaking of a magnitude so worthy of the concern of a grand empire . . . over whose progress the eyes of every other nation envying the opportunity denied them will stand judge." The fact that that no such empire yet existed provided all the more reason to plan on a grand scale.[27]

2 / Speculating in Failure

In 1791, short on cash but flush with land, President Washington and Congress established the nation's new national capital as a speculative gamble. Lacking the funds needed to construct the federal buildings and the public infrastructure of the city, they tapped into the national fervor for land speculation. In addition to ceding territory for the city, Maryland and Virginia appropriated $72,000 and $120,000, respectively, to begin the public buildings. Beyond that startup money, the city was to be built with earnings from the sale of lots left over after the government divided the real estate in the city with the original landowners. Therefore, the success of those landowners also hinged on land speculation in the federal city. Similar ventures had allowed colonial and state governments to develop their interior and frontier land without heavy dependence on public financing. And, of course, since the Northwest Ordinance of 1785, both the federal and Confederation governments had advanced the American national project at the expense of Native Americans through sales of land in the Ohio Territory.[1]

Many states saw the sale of their unsettled land as an ideal mechanism for promoting settlement and paying off their war debt. Pennsylvania, for example, followed this model to clear some of its debt. When Secretary of the Treasury Alexander Hamilton proposed federal assumption of state debts in 1790, Pennsylvania's comptroller-general, John Nicholson, opposed the measure. He asserted that between tariff revenue from the Port of Philadelphia and acceptance of the Revolutionary war debt certificates by the state's land office as payments for land, the state had largely paid off its war debt. A speculator himself, Nicholson's position favored holders of land certificates because assumption might hinder direct exchange of certificates for land. Congress approved Hamilton's plan in June 1790 as a part of a compromise that brought the federal seat of government to the Potomac. However, assumption did not stop speculation in land warrants. Nicholson is proof enough of that. During his long tenure at the head of the office in charge of Pennsylvania's land distribution, the comptroller-general amassed title to about four million acres in the state by 1794. As Nicholson's actions suggest, land warrants fell easily into the hands of speculators. These men offered veterans and other recipients of land credits small but immediate payments in return for their rights to distant land that held only potential value. In total, these sales represented a government-backed transfer of wealth from the poor Americans who had done the fighting during the Revolution to wealthy speculators.[2]

The potential profits from land speculation lured many prominent Americans into the business, including Washington. Having explored the western frontier as both a soldier and a surveyor, he had firsthand knowledge of the land's value and potential. Early in his surveying career, he accumulated small tracts of land in Virginia's Shenandoah Valley. Over time, Washington purchased larger parcels west of the Appalachians. By 1790, he owned 52,000 acres, primarily in the Ohio Valley along the Ohio and Kanawha Rivers but also in southwestern Pennsylvania, central New York, and western Kentucky.[3]

To Washington and the other the leaders of the new republic, specu- lation represented the most logical and cost-effective means for local development. While many Americans had defied the British prohibi- tion on settlement west of the Appalachians, the inability to obtain legal title prevented speculators from buying large tracts. However, victory over the British in the revolution swept aside Parliament's limitations on settlement as well as royal rights to unclaimed land. In response, wealthy Americans, land companies, state governments, and even the Confedera- tion Congress began speculating in land. This change not only privileged the desires of European Americans over the region's Native population, but it also brought settlers into conflict with speculators who claimed ownership of large swaths of western land. In 1789, ratification of the Constitution reduced the risk associated with large investment in land by establishing greater national political stability and by preventing state governments from "impairing the obligation of contracts." The framers of the Constitution feared that such impairment by states might infringe on the rights of speculators in land or war bonds, mortgage owners, and other holders of private debt. In the aftermath of a costly war, many states needed the cash speculators could provide for large tracts of land in order to pay war debts while keeping taxes low. Five years later, in 1794, a military victory over Native Americans in the Northwest Territory improved security for western settlers. And American treaties with Great Britain in 1794 and Spain in 1795 reinforced American control of the region. Each of these developments fostered American confidence in western land speculation. In 1790, amidst this torrent of land dealing, Washington and Congress chose to fund the creation of the federal seat of government through speculation.[4]

Only a few years later, in the mid- and late 1790s, the fervor for land speculation began to decline. Before Congress took up residence on the Potomac in 1800, the failure of large land companies, the bankruptcy of major speculators, and a contraction in the credit market had dampened American enthusiasm for speculation in land. By that time, however, construction of the city had begun, and Congress lacked the political will to alter the plans for its funding.[5]

In many ways, Washington and Congress had little choice beyond reliance on speculation. Before his departure, L'Enfant had estimated that the first four years of the project would require $1 million over and above the $192,000 provided by Maryland and Virginia. The federal government simply could not provide such a sum. Largely gained from customs duties on imported goods, the total receipts of the United States only came to about $4.5 million for the period from 1789 to 1791. Of that, just over half went to pay interest on the national debt, which, after assumption of the state debts in 1790, stood at over $77 million. L'Enfant assumed that the nation would borrow the needed $1 million against its real estate holdings in the city.[6]

A little over a month after L'Enfant submitted his plan, Jefferson transmitted a different loan proposal to the commissioners. This one had been developed by Samuel Blodgett, a Bostonian who became entangled in a variety of development and investment schemes in the federal city. By his reckoning, a mere half-million-dollar loan could get work started. He offered to raise the loan money by selling shares to investors in Boston. Under this system, city funding would work very much like a joint-stock company, with investors fronting capital for a venture and hoping to be repaid by future profits. By the middle of the decade, earnings from lot sales would provide for city development and interest payments on the loan. Washington, Jefferson, and the commissioners agreed on the merits of Blodgett's plan. Unfortunately, by July, Blodgett had failed to find investors for the project and had deposited only $10,000 of his own money into the city's account. This setback left the commissioners entirely dependent on the startup funds provided by Virginia and Maryland and the potential earnings from lot sales.[7]

Reliance on lot sales to fund the city left Washington and his commissioners dependent on the idea of the inevitability of the American nation. Buyers attending auctions for city lots would need to buy into the vision for the city and the nation offered by Washington. Without that buy-in, the lots would be worthless. In addition, the federal city furthered the American national project. As a permanent seat of government rose along the Potomac, the United States became that much more tangible. After all, Maryland and Virginia had given over one hundred square miles of territory to be the exclusive domain of the new federal government. Each lot sold, home built, and masonry stone added to the Capitol increased the likelihood of the success for the new city and the young republic.

However, the new national government's attempts to tap into the speculative energies of early republic America backfired, stunting the city's growth. Dividing the land with the proprietors created a second set of entrenched speculators who competed with federal land sales. At the same time, efforts to engage some of the titans of American land speculation resulted in failed deals that tied up large swaths of the federal city in disputes over payments, titles, and building requirements. And, especially after the departure of George Washington, weakness at the local level and the distribution of power in the federal system prevented city officials from wielding the authority required to operate a speculative business venture.

Problems began with the very agreement used to obtain land for the city. Turning this land into a seat of government required buying out, forcing out, or bringing on board the several dozen owners of property in the area. Washington chose to pay the original proprietors $66.67 per acre for the areas in the city that would become federal property, such as the national mall and the lots for public buildings. In addition, the landowners freely turned over land set aside for streets and avenues. And, finally, the government and the proprietors evenly divided land that was to be sold for private development. For each square on the city plan, the commissioners evenly divided the individual lots with the owner or owners of that property (fig. 7).

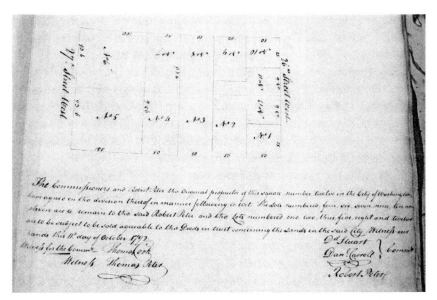

FIGURE 7. An entry from the Commissioners' Records showing the division of square number 12 between the city and the original owner of the land, Robert Peter. Peter retained control of lots 4, 6, 7, 9, 10, and 11. (Records of Squares, National Archives at College Park, Cartographic and Architectural Section)

By late 1800, the commissioners had completed division of the lots and transferred the rights to at least 95 percent of the lots reserved for the original owners. Of course, by this point, many of those proprietors had sold some or all of their land to speculators or settlers. In the end, the commissioners recorded transfers of proprietors' lots in the city to over three hundred individuals or interests. Through this complex process, the United States gained control of the 10,136 city lots that the commissioners would depend on for revenue. By combining appropriation, direct purchase, and division of land, the president gained access to the real estate he needed at a very low initial cost. The roughly 500 acres for public buildings and reservations cost a mere $36,099.35. And since the commissioners eventually paid that sum with profits from lot sales, the government had obtained the public land, the streets, and half of the city lots without spending a penny from the treasury.[8]

However, this arrangement locked the commissioners into an unbalanced relationship with the original landowners. Both sides became speculators, depending for success on the sale of lots in a city that had yet to be constructed. In most speculative land ventures, one land company, owner, or ownership group controlled all of the territory. In this case, the government acted as a land company but only controlled half of the salable real estate. In addition, the commissioners had responsibilities beyond those of a typical land company. They needed to construct public buildings and infrastructure sufficient for government business. The original landowners, meanwhile, could simply seek to maximize the return on their investment.[9]

Right from the start, this difference between the landowners and the commissioners led to conflict. The two groups disagreed vehemently about L'Enfant's role in the implementation of his plan. The proprietors felt that his grand vision represented the city's best chance for success and, consequently, their best chance for profit. Lamenting his departure from the project, a number of the largest landholders doubted "whether a successor can be found in this country, or indeed any country, qualified to be so eminently useful to the object which we are all so Interested." They believed that given a choice between keeping L'Enfant or the commissioners, Washington should have chosen L'Enfant. George Walker had even joked that the commissioners could not have acted more in the interest of the opponents of the Potomac capital if they had been paid by them directly. Later that year, another proprietor, the Georgetown merchant Samuel Davidson, blamed the commissioners' failure to obtain a loan for the city on their loss of the locals' faith in their abilities. Davidson went so far as to sign his letter, "with all *due* respect," suggesting none too slyly that the commissioners were due very little. Many of the proprietors clearly felt cheated by the president. It seemed that he had sold them a stake in a city that was to be built by a brilliant visionary but, in fact, it was in the hands of mere bureaucrats.[10]

From Washington's perspective, other attributes far outweighed artistic brilliance. The president knew that L'Enfant's prickly individualism and passion for the project would not have carried him successfully through negotiations with neighboring states or international lenders. He chose the first commissioners after consultation with Jefferson and Madison about the proper criteria for the appointees. The desired attributes began with experience managing, improving, and promoting land, something any large plantation owner in the Chesapeake region would possess. They also sought men with knowledge of the local political and legal systems so that complex local contracts and delicate political negotiations in Virginia and Maryland could be handled by the board.

Finally, the president identified men who had a personal interest in the success of the Potomac region but no large stake in any one area of the federal city.[11]

Each member of the first board possessed some or all of the attributes that Washington sought. Commissioner Carroll owned a large estate in Montgomery County, Maryland, and had served in the Maryland Senate, the Confederation Congress, and the U.S. Congress. Thomas Johnson had been elected Maryland's first governor in 1777 and had since served in the Maryland Assembly and been appointed by the president to be the U.S. District Court judge for Maryland. Washington also appointed Johnson to be a justice on the U.S. Supreme Court. Each of these Marylanders had also been active in the Potomac Company, proving their dedication to the region. Johnson had even served as president of the company after Washington took up the presidency of the nation in 1789.

The lone Virginian, Dr. David Stuart, boasted a less impressive political resume but made up for that with family connections. Living and practicing medicine in Alexandria, Stuart had invested in the Potomac Company and participated in regional efforts to win the capital. In 1783, when he married Eleanor Calvert Custis, Stuart found himself at the intersection of three prominent regional families. Born into one of Maryland's founding families, the Calverts, Eleanor had previously been married to John Parke Custis, a member of one of Virginia's powerful political families. Custis was also Martha Washington's son by her first husband. In 1781, Eleanor became a widow when Custis succumbed to illness during the siege of Yorktown. Therefore, a pair of second marriages brought Stuart and Washington together as family. And while marrying a man's stepdaughter-in-law might not necessarily create a close family bond, shared concern for the children from Eleanor's first marriage—Martha's grandchildren—brought the two families together. Stuart represented a close personal connection between Washington and the board. And the pairing of one Virginian with two Marylanders reflected the importance of the Maryland side of the District where the federal city lay.[12]

Three years into the project, the board began to change radically. Both Johnson and Stuart resigned in 1794. The following year, Commissioner Carroll also left the board. Now in his sixties, Johnson hoped to retire and reap the fruits of decades of effort promoting the Potomac region by selling his land in northwestern Maryland and purchasing land in the city. Leaving his public obligations allowed Johnson to care for his wife, who had taken ill. Stuart, meanwhile, had moved to western Fairfax

County, Virginia, since joining the board and had grown tired of the commute. After Johnson and Stuart left the board, Commissioner Carroll served for nine months before retiring due to poor health.[13]

Carroll's departure completed the transition to an entirely new board, one that would oversee the remaining preparations for the removal of the government to the city. Finding new board members proved difficult. The position offered little compensation. The first board earned only $6 for each day spent in Washington. To ensure their presence, the president chose to pay the second board an annual salary of $1,400 but also required that they reside in the barely developed city. Several promising candidates turned down the president when approached about the position, among them, Tobias Lear, Washington's trusted former personal secretary. Two men who did accept appointments fit neatly into the mold established by the president in 1791.

In August 1794, Gustavus Scott, a forty-one-year-old lawyer from Maryland's Eastern Shore, took Johnson's place on the board. Like the members of the first board, Scott owned land in the region and held shares in the Potomac Company. He had also served in the Maryland Assembly, where he made connections that would prove useful when the city sought financial assistance. Commissioner Carroll's replacement also brought political experience to the board. Appointed in May 1795, Alexander White had previously served in the Virginia House of Burgesses and in the U.S. Congress representing Virginia's northern counties, including those through which the Potomac meandered on its way to Chesapeake Bay.

The only commissioner appointed by Washington who disrupted the usual pattern was Stuart's replacement, Dr. William Thornton. A young man of only thirty-three, Thornton owned no land in the Chesapeake region. And, until 1793, he had no connection to the Potomac or the federal city. That year he submitted plans to the contest held by Washington and the commissioners to determine a design for the Capitol. Having dabbled in architecture and engineering, in addition to his primary career in medicine, Thornton had won praise for his design of a building for the Library Company of Philadelphia in 1789. His plan for the Capitol impressed Washington, who named it the winner. A year later, Washington tapped Thornton for a place on the board. With the public buildings under way, the eye of an architect might prove just as valuable as the skills of a well-connected local politician. As he had in 1790, Washington appointed men to the second board who shared his personal dedication to the success of the Potomac region and the federal city.[14]

This second board improved relations with the local population by increasing the stability and professionalism of the office. Washington had urged the new board members to reside within the District so that they could better attend to its needs. Thornton already owned a home in Georgetown, and Scott moved from the Virginia countryside to a home just outside the District's limits a few months after his appointment. Commissioner White, on the other hand, never moved from his home in Woodville, Virginia. After a three-week trial period, Mrs. White vetoed any move to the city. However, despite White's long commute, the commissioners established regular business hours for their office, remaining open to the public two days a week in the winter months and three days a week during the rest of the year. The new board also established regular procedures and processes for handling and recording the business of the city, all of which improved the public perception of it. Together this board remained intact until Scott's death in December 1800. His position passed briefly to two additional commissioners before Congress dissolved the board in 1802.[15]

Lacking dedicated funding for the public buildings and city infrastructure, the commissioners needed to maximize their revenue from the sale of city lots. They attempted to add value to city real estate in three ways. First, they enforced a set of regulations for construction in the city. Among other things, these regulations stipulated that all buildings be erected parallel to the streets; that no cellar doors, stoops, porches, or any other part of a building obstruct the footways along the streets; and that no temporary lodgings be constructed without the board's approval. The original terms also declared that "the outer and party walls of all houses within the said City shall be built of Brick or Stone" and that houses built on the avenues should stand between 35 and 40 feet high to the roof. Some of these rules originated at a September 1791 meeting between Jefferson, Madison, and the commissioners. During the meeting, Jefferson asked the commissioners, "Ought there to be any wood houses in the town?" The secretary of state recorded their reply as a simple "No," and the discussion turned to the proper regulations for the brick and stone homes to be permitted. As settlement of the city had not yet begun, these regulations reflect Washington's and the commissioners' idealized vision for the city rather than a reaction to the proliferation of actual wooden homes. In their minds, wood-frame shacks, storage sheds, and unsightly angles would have no place in the capital. Instead, stately, two-story brick and stone homes would line its avenues with no obstructed sight lines.[16]

Historians have long explored the role of the cities as regulators and a shapers of local commercial and social life. Through their physical forms and their regulatory structures, cities both reflect and affect the economic and social exchanges possible within their boundaries. The building regulations established by the commissioners asserted the desire to create a visually stable urban form, one that contrasted with the chaotic jumble of streets and buildings found at the core of many colonial seaport cities. City planners at the turn of the nineteenth century harnessed the regularity of grid systems to ease the sale of city lots and also to create a mechanism by which they could regulate the functions, and consequently the residents, of different segments of the city. Filling out L'Enfant's grand city plan with stately homes of brick and stone would prevent poor laborers, beggars, drunkards, and other unseemly types from settling there while sending the aesthetic message that the federal city belonged to the type of respected gentlemen chosen by their states to serve in Congress.[17]

In Philadelphia, an older city with a more mature economy, the rapid population growth experienced after the revolution resulted in a mingling of upper- and lower-class housing where stately row houses stood in close proximity to dirt-floor shacks and wooden homes packed tight with the city's poorest residents. The commissioners hoped to prevent such a situation from developing in Washington. Jefferson had assumed that commercial activity would be concentrated at the edges of the city by the Eastern Branch and the mouth of Rock Creek. The commissioners likely made the same assumption and hoped that they could reserve the governmental core of the city for genteel local elites and federal officials.[18]

Unfortunately, the reality of life in the infant city conflicted with these idealized regulations. Few residents in the federal city could afford to build two-story houses fronted with brick or stone. By 1796, Washington and the commissioners recognized the need to alter the regulations. After all, the primary economic activity in the city was the construction of public buildings, requiring a constant supply of skilled and unskilled laborers. The board suspended the height requirement and the mandate for outer walls of brick or stone, making legal the wood-frame housing that had already been erected for the city's labor force. After the initial suspension expired in 1800, successive presidents provided additional suspensions through 1818. Finally, in 1820, the federal government turned over control of such regulations to the city government. By extending the suspensions rather than abolishing the rules altogether, four presidents expressed hope that the capital would soon develop to the point where they could achieve an orderly separation between the laboring classes and the city's elites.[19]

The board also promoted construction of substantial homes and buildings at the point of sale. To accomplish this, they discounted the purchase price of lots for buyers who agreed to build such homes within a set period of time. In one December 1794 sale, the purchase price was contingent upon the buyer improving the lots by "erecting and finishing thereon one good brick or stone building two Stories high covering at least 1200 square feet within the year 1795 and another of the same size in the year 1796." By 1799, the board regularly discounted lots sold with similar building requirements by 20 percent. They hoped to improve the long-term value of the remaining lots by influencing the overall real estate market in the city. In addition, the commissioners also sought to lay down some basic infrastructure for the city.[20]

Petitions rolled in for the government to fund construction of bridges, roads, wharves, and markets throughout the city. The commissioners acceded to these requests when they had the money, which was rare, and when the project also advanced their primary goal of preparing the city for the government. The first board expressed a particular interest in building up the city's infrastructure, but poor lot sales limited the funds available for such projects. Before the city plan had even been published, for example, Georgetown mayor, Robert Peter, and several proprietors proposed the construction of wharves at the western edge of the city, just east of Georgetown. The commissioners agreed that wharves would increase the value of the lots in the area, possibly even enough to defray their cost. However, having yet sold no lots, the city could not begin such a project. By November 1795, the commissioners had spent about $30,000 on wharves, roads, canals, and bridges around the city, about 9 percent of the board's total outlays to that point.[21]

Occasionally local landowners offered to share the cost of projects with the commissioners. A wealthy Briton who had moved to Washington in 1794 and become one of the more successful developers there, Thomas Law, proposed a toll on carts and carriages to pay for the upkeep of city streets in July 1796. The board rejected this idea. However, the following month they gave Law $50 to aid the construction of a bridge between two hills along New Jersey Avenue. That September, two of the city's most notorious land speculators, Robert Morris and John Nicholson, offered to pay half the cost of a bridge over Tiber Creek on Virginia Avenue if the commissioners would deduct the other half from the large sum they owed the city. Famous for his financial support of the revolution, Morris was one of the wealthiest men in the new nation. He and his young partner, Nicholson, the former comptroller general of Pennsylvania, speculated heavily in New York, in the Ohio country, and on the southern frontier. The board rejected their proposal, preferring payment from them in cash. In a delightfully ironic response, the heavily indebted speculators offered to loan the city money for this and other public works. Not surprisingly, the commissioners had no interest in this offer either. As time went on, the board focused its limited funds and attention on its primary mission, preparing a seat of government. [22]

They did not rule out infrastructure projects entirely. Responding to requests from residents in 1801, for instance, the board pledged $500 for the establishment of a market along Pennsylvania Avenue between the President's House and the Capitol. They could justify this expense because the market straddled the primary corridor of government business and because it brought order to the city's retail enterprises by placing them under the regulatory purview of the board. When a prominent resident requested road improvements in 1802, the commissioners wrote that it was true that "we have expended considerable sums on the Streets to facilitate the access of the Members of the Government to the houses where their respective duties require their attendance; but it is equally true that we have resisted every application to deviate from that principle." For the board, any significant outlay of funds required a direct benefit to the government. The city's persistent penury prevented adoption of any other interpretation of its mission. The board's responsibility for projects like these exemplifies the imbalance in its relationship with the original landowners who benefited from the commissioners' work but bore none of the cost. [23]

The board's efforts to sell lots at discounted rates to those willing to build large homes also set it apart from its competitors in the sales market. The original proprietors had considerably more flexibility in the terms they could offer potential buyers. They operated freely in the market while the commissioners struggled with their broader responsibilities. Reporting the state of its affairs to President Jefferson late in 1801, the board noted that its recent sales had netted an average of $470 per lot while the proprietors were earning $579 per lot for cash sales and $921 per lot for sales on four, five, and six years' credit. The commissioners typically demanded one-third of the purchase price for lots within sixty days of the sale, with the other two-thirds paid in equal annual installments, without interest, over the next two years. Not needing immediate cash for public works, the proprietors could earn nearly twice as much for a lot by offering longer-term credit. In this way, the division of land with the proprietors prevented the commissioners from controlling the terms and conditions of the market for city lots. As a result, income from lot sales continually fell short of their needs. In 1800, Commissioners Scott and Thornton linked their lack of money and their low opinion of lot sales as a source of revenue: "We have in vain tried Sales; they produce nothing but bad paper and perplexity."[24]

Complications for the commissioners caused by the original landowners paled in comparison to the damage done to the city by land speculators. In September 1793, a young investor with connections to Dutch banking interests named James Greenleaf approached Washington and the commissioners about a large-scale purchase of lots. Greenleaf initially proposed a purchase of three thousand city lots. Within a few months, Greenleaf had brought on board two additional investors with considerable land speculation experience, Morris and Nicholson. Together the three men doubled the scope of the proposed deal to include a total of six thousand lots, 60 percent of the total held by the government. Greenleaf, Morris, and Nicholson agreed to pay $80 per lot, a total of $480,000.[25]

This price represented a marked discount for the speculators. The most recent sales in the city had netted $266.67 per lot. The commissioners issued the first thousand lots on the bond of the three men. The speculators agreed to pay the remaining purchase price in six equal annual installments without interest starting on May 1, 1795. Keen to see the city develop, the board required them to build "twenty Brick Houses annually, two stories high and covering 1200 square feet each." And to prevent the speculators from undermining the real estate market by quickly selling these low-cost lots, the commissioners forbid them from selling any land until January 1, 1796, unless they had completed one substantial house for every third lot. Greenleaf planned to use the rights to the first thousand lots as collateral for a Dutch loan. That money would cover the partners' annual payments and the cost of construction. In this way, the board pinned its hopes for locking in a steady stream of funding for the public buildings on Greenleaf's ability to secure Dutch financing and on the reputations of Morris and Nicholson.[26]

It soon became clear that their plans would falter. Despite his connections, Greenleaf failed to secure Dutch financing. Early in 1795, construction halted on the buildings they had been erecting in compliance with the contract. Then the May 1 deadline for the first payment came and went without any action from the investors. The following month, two of the commissioners complained to Secretary of State Edmund

Randolph that the investors had made $95,000 on the sale of city lots purchased from the original proprietors but claimed to be unable to pay their first installment of $68,500. The commissioners concluded "that those Gentlemen think their funds can be better employed than by complying with their Engagements with us." It would become apparent to the board as the years went on that the speculators ranked their debts to the city quite low on their list of financial priorities.[27]

Over the course of the 1790s, the failure of their many land speculation ventures drove Greenleaf, Morris, and Nicholson into bankruptcy. The three-man partnership broke apart in the summer of 1795 after Greenleaf defaulted on notes that Morris and Nicholson had endorsed for him. In response, the two professional speculators attempted to rid themselves of Greenleaf. After struggling to iron out the various debts that linked the three men, Morris and Nicholson bought out Greenleaf's shares of their federal city venture. However, since they lacked cash for the buyout, they paid Greenleaf with notes backed by their city lots and by shares in the North American Land Company, a corporation they had created to combine their many speculative landholdings. Even this partial separation from the weakest member of the investment group could not prevent the collapse of Morris and Nicholson's finances. As one historian has described it, their speculation resembled "a giant pyramid scheme." The men desperately sought new investors to pay dividends promised to prior investors. They also attempted to generate cash by selling shares in the North American Land Company. Eventually the two men resorted to cross-endorsing notes for one another, in effect creating their own currency backed solely by their reputations as wealthy men. Totaling as much as $10 million, these notes depreciated in value and eventually became the object of speculation by others. When America's speculative bubble burst in 1796–97, Morris and Nicholson could no longer sustain their paper empire. By late 1799, Greenleaf, Morris, Nicholson and many other prominent American land speculators had been imprisoned as debtors.[28]

Early republic Americans witnessed the dramatic rise and fall of many men like Morris, Nicholson, and Greenleaf, along with the bursting of various speculation-fueled economic bubbles. Relatively new and particularly risky forms of wealth proliferated rapidly after the revolution. Freed from the British regulations and restrictions designed both to prevent economic bubbles and to keep financial power centered at the heart of the empire, Americans dealt freely in bank shares, corporate stocks, and land certificates. With little way to determine the safety of any given investment, Americans allowed traditional social indicators such as honor and reputation to guide their investments. Widely respected for his financial support of the revolution, Morris, in particular, benefited from this aspect of early American capitalism. Trading on their reputations, Morris and Nicholson managed to keep their company afloat until the market for shares in speculative land began to contract. When a major investor like Morris or a whole market came crashing down, both the tremendous complexity and the great weakness of the economic system that had fueled the nation's postwar growth were revealed. Unfortunately, for the District commissioners, the bubble burst on Morris's financial empire only after the majority of the government lots in the city had been legally entangled with his investments.

For their part, the commissioners spent seven years trying to cajole payment from the three speculators and from the creditors who took up the tattered remains of their portfolio. At times they attempted to play on the speculators' sense of morality and patriotic duty. Laying bare the desperate state of the city's finances, the board pleaded with them to pay the money they owed. In September 1795, for example, the commissioners told Morris, "Without a payment of at least fifteen thousand Dollars in ten Days our Operations must totally cease." And in July of the next year, they declared, "There is a certain point beyond which forbearance becomes folly and a total dereliction of public trust. How far in the present Instance we have broken in upon this Rule is a subject of which we ought not to seek a description." At other times the board offered to establish monthly payment plans for the speculators. Hinting that it was the only way for Morris to avoid legal action, they proposed payments of $12,000 per month until the entire debt was paid. Over the years, they occasionally received partial payments from the speculators or their eventual creditors. In general, however, these efforts produced few results.[29]

Behind all of these efforts to coax payment from Greenleaf, Morris, and Nicholson lurked the threat that the commissioners would declare their purchase forfeit and sell the lots at auction to recoup the purchase price. Just a few days after the board sealed its deal with the speculators, the Maryland Assembly passed a law regarding land sales in the federal city stating that "if any sum of the purchase money or interest shall not be paid for the space of thirty days after the same ought to be paid, the commissioners, or any two of them, may sell the same lots at public vendue, in the city of Washington, at any time after sixty days' notice of such sale, in some of the public newspapers of Georgetown and

Baltimoretown." Money earned from such sales would be used to cover the original sale price plus interest and the cost of advertising. Again and again, the commissioners warned the speculators that they could exercise this dramatic option.[30]

However, these threats had little impact on Greenleaf, Morris, and Nicholson. Despite Maryland's clear legislation, the speculators held all the cards in their dealings with the commissioners, and they knew it. The commissioners' pleadings had shown that the city desperately needed cash. They hoped that the threat of sale would coax full payment from the speculators. At the same time, however, they feared that at auction the lots would not raise the needed capital. Everyone involved could see that putting so many lots up for sale at one time would drag prices down. The commissioners also knew that the land would fetch higher prices after Congress took up residence in the city. As a result, they hoped to hold onto it as long as possible.[31]

Above all, the speculators knew they could undermine any resale by publicly asserting their rights to the lots and declaring that they would fight resale in the courts. In 1798, by which time Greenleaf, Morris, and Nicholson were each bankrupt or nearly bankrupt, their creditors employed this very tactic. Two of the commissioners complained to the Maryland Assembly in December of that year that when they offered lots for sale, "these gentlemen and their trustees have so alarmed the public as to defeat the object." Other claims to the lots also complicated matters. The speculators had resold some of their lots and used others as collateral for different loans and business ventures. Therefore, when the board initiated sales of these lots, a whole chorus of voices cried out in opposition. By 1800, when the government took up residence in the city, 1,350 of these lots remained in the hands of the commissioners, tied up for six years, generating little economic or social benefit for the city. The rest had either been sold at auction to recoup the low, $80 per lot purchase price or had been transferred to the speculators, their buyers, or their creditors when payments were made.[32]

Lacking the authority to handle difficult issues like this on their own, the commissioners often turned to the president for guidance. While in office, Washington remained personally involved in city business. He stepped in repeatedly to solve problems and mediate disputes. In 1791, for example, when L'Enfant tore down Daniel Carroll's home because part of it lay in what would eventually be a city street, Carroll complained relentlessly and demanded compensation. Washington suggested that the house be rebuilt in proper alignment with the street using the existing materials. The government would pay for the labor and additional materials needed to complete construction. Years later, on his way out of office, Washington instructed the board to concentrate its limited funds on the Capitol at the expense of the President's House. That Washington would engage directly in city business speaks to his dedication to and personal investment in the success of the city that would bear his name. After he left office, however, the federal city lacked a champion to lend authority to its cause.[33]

Although the board represented the federal government, it often turned to the State of Maryland for financial and legal support. Persuaded that their state had a "peculiar interest" in the success of the federal city, Maryland legislators provided emergency loans. Late in 1796, after failing to get loans from both Dutch bankers and the Bank of the United States, the commissioners obtained a loan for $100,000 worth of U.S. debt certificates that paid 6 percent interest from Maryland. To turn these into cash, however, they had to sell them at current market value rather than face value. Typically, the board held onto the shares and sold only what it needed each month in the hope that they might appreciate. In all, however, the board obtained only $79,000 in cash for its $100,000 in stock. And while this amount got it through the year, the coming of winter brought it back to the verge of insolvency.

Late in 1797, the commissioners turned again to the Maryland legislature for assistance. President John Adams authorized them to seek a loan of $150,000, an amount they felt would cover the year's expenses. However, they only obtained another $100,000 worth of U.S. stock. Late in 1799, Maryland loaned a final $50,000 to the city. Concerned about the city's ability to repay its debts, the legislature required the commissioners and a few prominent city landowners who had lobbied for the loan to sign on as personal guarantors. This placed the commissioners in the awkward position of risking their private fortunes on the success of this public venture. For the good of the city, they accepted the legislature's demands.[34]

With this requirement, the Maryland Assembly further obscured what were already quite blurry lines separating public and private interests in the District of Columbia. After all, Washington had established the federal city a mere stone's throw from his own estate. And many aspects of his vision for the national capital had begun as goals for his home region, some of which predated the American Revolution. And by hiring men connected to the Potomac region to serve on the Board of Commissioners, Washington had entrusted his vision for the region to those who would dedicate themselves to its success. Again and again over the ensuing decades, residents of the District of Columbia would follow Washington's example by dedicating private capital and energy to public city projects. This incident stands out because it involved a state government requiring that private citizens provide financial backing for a federal entity. However, the comingling of public and private interests that the Assembly required was not a new development in the federal city.

The commissioners also sought help from the Maryland Assembly in their dealings with Greenleaf, Morris, and Nicholson and their creditors. In 1796, the U.S. attorney general verified the commissioners' right to sell off lots whose purchasers had not fully paid the amounts they owed to the city. Facing resistance from the speculators and their trustees, the board sought additional legal assistance from Maryland because the laws of that state still governed land it ceded for the federal district. Late in 1798, the board requested a law guaranteeing both its right to sell defaulted land and the validity of sales it had already made so that there could be no legal interference from the original buyers. Unable to rely entirely on federal support, even the legal opinion of the U.S. attorney general, the board hoped Maryland might provide the unimpeachable authority it needed to effectively manage the sale of city lots. However, the legislature ignored its request for stronger default legislation.[35]

The distribution of authority between the federal and state governments and between the separate branches of the federal government handicapped decision making in the federal city. After Washington's retirement, the city lacked a champion committed to its cause. The Adams administration often responded slowly to the board's requests. Adams clearly placed a lower priority on the city than Washington had. The board often wrote Adams and his cabinet members begging for responses to previously submitted questions. In 1799, for instance, it sought executive branch input on a lottery to construct a canal organized by city residents. The board worried that little progress had been made on the canal and sought the authority to compel completion of the project. Two months later, in early August, it dispatched a letter to Secretary of State Timothy Pickering reminding him of its inquiry and requesting a reply.[36]

That fall, the board encountered similar delays when attempting to keep the city afloat financially. On September 25, it wrote to Adams at his home in Quincy, Massachusetts, providing the good news that, the Capitol would be ready for Congress in 1800. It also requested permission to seek a loan from Maryland to fund the next year's work. After a month of silence, the commissioners wrote to Adams again. Politely assuming the first letter to Quincy had been miscarried, they repeated their request. Polite as they might have been, it must have been clear that they could not expect Washington's hands-on style from this president.[37]

Adams seems to have been largely disinterested in the federal city. When Congress opened its first session in Washington, Adams delivered a message before the assembled representatives and senators, at one point reminding them that when it chose Congress could assume its constitutionally granted responsibility for the city. If they intended to do so, he urged them to "consider it as the Capital of a great nation advancing with unexampled rapidity in arts, in commerce, in wealth and in population, and in possessing within itself those energies and resources, which if not thrown away, will secure to it a long course of prosperity and self government." While Adams had reiterated the connection between the city and the expanding nation established by Washington, he clearly hoped that Congress would take management of the District off his hands. Adams's disinterest in the capital may have stemmed from his roots as a New Englander or simply from his attention to other matters. Some historians have noted that both Adams and his wife, Abigail, suffered from ill health during his term in office. That situation likely contributed to his decision to return home to Massachusetts each year when Congress was not in session, in order to gain physical and mental distance from the stresses of the presidency. In the end, however, Adams oversaw the successful removal of the government from Philadelphia to Washington and seems to have generally, if not very vigorously, supported the city.[38]

Although the city's initial designation as a project of the executive branch largely prevented legislative interference, its financial woes required engagement with the holder of the nation's purse strings: Congress. If the board wanted permission to obtain funding beyond revenue from lot sales, Congress would have to approve. In 1796, the board sought congressional permission to obtain loans using city lots as collateral. Commissioner White spent nearly six months in Philadelphia pressing Congress for passage of a loan authorization bill. He provided a detailed accounting of the money spent to that point and the expected costs and revenues for future years. But many congressmen still accused him of hiding the true state of the city's affairs. He reported back to the board, "Indeed so many unpleasant circumstances have attended this business that I can with great truth say the two last months have been the most disagreeable period of my life." Despite White's distaste for the business,

Congress eventually authorized the board to borrow up to $300,000. The loan bill required that the board, "semi-annually, render to the Secretary of the Treasury, a particular account of the receipts and expenditures of all monies intrusted to them, and also, the progress and state of the business, and of the funds under their administration; and that the said secretary lay the same before Congress, at every session after the receipt thereof." In effect, the board traded congressional oversight of the city for the ability to seek loans. Passage of the bill cleared the way for the loans later provided by Maryland. Unfortunately, neither the emergency loans nor the prying eyes of Congress did much to correct the city's wayward course.[39]

Desperately poor lot sales not only undermined the city's finances; they also reflected the public's lack of interest in settling or investing in the city. Greenleaf, Morris, and Nicholson had managed to tie up the majority of the government's lots. And the remainder sold poorly. By late 1800, the board had received full payment for about 3,600 lots, netting only about $350,000. Removing the three major speculators and their creditors from the calculations, the sales data shows that other investors contracted for about 1,250 lots, costing approximately $225,000. All together, these ordinary settlers and minor speculators paid for only about 10 percent of the government's lots by the end of 1800. More buyers certainly purchased lots from the original proprietors. But these low numbers speak to the Americans' unwillingness to risk investment in the city before the arrival of the government. Without a financial or commercial base for the local economy and only the promise of the government's arrival in 1800, the commissioners lured few settlers beyond the laborers who sought work on the public buildings.[40]

Revenues paled in comparison to the cost of the public buildings. During the building season (roughly spring through fall), operating costs ranged from $10,000 to $12,000 per month. Only in 1798 did sales earnings cover these costs. That year, payments generated over $145,000. In all other years up to and including 1800, revenue never totaled even half that amount. Also, the commissioners could not effectively recoup the more than $178,000 owed by the speculators and other buyers in default. This financial data highlights the difficulty faced by the board as it struggled to fund the public works. And by 1802, payments due on the Maryland loans threatened to undermine the entire endeavor. This addition to the city's balance sheet proved impossible to manage. In response, Congress called for the sale of the lots pledged as collateral for the loans unless the president determined that such sales would present an "unwarrantable sacrifice" of the property. In that case, Congress would appropriate the money for the loans. In the same bill, Congress disbanded the commissioners' office in favor of a single superintendent working out of the Treasury Department.[41]

Ultimately, the failure of the young federal government's foray into urban land speculation stemmed not merely from decisions made by the commissioners but also from the government's approach to the entire project. Aside from the hope of an eventual connection with the West via the Potomac, the government did little to promote the commercial appeal of the city. This approach protected the government from the influence of moneyed interests in Philadelphia and New York. However, the city's dim commercial prospects also dampened investment and settlement in the city. In addition, harnessing the real estate in the city in order to attract settlers and fund the public buildings would have required control of the sales market. Instead, the commissioners operated in a shared market with the original proprietors. And when they sought ironclad legal authority to enforce the terms of sale for lots and their contract with Greenleaf, Morris, and Nicholson, the commissioners encountered a diffusion of power among themselves, the president, Congress, and the State of Maryland. Caught between the executive branch, the legislative branch, and the state government and lacking representatives in Congress or a champion in the President's House, the board proved unable to navigate the new government's federal structure. Beholden to all but with authority over very few, the commissioners had succeeded in only their most basic mission, preparing public buildings and infrastructure just barely capable of hosting the federal government.

3 /   A Boomtown without a Boom

By the time Congress arrived in the autumn of 1800, the board had spent over $1 million on the city. The results of its efforts impressed neither Congress nor the American people. Nearly every government official or private citizen who arrived in the new seat of government mocked the city. Noting that she and her traveling companions had become lost in the woods between Baltimore and Washington, for instance, Abigail Adams famously wrote, "Woods are all you see, from Baltimore until you reach *the city,* which is only so in name. Here and there is a small cot, without a glass window, interspersed amongst the forests, through which you travel miles without seeing any human being." She added, "In the city there are buildings enough, if they were compact and finished, to accommodate Congress and those attached to it; but as they are, and scattered as they are, I see no great comfort for them." Connecticut congressman John Cotton Smith described a similar scene on his first approach to the city:

> One wing of the Capitol only had been erected, which, with the
> president's house, a mile distant from it, both constructed with
> white sandstone, were shining objects in dismal contrast with the
> scene around them. Instead of recognizing the avenues and streets
> portrayed on the plan of the city, not one was visible, unless we
> except a road with two buildings on each side of it, called the New
> Jersey Avenue. The Pennsylvania Avenue, leading, as laid down
> on paper, from the Capitol to the presidential mansion, was then,
> nearly the whole distance, a deep morass covered with alder bushes.

Smith at least admired the situation of the city, making note of views down the river and across the nearby fields. For most Americans, however, the slow development of the city, its small population, and its poor economy overshadowed whatever natural beauty the region might have to offer.[1]

Still more woodland than metropolis, the city contained only a smattering of brick buildings, few gravel-paved streets, and functional but still unfinished public buildings when Congress arrived in November 1800. By mid-May of that year, a paltry 109 brick homes were strewn across the length of city. Small clusters could be found near the public buildings, between them along the Pennsylvania Avenue corridor, between the President's House and Georgetown, and to the south of the Capitol toward the confluence of the two rivers. Congressman Smith also commented on the city's housing stock, noting that between the President's House and Georgetown stood a group of houses known as the Six Buildings. "There were also two other blocks," he said, "consisting of two or three dwelling houses, in different directions, and now and then an insulated wooden habitation." Between these buildings he described a city covered by "shrub-oak bushes" on high ground and by trees and other shrubbery in the lower marshy soil. Finally, he noted Greenleaf's many unfinished buildings in "ruinous condition," adding to the "desolate aspect of the place." All of the board's efforts to encourage construction of brick and stone homes had come to naught. The vast expanse of L'Enfant's city swallowed up its few buildings, obscuring any signs of progress and offering only a sense of emptiness.[2]

The lack of residents exacerbated the difficulties the board faced when attempting to spur city development. During the 1790s, few Americans relocated to the city. Although its promoters promised future prosperity, that future depended entirely on the government's arrival. And many Americans assumed what locals always feared, that come 1800, Congress would balk at the prospect of departing from the conveniences of Philadelphia. When the Residence Bill passed in 1790, many members of Congress doubted that that body would willingly move into the woods along the Potomac a decade hence. Uncertainty about the government's dedication to the location would dog city leaders for decades. Even after the government arrived, the anxiety remained. Residents feared that Congress would leave for greener—or perhaps better paved—pastures. During the 1790s, such uncertainty dampened migration into the District.[3]

The Federal Census of 1800 provides some details about those who made the city their home. In April 1800, 14,093 people lived within the District of

Columbia's ten-mile square. If this total represented a single city, it would qualify as the sixth largest in the United States at the time. However, that number included the residents of Washington City (the area covered by the L'Enfant Plan), Alexandria, Georgetown, and the rural areas around and between these urban centers. Although united by interest in the success of the federal district, residents of these three cities viewed them as quite separate. At this point in Washington City's development it is much more useful to examine it separately from and in comparison to its better-established neighbors.[4]

The census data show that Washington was stable and racially diverse but only thinly populated. These features link the town with patterns seen in other small Southern cities in early republic America. At the time of the census, just eight months before the arrival of Congress, 3,210 people lived in Washington City. The sex ratio of the white population was 1.18. This meant that for every white female, 1.18 white males lived in the city. The census returns also show that children under the age of sixteen made up nearly 42 percent of the city's total white population. Having a fairly balanced mix of the sexes and plenty of children afoot put the new city of Washington on par with Georgetown, which had been established forty years earlier. At this moment, the cities bore a considerable demographic resemblance. With a total population of 2,993, Georgetown lagged behind Washington by only a few hundred people. And compared to other urban areas, the cities ranked thirty-first and thirty-second in total population nationally.[5]

The great disparity in the physical size of Washington and Georgetown undermines this image of twin cities along the Potomac. The published plans for the federal city included nearly ten square miles of land. On the other hand, the small city of Georgetown hardly covered one quarter of a square mile. In this context, the census data reveals striking disparities. As critics like Abigail Adams made clear, Washington's population was so dispersed that the term *city* hardly seemed to apply. Most of the lots sold and buildings constructed lay south and west of Massachusetts Avenue. However, even if we exclude the area to the north and east of that line, Washington City still covered nearly six square miles. L'Enfant had hoped that separating the branches of government would spur wider settlement in the city and prevent growth from concentrating in a single place. At this early stage of development, however, the city plan encouraged the population to spread very thinly across all areas of the city. As the scatter plot shown in figure 8 suggests, Washington City's large size and small population set it apart from other American cities as well.[6]

Carved from two Southern states, the District of Columbia maintained a distinctly Southern feel in 1800. Although the government had also turned

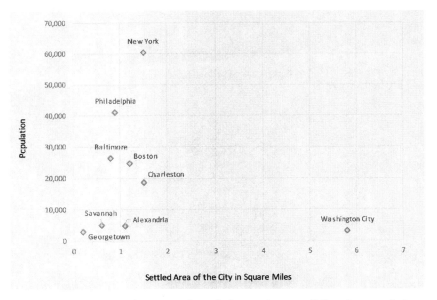

FIGURE 8. Urban populations and settled areas in 1800. When its population and settled areas are compared to other cities, Washington City stands apart as an outlier.

them into land speculators, the original proprietors remained Southern planters during construction of the city. Many resided in their original homes and worked their fields as the city grew up around them. Some of these landowners came into conflict with the commissioners when the board insisted that land be cleared or fences removed in areas designated for city streets or public use. In such situations, the proprietors often asked for the right to use the land until the government actually needed it. In 1799, for example, the board granted Daniel Carroll permission to plant a field of wheat on public grounds given the condition that he "do so subject to the hazard of our erecting and planting ornamental trees on [his] wheat field, though it is not at present very probable that the thing will be done." The board lacked funding for such trees but clearly wanted to be sure that Carroll understood that they controlled the land in question.[7]

The prevalence of slavery in the federal city reinforced its Southern nature. Nearly 40 percent of households in the city owned slaves, and blacks (both enslaved and free) accounted for 23 percent of the populace. Slaves alone made up around 19 percent of the total population. These percentages put the city in line with its neighbors in Maryland and northern Virginia: Georgetown, Alexandria, and Baltimore. Of the four,

	Total Population	Slaves	Free Blacks	% Black (Slave & Free) of Total Population	% Slave of Total Population	% Free of Total Population	% Slave of Black Population	% Free of Black Population
New York	60,515	2,876	3,506	10.55	4.75	5.79	45.06	54.94
Philadelphia	41,220	55	4,210	10.35	0.13	10.21	1.29	98.71
Baltimore	26,514	2,843	2,771	21.17	10.72	10.45	50.64	49.36
Washington City	3,210	623	123	23.24	19.41	3.83	83.51	16.49
Georgetown	2,993	731	201	31.14	24.42	6.72	78.43	21.57
Alexandria	4,971	875	369	25.03	17.60	7.42	70.34	29.66
Richmond	5,737	2,293	607	50.55	39.97	10.58	79.07	20.93
Petersburg	3,521	1,487	428	54.39	42.23	12.16	77.65	22.35
Norfolk	6,926	2,724	352	44.41	39.33	5.08	88.56	11.44
Charleston	18,824	9,053	951	53.14	48.09	5.05	90.49	9.51
Savannah	5,146	2,367	181	49.51	46.00	3.52	92.90	7.10

FIGURE 9. Washington City's free and enslaved black populations in comparison to neighboring cities and others to its north and south.

Georgetown ranked highest in these categories, with all blacks accounting for 31 percent of the population and slaves making up over 24 percent of the total. By comparison, slaves constituted a far smaller share of the total population in Northern cities. In New York, slaves made up nearly 5 percent of the city population, while in Philadelphia they accounted for only 0.13 percent of city inhabitants. (See figure 9 for full population details of these two Northern cities and nine Southern cities.)[8]

With one-fifth of its population held in bondage, Washington exhibited distinctly Southern economic and cultural characteristics. Northerners who visited often noted slavery's peculiar hold over the Southern psyche. Writing home to his wife in 1803, for instance, Massachusetts congressman Thomas Dwight observed that there was "no one thing of which the people universally in this part of the Country are so fond of as owning slaves." He marveled that even poor whites and free blacks invested their money in human chattel and that they would continue adding to their stock of this property as often as their earnings permitted. As an example, he explained that the owner of his boardinghouse hired slaves to work as servants from a free black woman who owned as many as eight slaves. This type of "hiring out," common in the urban South, allowed Southerners to achieve some of the efficiency and flexibility of a wage labor system while retaining their right to the ownership of others. Examination of newspaper want ads in Washington has shown that employers remained open to hiring both black and white laborers, freely mixing hired-out slaves with poor white and free black workers. Expressing his disgust with the entire system, Dwight praised God that his home was "in a section of our country where slavery is looked on with abhorrence."[9]

The 1800 Census lists 501 households in Washington but tells us very little beyond the race of the inhabitants and, if they were white, their age and sex. The data show that the average household in the federal city contained 6.4 individuals, including any slaves. But the census does not give the occupations or social status of the heads of these households. Examining the names of the heads of Washington households, we find nineteen original proprietors who signed their land over to President Washington in 1791, as well as many of the smaller landholders from that time. The largest owner of land, Daniel Carroll, is listed as the head of a household consisting of himself, one adult white female, two male and two female white children, and twenty-five slaves. The lists also include land speculators like Thomas Law. Unlike most wealthy developers, Law chose to reside in the city and personally oversee his investment. Those speculators who operated from a distance often sent agents and other employees to manage their operations. For instance, Morris and Nicholson employed William Cranch, a nephew of John and Abigail Adams, to act as their agent in the city. Nicholson also employed a team of men who lived with their families in the city and oversaw construction and supply of his buildings there. The city also attracted some professionals. The heads of household list includes a handful of men known to be lawyers, doctors, and pastors as well as architects and artists interested in the federal building projects. Three hundred to four hundred laborers and mechanics round out the list of Washington householders. This group included at least twenty-six households headed by free blacks.[10]

These laborers recognized an opportunity other than speculation in the new city: steady work. Starting with the laying of the cornerstone for the Capitol on September 18, 1793, work commenced that required carpenters, bricklayers, stonecutters, and overseers. However, the lure of opportunity in the city proved disappointing. The presence of slavery probably dragged down wages. The board employed slaves hired out from local residents in the construction of both the President's House and the Capitol. In 1794, the commissioners resolved to hire out as many as one hundred "good laboring Negroes by the year." In this arrangement, the slaves' owners supplied them with clothes and blankets while the board provided their provisions. In exchange for a year of a slave's labor, the owner received $60. In 1795, reacting to the high wages paid to stonecutters in Philadelphia, Commissioner Thornton proposed hiring out "50 intelligent negroes" from local slave owners for six years and training them as stonecutters. The slaves would do the rough cutting while more experienced cutters did the finish work. He even suggested that if the slaves could be purchased (rather than hired out) and then freed after their service, it would improve the situation by preventing interference from their owners. Although the board did not accept Thornton's recommendation, his plan reflects the commissioners' willingness to rely on slave labor in the construction of the public buildings.[11]

For their part, free workers at the public buildings occasionally appealed to the commissioners for higher wages. In spring 1797, for instance, bricklayers, stonecutters, and their overseers received higher wages after making such a request. But an oversupply of carpenters in the city meant that they received no bump in pay. A year later, when stonecutters again requested a raise, the commissioners responded more forcefully, declaring, "As we have no intention of raising your wages we take the earliest opportunity of letting you know that we shall expect you to quit the public employment at the end of the present month." By early May, as the commissioners inquired about obtaining stonecutters from other cities, those in Washington decided that they were, in fact, content with their wage of $0.66 per day. The board allowed them to return to work and also reaffirmed the wages for other public employees. Stone fitters earned $1.66 per workday, and carpenters took home $1.20. The board set the wages for foremen at the public buildings at $2.00 per day. Their hard line on workers' wages reflects the strength of their control over the labor market in the federal city.[12]

By and large, laborers and poor wage workers in early republic America held little power over their pay or the circumstances of their employment. Despite the rhetoric of freedom employed during the revolution, Americans labored under a system that permitted a wide variety of unequal economic relationships. The enslaved blacks who worked on the public buildings and in the homes and fields of many elite Washingtonians provide the most obvious example of such inequality. However, laws governing apprenticeships, indentures, and the punishment of debtors all created economic relationships that resulted in varying degrees of unfreedom. Likewise, for free married women coveture laws subsumed their legal and economic status to that of their husbands, allowing these men to govern the economic connections forged by their wives. And the lack of social standing of free unmarried women in the community hindered their very ability to take part in economic transactions. The board's summary dismissal of stonecutters who asked for higher wages was a stark reminder to the workers of their tenuous place in the economy. With this action, the board also confirmed its standing as an arbiter of economic relationships within the District, a role many municipal authorities had held since before the revolution.[13]

When the local or regional workforce proved insufficient in numbers or skill, the board looked abroad for workers. During the 1790s, the commissioners inquired about importing Scottish, English, Palatine German, Dutch, and French stonecutters, masons, and bricklayers. If imported as indentured servants, these men would have worked for twenty months to pay the cost of their passage. In July 1792, the commissioners offered to pay the passage of up to one hundred Scottish laborers on their arrival in Georgetown. They proposed paying skilled laborers 20 shillings, or approximately $4.44, per month; unskilled laborers would receive 12 shillings, or $2.66, per month. The commissioners offered these terms to "able single men only." In early 1793, they reconsidered and determined that in some instances they would pay for the passage of the wives of skilled laborers.[14]

The board's willingness to consider passage for wives may have been spurred by the discouraging reports they were receiving from Europe. In September 1792, their contacts in Amsterdam reported that it was "seldom possible to obtain single men without wives, children or aged parents." Two months later, their contact in Glasgow stated that the demand for labor was so high in Scotland and England that few laborers would accept their terms. He pointed out that skilled workers currently earned 21 shillings per day and unskilled workers earned 16 to 18 shillings. He concluded that "good men could not be engaged to go to America unless they were assured of near double the wages which they get here." In April 1793, the board received similar bad news from France, where war and rigid laws against emigration prevented their contact from sending workers to Washington. After these failures, efforts to lure labor from Europe waned. But the commissioners remained open to the prospect, entertaining at least one additional plan for the importation of skilled laborers in the ensuing years. In addition to labor shortages, residents of the new federal city faced cash and supply shortages that contributed to the general sluggishness of the economy.[15]

Early on, the city suffered with the rest of the nation from the lack of hard currency in circulation. In 1792, Secretary of State Jefferson informed the commissioners that a "crush" had occurred in New York and Boston affecting men dealing in paper and those "good merchants and others who had dealings with paper-men." This resulted in "a general stagnation of money contracts." Because it would be unwise for the city to seek a loan during this crisis, they delayed some of their operations. By late 1793, local promoters and the Maryland Assembly had taken a step to improve the supply of money and the broader economy in the District. On December 25, responding to a request from a group of local investors, the Assembly approved the charter for the Bank of Columbia. The charter authorized the bank to enlist subscriptions for capital totaling $1 million over the next seven years. The bank's first president, Samuel Blodgett, later listed the increase of money in circulation as one of the primary benefits of banks like his. Although Washingtonians hoped that the bank would remedy the lack of hard currency available in the city, the shortage continued. In 1797, one of John Nicholson's agents complained, "I am afraid I Shall never be able to carry my Business on, for money is so Scarce here I am not able to sell my bread for ready money."[16]

Two years earlier, Nicholson had hired a local merchant named Lewis Deblois to supervise his construction projects in the city. Right away, Deblois fell victim to Nicholson's mismanagement and the city's difficult economic circumstances. Their workers demanded better pay, something Deblois could not afford. His debts mounted as he attempted to keep the operation up and running. In March 1795, he complained that without funding from Nicholson he would have to abandon the business. Creditors took goods from his store and confiscated any revenue it produced. By the end of the month, Deblois's wife wrote to Nicholson that the stress of indebtedness had "agitated his Spirits to that degree that it has flung him into a most Violent Fever, that rendered him unable to do anything and God only knows how it may End." Another letter followed from Mrs. Deblois, thanking Nicholson for sending $1,350. She assured him that when her husband was well enough to hold a pen, he would thank Nicholson personally.[17]

Lacking connections, supplies, and capital of his own, Deblois became completely reliant on Nicholson. His letters over the next two years detail a downward spiral of debt and poverty. Deblois repeatedly requested money and supplies from Nicholson, who only occasionally obliged. By June 1797, Deblois complained that his shop had been closed for nearly a year and he now had no money left to support his household, which included eight children under sixteen as well as a slave. By this point, however, Nicholson was near bankruptcy and could do nothing to help Deblois or the other agents and laborers he had failed to pay.[18]

Desperate pleas like those of Mr. and Mrs. Deblois were all too common in the federal city at the close of the eighteenth century. Agents of absentee speculators, laborers at the public works, landed proprietors, speculators, and the city commissioners all spent considerable time requesting, demanding, cajoling, convincing, and downright begging others for money. Comparing the state of the city on the government's arrival in fall 1800 to the grand vision put forth by President Washington and symbolized by the L'Enfant plan, the obvious question arises as to what had gone awry on the banks of the Potomac during the previous decade. The reactions of visitors and the economic and demographic realities of city life suggest major flaws in both the plan and its execution.

L'Enfant's plan offered a metropolis appropriate for the dynamic and powerful empire he hoped the American republic would become. However, neither of those characteristics accurately described the United States in 1791 or in 1800 when Congress removed to the city. Meager revenues ensured that the federal government could not fund construction of the capital on its own. At the same time, a tight credit market and the failure of Blodgett's joint-stock scheme further restricted the funding options for the city. In response, President Washington and his commissioners followed the irresistible siren song of American land development and turned to speculation as a means of funding city development and the public buildings. They defrayed the cost of acquiring land by folding the original landowners into the speculation scheme. And finally, they allowed professional speculators to entangle thousands of city lots in a nationwide web of worthless landholdings and false promises. The federal government's weakness and penury exacerbated the problems caused by these decisions. Rendered almost powerless by a federal system from which their district had been expressly excluded, the commissioners grasped in every direction for assistance and for the authority to make the best of their difficult situation.

This decade-long struggle resulted in the transfer of the U.S. government to a barely developed and sparsely populated town inside the shell of a grand metropolis. The federal city seemed comically, even grotesquely, underdeveloped. But in the end the government did relocate to the shores of the Potomac in 1800. And because they took the reins of power in 1801, it would be up to Jefferson and his fellow Democratic-Republicans to guide future development in the federal city.

PART II

A "Federal Town" on the Potomac

In spring 1803, workers began planting five hundred Lombardy poplar trees along Pennsylvania Avenue between the President's House and the Capitol. The trees were aligned in four rows along the mile-and-a-half stretch of road. According to President Jefferson's specific instructions, workers planted the outer two rows 24 feet from the edges of the avenue and placed the inner rows an additional 33 feet toward the road's center. The rows of trees divided the 160-foot avenue into three carriageways: two paths 33 feet wide flanking a 46-foot-wide central passage (fig. 10). Together the tree planting and road improvements cost nearly $12,000 and took three years to complete.[1]

Recently introduced into the United States from Europe, the Lombardy poplar quickly became a favorite of American gardeners and estate owners. Jefferson added the trees to the carefully planned landscape of Monticello, his Virginia plantation. America's amateur arborists and landscape architects appreciated the trees for their height, rapid growth, and exceptional straightness, characteristics that made them excellent privacy hedges and attractive complements on avenues.[2]

Along this primary corridor in the federal city, the trees served both purposes. A citizen of the young republic could stand along this stretch of Pennsylvania Avenue and look from the elegant President's House to the northwest to the unfinished but still grandiose Capitol building rising on its hill to the southeast. Within a few years of their planting, the trees provided an elegant frame for these views, drawing the eye toward these symbols of American republicanism. At the same time, the

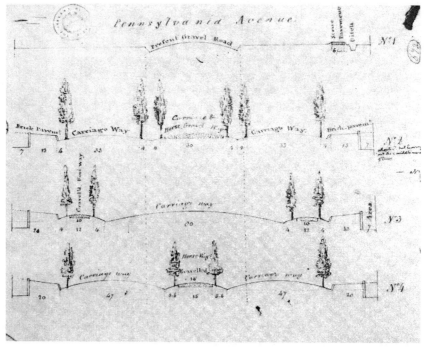

FIGURE 10. *Jefferson's Planting Plan for Pennsylvania Avenue*, 1803, by Nicholas King. Jefferson selected the second option but omitted the two innermost rows of trees. (Library of Congress, Manuscript Division)

trees would have prevented the same observer from seeing much of the sprawling, thinly developed areas that lay beyond the government buildings at the city's core.[3]

The twin effects of beautifying Pennsylvania Avenue and obscuring the rest of the city fit neatly into Jefferson's vision for what he sometimes called the "federal town." Jefferson earnestly supported the establishment of impressive and architecturally significant public buildings along with improvement of their grounds and the roads that connected them. On these issues his long-held interests in architecture and landscape design complemented his desire to adorn the capital with classical republican symbolism. Using the poplars, therefore, Jefferson provided ornamentation for the governmental core of the city while also separating it from the surrounding urban area. And since they cost only $0.125 each, the poplar saplings accomplished these aesthetic chores at minimal government expense, keeping the project in line with Jefferson's political ideology, which called for a federal government with limited power over the states and the citizenry and an even more limited fiscal impact on the nation.[4]

Jefferson and his political party, the Democratic-Republicans, promoted an agrarian vision of the United States in which independent farmers and artisans provided a solid foundation for a virtuous republic. In his *Notes on the State of Virginia*, Jefferson famously wrote that "those who labour in the earth are the chosen people of God, if ever he had a chosen people, whose breasts he made his peculiar deposite for substantial and genuine virtue." For the Virginian, virtue was vital to the republic because it allowed citizens to set aside their personal desires and vote and act in the best interests of the community. He worried that wage laborers might sacrifice their virtue and become subservient to the employers or customers on whom their livelihoods depended. Because manufacturing operations and large urban areas fostered such unequal relationships, Jefferson rejected the establishment of manufacturing in the United States, and he hoped that the "mobs of great cities" would remain in Europe. In 1800, he even suggested that a recent outbreak of yellow fever might discourage the growth of large cities, which he regarded as "pestilential to the morals, the health and the liberties of man." This antiurban sentiment proved popular and politically effective in the early republic period, as rural voters predominated. Consequently, Democratic-Republicans who shared Jefferson's views controlled Congress and the presidency for decades after Jefferson's election in 1800. Jefferson preferred to keep the federal city small to protect the government from the corrupting influences of the manufacturers, wage laborers, wealthy aristocrats, and ragged beggars who infested the large capital cities of Europe. Just as Washington and L'Enfant's grand plan for the city had reflected their vision for the new republic, the limited role played by the federal government in the District of Columbia between Jefferson's election and the War of 1812 reflected the vision of Jefferson and his party.[5]

However, many leading District residents sought to revive Washington's grand vision. Newcomers drawn to the seat of government joined together with longtime residents and attempted to establish municipal services and fund infrastructure projects. These divergent visions for the city pitted local residents against federal officials in a contest to determine whether a grand metropolis or a simple town would rise along the shores of the Potomac.

4 /   Jeffersonians and the Federal City

With the possible exception of Washington, no individual had more influence on the development of the national capital than Thomas Jefferson. As the republic's first secretary of state (1790–93), Jefferson served as an adviser and mediator for Washington. In this capacity, he had a hand in passage of the Residence Act, which established the seat of government on the Potomac; negotiations with the original landowners over the terms of their land cession to the government; management of the troublesome architect Peter Charles L'Enfant; and implementation of the city plan. In all of these roles he deferred to the will of the president, setting aside his own ideological dislike for large urban areas and actively supporting the growth and development of the federal district.

In 1790, the issues of federal assumption of state war debts and location of the national capital divided the new American government. According to Jefferson, he played a crucial role in fostering a compromise by bringing Alexander Hamilton and James Madison together for a dinner at his residence in New York in June 1790. As Washington's secretary of the treasury, Hamilton had proposed a national financial system in which the federal government would assume the war debts of the state governments. This plan met opposition from representatives of states, largely but not exclusively in the South, that had already retired their debts and from those who feared that the plan gave too much fiscal power to the federal government. As an influential congressman from Virginia, Madison could sway Southern support behind Hamilton's plan. In exchange, according to Jefferson, Hamilton agreed to make

minor alterations to the assumption bill and to support a bill establishing a permanent seat of government on the Potomac, the southernmost
site then under consideration.[1]

After the passage of the Residence Bill, Jefferson served as Washington's most important adviser on matters relating to the federal city. In
spring 1791, the secretary of state conveyed Washington's instructions
for laying out a city plan to Major L'Enfant. Jefferson appreciated the
opportunity to provide input on the city's architectural and design
elements, two subjects quite close to his heart. Before long, however,
L'Enfant's refusal to cooperate with the commissioners created considerably more vexing chores for the secretary of state. Both Washington
and Jefferson attempted to convince L'Enfant to submit to the oversight
of the commissioners in late fall and winter 1791–92. In February 1792,
Jefferson told L'Enfant that his position must be "in subordination to the
Commissioners." L'Enfant responded with a long critique of the commissioners' actions and resolutely asserted that he could not, and would
not, submit to their authority. Washington then dispatched his personal
secretary, Tobias Lear, in a final effort to change the Frenchman's mind
in person. After the visit from Lear proved fruitless, Jefferson communicated the president's decision that despite his desire "to preserve [his]
agency in the business," L'Enfant's service to the government was at an
end.[2]

Jefferson also represented Washington's views in dealings with local
officials and elites. In September 1791, Washington sent Jefferson and
Madison to Georgetown for meetings with the commissioners and some
of the original proprietors of land in the city. Washington wanted their
input on the sale of lots, the payment to the landowners, building codes,
and the naming of the streets, the city, and the federal district. Jefferson
reported back to Washington that having been "preadmonished that
they should decide freely on their own view of things," the commissioners concurred on every point "with what had been thought best in
Philadelphia." Jefferson and Madison also encouraged the landholders
to pressure the Virginia and Maryland Assemblies to endorse the Residence Bill and to appropriate the money needed to get the project under
way.[3]

In July 1793, Washington placed Jefferson at the center of a dispute
between the architects involved with construction of the Capitol. A self-
taught architect, William Thornton, had won the contest held by the
District commissioners to determine the design for the building. Thornton's Capitol featured a columned portico and central dome flanked by

two ornately decorated wings, one for each of the two houses of Congress (fig. 11). Washington called the plan "much superior" to any he had seen, and Jefferson cheered Thornton's Capitol as "simple, noble, beautiful, excellently distributed, and moderate in size." Unfortunately, the professional architect hired to implement it, Stephen Hallet, found numerous flaws in Thornton's plan. Along with James Hoban, designer of the President's House, Hallet insisted that the Thornton design would result in architectural instability, displeasing aesthetics, and high building costs. Learning of these objections, Washington instructed Jefferson to get the parties together and "after hearing the objections and explanations report [his] opinion on the case and the plan which ought to be executed." Meeting with Thornton, Hallet, and Hoban, as well as two additional Philadelphia builders, Jefferson oversaw the creation of a compromise plan that mitigated most of the structural and aesthetic issues raised by the professional architects and cut expected construction costs in half. Jefferson described the new plan as Dr. Thornton's "reduced into practicable form." As a connoisseur of classical architecture, Jefferson no doubt relished the opportunity to influence the Capitol. And as a public servant, he dutifully followed Washington's instructions for handling the dispute.[4]

After he left public office in 1793, Jefferson's influence on the development of the federal city declined considerably. During his brief "retirement," coinciding with Washington's second term, and during the four years he endured as vice president to John Adams, 1797 to 1801, Jefferson seldom engaged with the national capital. After his defeat of Adams in the election of 1800 and assumption of the presidency in 1801, however, Jefferson took up Washington's mantle as the key decision maker for the city. As chief executive for the District, Jefferson implemented an approach to city policy more deeply rooted in his own political ideology.

Unlike President Adams, who delegated most city issues to his cabinet, Jefferson personally addressed many of even the most minor decisions. In June 1801, for instance, Jefferson approved a request from the District commissioners to expand the area allowed between a private dwelling and the street to seven feet, as the previous five-foot span had been deemed "too confined." Similarly, in summer 1802, the marshal for the District, Daniel Brent, asked for input from the commander in chief regarding the method for affixing bars to the windows of the city jail. When Congress appropriated $8,000 for the jail's construction in spring 1802, Jefferson issued instructions for fixing the bars in iron frames. Encountering resistance to that technique from the builder,

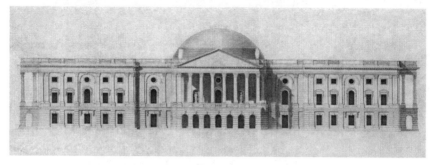

FIGURE 11. Detail of Thornton's original design for the Capitol. (Library of Congress, Prints and Photographs Division)

George Hadfield, Brent sought clarification from the president because he did not feel "at liberty to make a change without [his] directions." Brent's unwillingness to disobey Jefferson's instructions speaks to the president's control over federal architecture in Washington. And when it came to the President's House and the Capitol, no aspect of those projects escaped his notice.[5]

In March 1803, Jefferson appointed Benjamin Henry Latrobe to the position of surveyor of the public buildings. From that point until 1812, the British-born architect oversaw construction of the two buildings, dramatically improving the quality and pace of work. Still unfinished more than a decade after the cornerstone had been laid in 1792, the president's residence suffered from a leaky roof and crumbling plaster. During the Jefferson and Madison administrations, Latrobe repaired, expanded, and adapted the building to suit the needs of its occupants. He corrected flaws caused by shoddy construction, built fireproof office areas, added badly needed stables, and began work on grand porticoes that he designed for the north and south entrances.[6]

Latrobe also improved the mansion's grounds. In 1800, a local resident described them as a "great confusion" of old brick kilns, water pits, and rubbish. Latrobe surrounded the area with a stone wall, constructed a circular road around the building, and landscaped the unsightly grounds in the style of an informal English garden. Each of these projects received close attention from and inspection by Jefferson who lived on-site. And while he did not often visit the Capitol, the president also kept careful watch over the work being done there through frequent correspondence with Latrobe.[7]

The president hoped that Latrobe could complete the Capitol in the course of two building seasons. In the same bill that established Latrobe's position, Congress appropriated $50,000 for repair and alterations to the Capitol and other public buildings. Jefferson told Latrobe that he expected that $5,000 or $10,000 might be required for "covering the north wing of the Capitol and the president's house" and that the remaining funds would be applied to raising the south wing as far as could be completed that first season. He had no doubt that Congress would appropriate a similar sum the following year and that the building could be completed by the end of 1804.[8]

Unfortunately, neither the two-year time line nor the $100,000 budget proved adequate for completing the public buildings. In December 1804, Latrobe told Jefferson "that a sensible portion of the appropriation by Congress has necessarily been expended in pulling down or repairing what was done insufficiently, previously to the Year 1803." Discovering flawed materials and workmanship at every turn, Latrobe ordered the south wing of the Capitol pulled down to the foundation so that work could begin anew. In the north wing, he learned that insufficient light and poor air circulation had caused timbers in the ceilings and walls to decay. Four years later, Latrobe forwarded to Jefferson a sample of what he called the "strongest specimen" of dry rot that he had ever encountered. The sample came from the timbers that supported the Senate chamber in the north wing. He estimated that within two or three years the Senate chamber would have collapsed if the problem was not corrected. Of course, all of these problems created significant delays and cost overruns. Latrobe blamed the previous superintendents of work at the Capitol, Stephen Hallet, George Hadfield, and James Hoban, and the original designer, William Thornton. As a city commissioner, Thornton had held authority over each of the three superintendents. And, one by one, each came into conflict with Thornton and resigned. Working from the designs of an amateur that had been interpreted and altered by three other architects, Latrobe had inherited a Capitol riddled with architectural flaws.[9]

As Latrobe requested additional time and funding to complete the Capitol, Congress grew impatient with him. After the arrival of the government in 1800, the discomforts of the incomplete Capitol became an everyday issue for the members of Congress. In addition, during the 1790s, the city commissioners had funded construction of the Capitol with money from the sales of city lots, from the initial donations by Maryland and Virginia, and from loans they had acquired for the capital.

When seeking funding directly from Congress in March 1798, the commissioners reported that the work on the Capitol to that point had cost $229,223.97 and that an appropriation of $200,000 would allow them to complete it and other public buildings. Rather than appropriate the funds, however, Congress merely approved a loan of $100,000 for the commissioners. Now that Congress had taken control of the city, funding the public works required appropriations from the Treasury. And despite their frequent complaints about the pace of Latrobe's work and the cost the building, members of Congress appropriated more than $495,000 for the Capitol between 1801 and 1813.[10]

Throughout these many setbacks, Jefferson closely followed the Capitol construction project. When negotiations between Latrobe and Thornton over proposed changes to the House chamber soured early in 1804, Jefferson stepped in to decide on a course of action. He reminded Latrobe that Washington and the commissioners had selected Thornton's plan in the original competition, and he instructed him to adhere to the plan as much as was possible, asserting that it was "to overcome difficulties that we employ men of genius." The president regarded the completion of Thornton's neoclassical Capitol as a project of the utmost importance for the nation. Jefferson believed that public buildings carried great symbolic and aesthetic power and that they "should be more than things of beauty and convenience; above all, they should state a creed." Thornton's use of classical Greek and Roman architectural features provided an unmistakable link between the American republic and its classical precursors.[11]

In 1807, Jefferson displayed his strict dedication to classical architecture at the Capitol when he vetoed Latrobe's request to add a small, open structure to the top of the dome above the House chamber to allow in light and air. The architect hoped that the addition would prevent water vapor from gathering on the skylights and causing condensation to rain down into the chamber. Today the central dome of the Capitol includes just such an architectural feature, called a lantern, immediately below the Statue of Freedom. Reminding Latrobe of his reverence for Greek and Roman architecture, Jefferson insisted that he did not "recollect ever to have seen in their buildings a single instance of a lanthern, Cupola, or belfry." Consequently, he forbade Latrobe from erecting any such "degeneracies of modern architecture." The president's unwillingness to permit even this minor alteration speaks to the symbolic value he placed on the use of classical architectural forms for public buildings.[12]

The classic texts of ancient Greece and Rome had served as the foundation of the educations of Jefferson and all liberally educated members of his generation. And many of the ideological origins of the American Revolution had their roots in the classical Greek and Roman republics. Jefferson and the members of his party believed that the promotion of agriculture and widespread landownership would allow Americans to adapt this classical model to their larger and more populous republic. Even at the very outset of the revolution, Jefferson had advocated giving physical form to the ideals of the republic by designing public buildings in the classical style. When serving as governor of Virginia in 1776, for example, he proposed moving the state capital from Williamsburg to Richmond and provided the plans for a new state capitol building modeled after a Roman temple.[13]

Despite occasional disagreements with Jefferson, the unexpected costs, and the steady stream of difficulties, Latrobe made considerable progress at the Capitol. Crediting the president for these accomplishments in 1807, Latrobe declared, "The works already erected in this city are the monuments of your judgment and of your zeal and of your taste." He added, "I am not ashamed to say that my pride is not a little flattered and my professional ambition roused when I think that my grandchildren may at some future day read that after the turbulence of revolution and of faction which characterized the two first presidencies, their ancestor was the instrument in your hands to decorate the tranquility, the prosperity, and the happiness of your government." These effusive sentiments no doubt stemmed in part from the fact that the cost overruns at the public buildings had significantly degraded Latrobe's reputation and, consequently, his job security. However, Latrobe's words also reflected the president's goals for the public works. For Jefferson, the rapid rise and external beauty of the President's House and the Capitol symbolized exactly "the tranquility, the prosperity, and the happiness" he hoped his policies would bring to the nation. While he may well have been flattering the president to keep his job, Latrobe knew precisely what chords to strike with Jefferson on the subject of the public buildings. This Jeffersonian vision for the nation guided the work not only at the Capitol and the President's House but also at the city's other major government facility, the Navy Yard.[14]

Established in 1799, the Washington Navy Yard underwent a rapid transformation from representing the military might of the young republic to embodying Jefferson's desire that the nation avoid military conflict. Congress established the yard during the Adams administration at the height of America's Quasi-War with France. During this dispute, American naval ships engaged the French at sea in an effort to prevent the French seizure of American merchant ships bound for Great Britain. A 1799 act of Congress appropriated $1 million for the construction of six large frigates. Washington booster and secretary of the navy, Benjamin Stoddert, elected to use some of that funding to establish navy yards in Boston, New York, Philadelphia, Portsmouth, Norfolk, and Washington. Stoddert envisioned the yards as places to build, repair, and equip the rapidly expanding U.S. Navy. But before Jefferson took office in 1801, the Adams administration negotiated an end to hostilities with France. And, once in office, Jefferson began to reduce the size of the navy.[15]

In March 1801, Congress instructed the president to reduce the navy to peacetime levels. The act providing for a "Naval Peace Establishment" designated six frigates for continued service and relegated the remainder of the fleet to be laid up in dry docks, a process by which the ships would be dismantled and their pieces stored for reassembly in a time of war. Two years before appointing him surveyor of the public buildings, Jefferson hired Latrobe to construct the dry docks at the Washington Navy Yard. Never one to miss an opportunity to micromanage an architectural endeavor, Jefferson immediately sent Latrobe detailed plans for dry docks similar to those used in Europe. After his promotion to the surveyor's position in 1803, Latrobe developed a full plan for the yard that included a stone gate building, shipbuilding slips, work and storage sheds, and housing for the commandant and other officers. Gradually Latrobe put much of this plan in place in the years prior to the War of 1812. Like his work on the other public buildings, his conversion of the yard from a construction facility to one designed to store a largely mothballed fleet represented a physical manifestation of Jefferson's Democratic-Republican ideology. During the early years of his presidency, Jefferson held true to traditional republican philosophy, which assumed that a large standing army and navy threatened the stability of the nation by draining limited resources and by allowing the military to promote its power over the public.[16]

When making decisions concerning the city beyond the public buildings, Jefferson generally approved only those requests that required little to no federal spending. This conditional support for public infrastructure in the city also matched the president's ideological goals of limiting the size of both the city and the federal government. In November 1802, for example, a committee representing residents living west of the President's House asked Jefferson to establish a market site in their neighborhood. The previous year, the board had provided some funding for the establishment of a market along Pennsylvania Avenue between the President's House and the Capitol. These citizens now hoped to create a market on that same thoroughfare approximately halfway to Georgetown. In response, Jefferson issued a proclamation appropriating the land at the intersection of Pennsylvania Avenue, I Street North, and 20th Street West. He made no mention of funding for the market. If the residents did request funds, they were likely rebuffed by either the president or the commissioners because the market was too far from the city's governmental core. Three years later, in 1805, Jefferson issued a similar proclamation establishing a market near the intersection of Georgia and Virginia Avenues in the south of the city. And once again, he provided no funding for the project.[17]

As the federal city gradually became transformed from a landscape of plantations, orchards, and woodlands to the urban form promised by the published city plan, the president chose passive, low-cost methods for guiding the city's transition. For example, the subject of enclosed land often dogged city relations with the original proprietors. By the terms of their agreement with Washington, the landowners retained the right to utilize and enclose, or fence in, their land until it was sold to a third party or it was needed for city or federal use. Jefferson respected these rights but also endeavored to wean the landowners off of their enclosures. In particular the president complained of enclosures in the northeastern quarter that inhibited travel in and out of the city and were "not employed in raising garden stuff or grass or any other article which might accommodate the City, but are worn down in Indian Corn." In February 1806, he decided that when landowners removed their fences for any reason from land designated for streets, they lost the right to enclose the land again.[18]

Jefferson wanted the land opened and used as common grassland to support cattle owned by the city's poor. Setting aside common land in this way would have put city policy in line with urban planning practices common throughout the nation. During the previous two centuries, British colonists and city planners had set aside parcels of land within and just outside cities like Plymouth, Philadelphia, and Savannah. Modeled after similar commons found in British cities, these areas provided pasture and woodland for the use of city residents as well as for the city itself in order to expand.. But unlike the agricultural commons of rural England, which landowners had gradually enclosed since the 1500s, some urban commons remained open to the public into the nineteenth century. In this way, Jefferson sought to act as a good steward for the city but also to limit the federal government's role in its development. In his view, federal responsibility ended with the provision of a basic foundation on which locals could later improve.[19]

In March 1807, Washington mayor Robert Brent politely wrote to President Jefferson with a request. Brent noted that the last Congress had appropriated $3,000 to be applied at the president's discretion to improve roads, streets, and avenues in the District. Brent asked "the favor of you, if you do not deem it improper, to direct an application of a part of that fund to the opening and improving the Delaware and Maryland Avenues from the Capitol to their intersection with the potowmack." Delaware Avenue connected the Capitol to the deepwater wharves of the city's southern peninsula. Within a few years, Maryland Avenue would extend over the Potomac via a bridge onto the Virginia side of the river. The mayor explained that, in addition to improving the city's connection to nearby communities, opening these avenues would help ensure that the "Houses which have so long been in a ruinous state" at the river's edge would be occupied by "respectable and Reputable Inhabitants." Finally, Brent reminded the president that investment in the area would benefit the family of Notley Young, who had given up much of his land to the federal government. Brent felt that improving the connection of this area to the center of the city would reward Brent's sacrifice.[20]

Jefferson replied the very next day. Using language as dismissive as Brent's had been humble, he explained that he would not use federal money to open and improve the streets in question. Although Congress had appropriated funds for the avenues and roads of the District of Columbia, that body had no intention of paying for any roads other than those that connected the government's buildings. Jefferson argued that the broad language in the appropriation stemmed not from Congress's desire to expand its role in the District but from a lack of time to craft more specific legislation before the close of session. He stated flatly, "We cannot suppose Congress intended to tax the people of the U.S. at large for all the avenues in Washington & roads in Columbia." In any case, Jefferson supposed, the entire appropriation would be needed for improvements to the stretch of Pennsylvania Avenue between the public buildings. Brent and the city would receive no federal funding for Maryland and Delaware Avenues.[21]

Both Brent and Jefferson promoted differing views of the city. Their conflict represents a small piece of a much larger process occurring in the early republic in which Americans developed what architectural historian Dell Upton has called a "republican spatial imagination." This term refers to the complex and conflict-ridden process by which American politicians, elites, and city officials translated social, political, and economic goals into physical and spatial forms. For example, the efforts of city planners to establish gridiron street plans in American cities reflected their preoccupation with order and established the means by which city officials could organize, separate, and classify residents. This rational organization of the cities paralleled the republican efforts to create a rational and orderly system of government. Although both Brent and Jefferson participated in the social construction of this republican spatial imagination, their disagreement highlights their differing goals for the federal city.[22]

For Americans in the early republic, the idea of improvement carried connotations beyond the simple act of making something better. Starting in the second half of the eighteenth century, Britons began to use the term in reference to public or private projects designed to rebuild, reform, and revitalize different parts of London. As one historian's examination of the term's definitions as printed in Noah Webster's 1828 dictionary has revealed, the idea of improvement "blended work, productivity, progress, and righteousness." For example, in upstate New York when wealthy merchants funded the construction of new cities and transportation infrastructure, they viewed the cities as agents of improvement because they brought positive social change to the Native Americans and unruly settlers of the frontier. Brent's desire to attract "responsible and Reputable Inhabitants" to the southern tip of the city shows the same logic. Supporters of urban improvements, therefore, sought to mitigate and even reverse the negative effects of urbanization that Jefferson viewed as reasons to avoid settling large numbers of Americans in urban areas.[23]

In general, Congress followed Jefferson's lead when it came to development and improvement in the federal city. After it took up residence in Washington in the waning months of the Adams administration, Congress quickly exercised the right to "exclusive legislation" over the federal district guaranteed to it by the Constitution. In early 1801, the Federalist-dominated, lame duck Sixth Congress established a legal system for the District. Laws in force in Virginia and Maryland on December 1, 1800, became the legal codes for the areas that had previously belonged to those states. Congress also authorized the president to appoint judges, marshals, and justices of the peace for the District. However, the Federalists failed to create a local government for the federal city before their time in office ran out.[24]

Many District residents objected when the laws passed in 1801 provided no means for them to vote in national elections. Without the umbrella legal authority of a state, District residents found themselves disenfranchised from the federal electoral system. Locals argued over whether the benefits of federal jurisdiction over the District outweighed the loss of their voice in congressional and presidential elections. As it had been merely a quarter century since the nation had declared its independence from Great Britain, the irony that Congress expected residents of the federal district to accept taxation without representation was lost on no one. In Congress, however, most members accepted the logic that having a federal district prevented any single state from unduly influencing the federal government. During an 1803 debate over retrocession of the District to Maryland and Virginia, for example, the Delaware Federalist James Bayard argued that their lack of voting rights did not reduce the residents of the District to the status of slaves as some had argued. Instead these Americans were free and "willing to live under the protection of Congress." And he noted that the retrocession debate carried a "more serious consideration relative to the people of the Territory," the fact that without a federal district, the government would have no obligation to remain in Washington. Agitation by Northern lawmakers, financiers, and businessmen to move the seat of government back to a Northern city had begun even before the arrival of the government in Washington. In 1798, for example, the Massachusetts Federalist Benjamin Goodhue had warned Commissioner White that once established on the Potomac, the government had no obligation to stay. Since the fortunes and livelihoods of most District residents hinged on the government remaining in Washington, they did not feel comfortable complaining about the loss of their rights.[25]

With the city established and a charter for a local government making its way through Congress, the federal government no longer needed a full board to oversee the District. On May 1, 1802, Congress abolished the Board of Commissioners. Decisions regarding the sale of government lots and the construction of public buildings shifted to a single superintendent of the city. Jefferson chose the commissioners' clerk and postmaster of Washington, Thomas Munroe, for the position.[26]

In the same bill, Congress began cleanup of the city's financial mess, directing the superintendent to sell off city lots in order to make the payments due on the Maryland loans. In effect, Congress overturned the board's long-standing policy of avoiding a large public sell-off and of holding onto lots in the hope that in the future they would sell at a higher price. Jefferson allowed the sale to proceed, and Munroe began advertising in June 1802. Sales began on August 30 and continued until October 29. During these two months, Munroe sold 866.5 lots and netted $26,848.10. He reported to Jefferson that the number of lots for sale was "much greater than the demand" and that selling so many lots in such a brief period disadvantaged the sale. However, they did raise enough money to pay the installments due on the Maryland loans.[27]

Two days after establishing the superintendent's office, Congress incorporated Washington City, giving Washingtonians a degree of self-government. The new city government consisted of a presidentially appointed mayor and a two-chambered city council. Taxpaying free white men twenty-five years of age and older who had resided in the city for at least a year gained the right to elect the twelve-man city council. After a general election, the council members would choose five of their ranks to serve as an upper council. The remaining seven made up the lower council. Ordinances passed by the council could be vetoed by the mayor, but a veto could be overturned by a three-fourths majority vote in both chambers.[28]

A holdover from English feudal tradition, chartered municipal corporations provided local elites in commercial areas with a means of organizing their own affairs. By providing for presidential appointment of the mayor and by retaining a property requirement for voting rights in Washington, Congress offered residents a less liberal city charter than other cities received from their states in this period. In doing so, Congress retained more authority over its federal city. And as it had the year before, Congress continued to exclude District residents from federal elections.[29]

The city charter defined Congress's relationship with Washington. Exclusive jurisdiction meant that Congress could assign discrete tasks to the local government but retain the right to interfere. In the charter, Congress delegated responsibility for construction and development of the city to the newly incorporated local government. The act gave the corporation "full power and authority" to impose and collect taxes; protect public health and safety; regulate and license various industries, including liquor sales, hackney carriages, and public amusements;

prevent and extinguish fires; restrain or prohibit gambling; and even "establish the size of bricks" in the city. The long list of powers also included authority "to erect and repair bridges; to keep in repair all necessary streets, avenues, drains and sewers, and to pass regulations necessary for the preservation of the same, agreeably to the plan of the said city." In 1804, responding to requests from local officials, Congress amended the articles of incorporation, providing for direct election of both council chambers and adding to the city's enumerated responsibilities. In 1812, again responding to petitions from the city government, Congress expanded the council to twenty men who would represent four newly drawn wards in the city and turned the appointment of the mayor over to that body. These changes put the city's charter more in line with those of other early republic municipalities.[30]

The committees for the District of Columbia in both the House and the Senate received numerous requests from city officials and local residents. Congress typically approved charters for private development projects and new city institutions such as turnpike, bridge, and insurance companies, as well as several banks. Unfortunately, the congressional records provide little detail of the debates over these bills. In addition, the few existing vote tallies suggest that neither party, nor section clearly determined the voting pattern. When discussing the erection of a bridge over the Potomac in 1806, for example, representatives focused on its possible benefits to national commerce and the chance that Georgetown's markets would be hurt. A House vote on the bill resulted in sixty-one votes in favor of the bill and forty-nine against. Majorities in both parties favored the bill but not without significant dissent. Among Federalists, six of the twenty-two voting members, 27 percent, voted against bill, and thirty-three of seventy-seven voting Democratic-Republicans, 43 percent, also opposed the measure. Examination of the vote by state delegations paints an equally muddled picture. Every state delegation with more than two members split its votes on the bill. And, by and large, the various sections of the country voted for and against the bill in similar proportions. When it came to providing actual appropriations for work in the city, Congress limited funding to the public buildings and improvements to Pennsylvania Avenue. In 1810, for example, Congress passed an act making "a public highway" of a road leading through county lands north of Washington City to the Eastern Branch. It assigned to the levy court of Washington County, the governing body of the unincorporated parts of the District on the Maryland side of the Potomac, the power to appoint a three-man commission to survey the road and determine the appropriate compensation owed to its original owners. However, Congress left responsibility for payment to the landowners and upkeep of the road to the county authorities. Even when Congress acted in the interest of the District, its unfunded mandates increased the burden borne by its residents.[31]

After taking office in 1809, Madison maintained Jefferson's spending policies in regard to the federal city. In his first term, federal outlays remained limited to the federal buildings and their immediate surroundings. Latrobe's work advanced rapidly at the Capitol. In addition, Madison and his wife, Dolley, authorized resumed work on the President's House. Jefferson had largely ignored the residence after the initial spurt of improvements made early in his presidency. Dolley Madison collaborated closely with Latrobe to redesign and furnish the executive mansion, which, by this point, locals referred to as the White House thanks to the whitewash applied to its sandstone exterior. Just months after the Madisons moved into the residence, the first lady and the architect completed a small sitting room (now the Red Room) designed for the reception of ladies who came calling during the rounds of visiting that defined the social scene of Washington elites. By January 1, 1810, they had completed a larger oval drawing room, which was used for more formal events. The pair then launched work on a large dining room suitable for the grand state dinners that the Madisons had reinstated. From this newly renovated residence, James and Dolley Madison altered the social practices of elite Washingtonians and government officials by expanding the number and size of public interactions with the president and the first lady. In these events the first lady promoted what one historian has called her "nationalist mission." For the oval drawing room, for instance, Dolley commissioned Greek-style furniture, including thirty-six chairs with the insignia of the United States on their backs, making simultaneous use of the classical aesthetic tradition and distinctly American symbols. And throughout the executive mansion, she selected artwork that conveyed this nationalist ideal, including portraits of American heroes and examples of domestic manufactures.[32]

In July 1812, Congress authorized President Madison to lease public land in the city, including the National Mall, on terms that would "best effect the improvement of the said grounds for public walks, botanic gardens, or other public purposes." Congress hoped that leaseholders might accomplish what it refused to attempt: namely, development of neglected areas of the city. A month after the bill's passage,

Superintendent Munroe received the first inquiry about the program from John P. Van Ness, who expressed interest in portions of the president's square (now known as Lafayette Square), the National Mall, and Capitol Square. Van Ness had come to the city as a congressman from New York in 1801 and married Marcia Burnes, the daughter and heiress of David Burnes, the original owner of much of the land between the President's House and the Capitol. Van Ness relocated to the federal city and became a leader in local society. He hoped to lease all available government lands previously owned by his father-in-law. However, Van Ness would not commit without knowing the president's terms and conditions for such leases. Unfortunately, the superintendent's records do not show whether Van Ness added any of the former Burnes land to his real estate portfolio.[33]

The records do contain paperwork submitted by Mountjoy Bailey to lease the easternmost portion of the Mall, roughly from 1st Street to 7th Street West. Approximately half of this land once belonged to Burnes. The other half had been sold to the government by another large proprietor, Daniel Carroll. Bailey paid $1,000 to lease the land for ten years, the maximum term allowed by the law, and immediately rented part of the property to a third party for $400. Presumably, Bailey intended to seek other renters for the remainder of the property or to make use of it himself. The lease required Bailey to improve the land by "draining, clearing & cultivating the same in such manner as to render it dry & level & prepared it for future public purposes, for public walks, or pleasure grounds." Following the advice of Congress, Madison and Munroe encouraged the use of private capital to develop this public land.[34]

Jefferson and Madison shared the goal of turning the young republic into an empire of liberty. Their vision required a federal government incapable, either militarily or economically, of oppressing its citizens or of dominating the states of the union. At the same time, the citizens in this empire would need reminding not of the power of their government but of the powerful ideals upon which the revolutionary generation had founded it. Jefferson's willingness to endure Latrobe's delays and deficits and his insistence on strict adherence to classical traditions reveal the importance of this symbolism to him. He hoped that the public areas in the city would provide a showcase of classical republican imagery set amidst a virtuous and decidedly unpretentious local population. This classical imagery not only linked the republic to those of antiquity but also bolstered the Jeffersonian political ideology by privileging the classical over the modern and the virtue of the agricultural republic over the depravity of the manufacturing empire. The Democratic-Republicans in Congress and Madison followed Jefferson's example. Without any say in the federal electoral system, District residents could expect oversight from federal officials but little in the way of concrete support.

5 /   The Limits of Local Control

Despite the Jeffersonian shift away from federal support of the District of Columbia, local residents stepped up their efforts to promote and develop the national capital. By 1812, locals had taken the reins of city governance, enacting city ordinances, establishing property taxes, regulating economic activity, and providing minor infrastructure repair and development. The local government also created a social safety net to feed, wash, and clothe the city's poorest white residents. At the same time, elite Washington residents sought to improve the appearance and reputation of the city by building impressive new houses. For larger improvement projects such as bridges and toll roads, local elites pooled their available capital to charter companies to and administer infrastructure projects such as bridges and toll roads.

However, the antagonistic attitude of some members of Congress toward the District of Columbia created an atmosphere of uncertainty and fear among the local leaders. In March 1804, for example, Senator Robert Wright, a Democratic-Republican from Maryland, explained that he had proposed a bill calling for the removal of the seat of government to Baltimore not with the intention that it should pass but instead so that it would act "as a spur to the inhabitants of Washington to effect a more complete accommodation of Congress." In addition, he proposed postponing further consideration of the bill until May, which would, "by hanging the bill over their heads, most powerfully tend to produce the desirable result of a concentration of the city, and an augmentation of accommodation." Although Wright's proposal did not win enough votes to pass, his efforts reflect the drastic imbalance of power that defined the relationship between the local population and the federal government.[1]

Once Congress delegated responsibility for city governance in 1802, local elites quickly assumed political leadership. The first twelve-man council included several original landowners, prominent members of the business community, and professionals who had worked for the city commissioners. The president of the First Chamber, James Barry, had come to the city during the mid-1790s and operated a wharf and store along the Eastern Branch. Meanwhile, Daniel Carroll led the Second Chamber. Other notable figures included James Hoban, the designer of the White House and a superintendent at the Capitol, and the city surveyor, Nicholas King. Although the council had considerable turnover each year, the pattern of prominent locals holding these elected positions continued.[2]

The presidentially appointed mayor provided a degree of stability and continuity, which contrasted with the turnover within the city council. To serve as the first mayor of Washington, Jefferson appointed Robert Brent, whose father's family had owned land in nearby Aquia, Virginia, where the federal government leased rights to the quarries that provided the sandstone for the government buildings. His mother, meanwhile, came from the prominent Carroll family of Maryland. In 1787, Brent cemented his personal connection with the land that would become the federal district when he married Mary Young, eldest daughter of Notley Young, the second largest original proprietor of land in the city. After first appointing Brent in 1802, Jefferson, and later Madison, kept him in the mayor's office for the next nine years.[3]

During the ensuing decade, Brent and the council members made the most of the limited authority granted to them by Congress in the city's charter. In October 1802, the council levied a tax of $0.25 per $100 in property including real estate. The next year the city government expanded the personal tax burden to include duties on dogs and enslaved people. Owners or employers of enslaved women between the ages of fifteen and fifty owed a yearly tax of $0.50 per woman. Male slaves in the same age range cost $1.00 each per year in taxes. The same rate of $1.00 per year applied per animal to dog owners. If found to have falsified their count of either slaves or dogs, residents faced a tripling of the original charges. Two years later, in September 1804, the council passed an additional tax of $0.07 per $100 for the specific purpose of supporting the poor, infirm, and diseased in the city. Although these ordinances do not mention race, a lack of detailed city records makes it difficult to determine whether or not some of the city's poorest and most vulnerable residents, free blacks, qualified for such relief. Finally, additional city revenue came from license fees charged to retailers, carriage drivers, and peddlers, as well as the operators of theatrical performances, amusements, and billiard tables.[4]

Over the next decade, the council increased the general property tax as well as the fees levied on slaves and dogs. The taxes on slaves increased in November 1808 to $1.00 per year for adult female slaves and $1.50 per year for adult male slaves. The corporation of Washington held steady the $1.00 per year tax on dogs until August 1809, when the cost of keeping a female dog jumped to $9.00 per year. This dramatic increase suggests that the city considered its dog population well over capacity. The same act also raised the reward for constables who killed and buried dogs lacking collars that identified their owners from $0.20 to $0.30 per animal. Finally, the $0.25 per $100 base property tax rate remained in effect until 1810, when the council increased it to $0.50 per $100.[5]

When compared to the property tax rates established by other cities over the next decade, Washington's rate ranked near the top of the list. Only Baltimore's 1816 rate of $0.75 per $100 and Boston's 1818 rate of $0.82 per $100 topped the federal city's rate. However, differences between the value of real estate in the various cities and the practice of local assessors in both Boston and Baltimore of assessing property at levels well below its market value meant that both of these cities ranked below Washington in per capita tax assessment. Despite setting their tax rates at $0.275 and $0.245 per $100, respectively, only New York and Providence had higher per capita assessment than Washington, suggesting that those cities might have used less lenient assessments than Boston and Baltimore and that Washington's assessment practices, like its rates, may have fallen at a point in between the two pairs of cities. Washington's high tax rates and its high per capita assessments likely resulted from the federal government's ownership of its public land and lots. Other municipalities could supplement property tax revenue with the sale of city property. Holding little property of its own, the corporation could not do the same.[6]

Most important, the council exempted U.S. government property from taxation. This meant that Washington City earned no revenue from taxation of federal land, buildings, or other property. While it gave "exclusive legislation" over the federal district to Congress, the Constitution did not specifically forbid local taxation of federal property. The Residence Act, which established the federal district, and the city's congressional charter also made no mention of federal tax liability. Seventeen years later, in 1819, Chief Justice John Marshall and the Supreme Court ruled in *McCulloch v. Maryland* that states could not tax the means by which Congress fulfilled its constitutional obligations. However, even that ruling affirmed the legality of state taxation of federal property "in common with the other real property in a particular state." Presumably, city officials exempted federal property to avoid antagonizing Congress and giving the enemies of the Potomac capital reason to agitate for the government's departure.[7]

Unfortunately for the city government, revenues from local taxes proved disappointing. For example, when the treasurer's initial assessment of property in the city for 1802 came in at $1,569,600, the council expected the tax to yield nearly $4,000. However, the city collected only $1,431.03. The root of this discrepancy lay in a section of the city's congressional charter that forbade city authorities from confiscating and auctioning off the property of landowners who failed to pay their taxes if the land in question was unimproved. Thus protected, owners of unimproved land felt no obligation to pay their city taxes. Even the city council's assertion in the tax code that it did, in fact, have the authority to seize and sell the property of tax delinquents failed to coax payment from these property owners. Until the passage of a new city charter in 1812, owners of unimproved property in Washington City remained effectively beyond the reach of the city tax collector.[8]

Augmenting its limited tax revenue with money borrowed from local banks, the city government funded many small infrastructure projects to promote development. In August 1804, the council provided small sums for street or bridge work at eleven different locations. Most of these projects received only $40 to $65, with a few more receiving $150 to $250. Together these appropriations totaled $1,005. Between June 1804 and May 1805, the council provided another $1,360 for street and bridge projects and authorized the mayor to borrow another $1,000. The reliance on borrowing and the small sums granted to projects reflected the council's desperate financial situation.[9]

Each year the city paid for the digging of new wells and the maintenance of old wells, pumps, and water pipes. The approximate cost to the corporation for these efforts ranged from $500 to $1,000 annually from 1803 to 1812. In addition, the council occasionally appropriated funds for the clearing and preservation of springs. Their efforts to control water in the city also included digging gutters and culverts in and along streets to improve drainage. Between these water projects and the work on streets and bridges, basic improvements to the city's infrastructure required significant portions of the city's annual budget.[10]

The council also funded several wharves on Tiber Creek and the Potomac River, as well as construction of a tobacco warehouse. In 1804, the council authorized the mayor to appoint a three-man commission to raise $200 in donations for the construction of a wharf on Tiber Creek at its intersection with 12th Street West. Once the commissioners raised these private funds, donors to the project chose two representatives from their ranks to join in the oversight of the project. The council also set aside another $300 for the construction of the wharf, pledged that the city would keep it in repair, and reserved the right to impose wharfage fees on articles landed there and not removed within twenty-four hours. Finally, that December, the council earmarked another $370 to complete the wharf.[11]

To overcome the limitations imposed by their limited tax revenue, city officials showed creativity and flexibility by combining public and private funding for projects like this one. In other American cities, local governments typically granted waterlot rights to individuals seeking to erect a wharf, relying entirely on the private sector to fund and maintain the structure and to pay an annual rent to the city. Through grants like this, for example, New York City controlled the development of its wharfs and improved both the city's infrastructure and its economy. And in the early republic period, the corporation of New York began purging city arrangements that combined private and public capital or efforts. In 1800, for example, the city replaced private volunteers who had organized the city's almshouse with paid city employees so that the public good would not hinge on private sacrifice and so that the corporation could exert more complete control over the poor relief system.[12]

In 1806, Washington's council secured private assistance to construct a tobacco warehouse in the southern section of the city on 3rd Street East between M and N Streets. The city received a donation of two city lots in square 801 from Daniel Carroll. As he had for the 12th Street wharf project, the mayor appointed a three-man commission to oversee the construction of a "good and sufficient warehouse, of brick or stone, covered with tile, slate, or iron, capable of containing at least six hundred hogsheads [large barrels] of tobacco." To complete the building, the council set aside $2,000 from the city's budget, nearly 20 percent of the total revenues received the previous fiscal year. And in case the city treasury could not support this expenditure, the council authorized the mayor to borrow additional funds. City leaders hoped that this warehouse would encourage local farmers to ship their tobacco through Washington's wharves rather than the busier and longer-established wharves in Georgetown and Alexandria.[13]

In December 1804, the council appropriated $500 for the purchase of a lot and its adjacent wharf on the Potomac. The riverfront lot sat between 21st and 22nd Streets about a mile downriver from Georgetown. The council planned to purchase this real estate from the federal superintendent in charge of selling off the remaining government lots in the city. Noting that the $500 offer fell far below what he would consider selling the lot for to a private buyer, Superintendent Munroe accepted the city's offer because the council wanted the lot for public use and because his office needed the income "to satisfy some pressing claims." However, he stipulated that the city pay by January 1 instead of March 1, as they had proposed. The records suggest that the city did not complete the transaction. The council's annual summary of revenue and expenditures from the following year lists no such purchase. Also, later records indicate that the superintendent sold the lot in question to Andrew Way & Co. in May 1807 for $1,000. It may well have been that the city could not manage the payment on the superintendent's time line. Clearly, however, the city had come to expect no funding appropriations or even donations of land from the federal government for local infrastructure projects.[14]

Beyond these physical investments, the council regulated many aspects of the city economy. In its first session, the local government established permanent markets in the eastern and western portions of the city. It also laid down a set of standard weights and measures for economic transactions. By 1810, the city government had established rules and standards for the sale or quality of products sold in the city such as bricks, hay, coal, flour, lumber, tobacco, and swine. In April 1806, for example, it passed regulations regarding the weight, quality, and cost of bread sold in the city. These regulations mandated that bakers use only city-inspected flour and that they stamp their loaves with their initials and the quality of flour used. The council then pegged the weight of bread loaves to the cost of the various flour types available. As flour prices rose, loaves for sale would weigh less, ensuring a stable price per loaf. Finally, the act required that the mayor make a monthly survey of flour prices so that the appropriate weight for loaves could be determined. City regulation of the local economy had been common in the colonial era. But since the revolution, most cities had eliminated laws regulating prices and commerce. The continued use of these tools in Washington suggests that the council sought to mitigate what it saw as weakness and fragility in the local economy.[15]

Through these efforts, city leaders offered a response to the protracted economic malaise experienced by residents since 1800. Contrary to the hopes of many locals, the arrival of the government had spurred little economic activity. In 1806, Benjamin Henry Latrobe wrote that the city abounded in cases of poverty and distress:

> The families of Workmen whom the unhealthiness of the city, and idleness (arising from the capricious manner in which appropria- tions for the erection of the public buildings have been granted, give to them for a short time high wages, and again perhaps for a whole season not affording them a weeks work) have ruined in circumstances and health, are to be found in extreme indigence scattered in wretched huts over the waste which *the law* calls the American Metropolis, or inhabiting half finished houses, now tum- bling to ruins which the madness of speculation has erected.

As for the master tradesmen fortunate enough to have purchased a lot and built a home in the city, Latrobe referred to them as "quite as wretched and almost as poor, tho' as yet not quite so ragged." Beyond the public building projects, the presence of the government provided little fuel for the city's economic engine. Only the printing industry flourished in the city thanks to contracts provided by the government. But the city could not solve its economic troubles via the printing press. The local govern- ment aimed to correct the problems described by Latrobe by regulating the economy and building up the local infrastructure to spur growth.[16]

Each year the council also devoted a substantial portion of its bud- get to relief and care of Washington City's poor and sick. In addition, it sought to provide for members of the community deemed insane. In 1802, the council hired an overseer and appointed three volunteer trust- ees of the poor, each responsible for a third of the city. The trustees deter- mined who required the assistance of the corporation and passed that information on to the overseer. Once notified about a person in need, the overseer would contract for that individual's "board, washing, and lodging." In this "out-relief" model, the city provided the goods and aid to the needy but did not require that they enter a poorhouse. The trustees could also order that the city provide an allowance of $2 weekly to any poor person having a family and a place of residence in the city.[17]

Between June 1802 and May 1803, the city spent $720 on the relief of the poor and the sick, 42 percent of its total outlays for that fiscal year.

The next year spending on such relief more than doubled, to $1,610.73. However, this amount represented only 28 percent of the corporation's total spending that year. During the remainder of the decade funding for poor relief fluctuated but remained a significant outlay for the city. Starting in December 1804, the council appropriated smaller sums for the "apprehension, security and maintenance of lunatics within the city." In 1806, the council appropriated $2,000 for the construction of an "Infirmary," designed to "constitute the poor house of the city, where poor, infirm and diseased persons who may not be otherwise provided for, shall be lodged and maintained." Additional appropriations for completion and maintenance of the Infirmary appeared in subsequent council records, including an 1809 provision for, among other things, "making secure a room of confinement." These efforts on the part of the city council to both assist and control the poor, sick, and mentally disabled suggest a desire to improve the image of the city. Washingtonians presumed that the more services, amenities, and signifiers of urban society they could provide, the less visitors and members of Congress could complain about the city. As it was, even the city's allies in Congress openly complained about its deficiencies. For example, in 1806, when defending plans to erect a bridge across the Potomac River, Virginia Federalist Joseph Lewis Jr. conceded that it was not "altogether unjust" to compare the federal city to a wilderness, but he hoped that the bridge would promote better markets and boardinghouses there. [18]

The city's comparatively early efforts to move away from an out-relief model to that of the poorhouse put it in line with reform efforts taking place in the North. In Boston, New York, and Philadelphia, civic and religious leaders established these institutions early in the nineteenth century in an effort to combine basic aid to the poor with efforts to address the moral failings that they assumed lay at the root of poverty. Typically, such institutions mandated labor from recipients of aid in order to provide moral uplift. In the South, on the other hand, the use of traditional forms of out-relief continued to dominate efforts to assist the poor throughout the early republic and antebellum eras. Where Southern states and municipalities did adopt the poorhouse model, they tended to do so as a cost-saving measure, hoping that it might prove more efficient than outrelief. In Washington, the council increased funding for poor relief with the establishment of the Infirmary, suggesting that their efforts had more in common with Northern reformers than their fellow Southerners. [19]

Similarly, the council created a public school system for the city after 1804, when Congress amended the city's charter to include, among other things, the right "to provide for the establishment and superintendence of public schools." However, not all city residents supported a public school system. In fact, the council's first attempt, in August 1804, to endow a public school failed when four of the seven members present in the Second Chamber voted against an act that had been unanimously passed by the First Chamber. Outside of New England, very few municipalities funded public schools. For example, neither of the previous two U.S. capital cities, New York and Philadelphia, had public school systems in 1804. And Southern tradition favored individual education via private tutors hired by well-to-do parents. Responding to the act's failure, one of the city's leading newspapers, the *National Intelligencer*, declared that the school system would have been "of incalculable benefit to the city, by enlightening the minds and improving the morals of the rising generation, by rescuing the metropolis from its darkest reproach, and by rendering it worthy the esteem of a rising nation." Clearly some locals felt that establishing public schools would improve the city's reputation and deflect some of the aspersions cast against it.[20]

In December, the council created a joint public-private educational system. To support the school, the council pledged its receipts from specific municipal taxes and license fees, including those levied on slaves, dogs, carriages, taverns, amusements, peddlers, and liquor. In addition, the city sought subscriptions from the public. Dozens of local residents pledged at least $5 to the effort. The largest donations, $200 each, came from President Jefferson, the wealthy and prominent John Tayloe III, and Samuel Harrison Smith, editor of the *National Intelligencer*. The school system also collected fees from some of its students.[21]

Rather than provide a free education to all pupils, the school system charged tuition to parents who could afford the cost and waived the fees for the children of poor whites. All pupils learned reading, writing, and arithmetic, as well as the branches of mathematics needed for their future professions or household duties. Paying students also studied geography and Latin. In the first half of 1806, the school system's board of directors admitted thirty-five children of poor parents, including one orphan and ten children of local widows. Six of those slots went to female students. It does not appear that the board allowed any free black children to attend the city's schools. By the end of 1806, the corporation had erected two schoolhouses, dubbed the Eastern and Western Academies. Unfortunately, the school board could not keep the system afloat. The trustees collected only about half of the money pledged by private citizens. And much of that money went to construction of the academies.

In addition, in 1806 the city reduced its pledge of funding for the schools from $1,500 to $750, citing complaints about the high percentage of city funds devoted to the system. The board also encountered difficulty locating qualified teachers willing to accept the low pay offered by the city.[22]

The school board lamented its penury, declaring in 1809 that the institution "could not be supported in anything like a state of respectability." Three years later, in November 1812, the council scrapped the system. Declaring their revenue inadequate for a school system, they passed a resolution instructing the mayor to seek approval from President Madison to operate a lottery designed to raise $10,000. With the money, they hoped to build two schools on the cost-saving Lancastrian model. Under this system, students of all ages studied together under one teacher, and the older students were responsible for instructing the younger ones. Presented with the request a few days later, Madison approved the lottery, signaling the end of the previous school system. Even under this less costly system, the city was able to educate only 130 students, about a tenth of the approximately 1,000 white children under fifteen living in Washington City as of 1800. Eventually elite Washingtonians realized that insufficient tax revenue and local unwillingness to increase already high taxes precluded establishment of a successful school system.[23]

A number of private educational intuitions did appear in the city, often serving populations excluded by the public system. Between 1807 and 1812, several schools opened to serve the city's growing free black population. In 1807, three former slaves from nearby Maryland and Virginia, George Bell, Nicholas Franklin, and Moses Liverpool, opened the first school for free black students in the District of Columbia. The school occupied a one-story wood-frame house in Southeast Washington at Second and D Streets. Uneducated themselves, the three men hired a white teacher named Mr. Lowe to lead basic instruction in literacy and arithmetic. Mrs. Anne Maria Hall, a free black woman from Prince George's County, Maryland, also ran a school in the city and served as its teacher.[24]

Other schools extended educational opportunities to young white women. In 1803, John Gardiner advertised that he and his wife were accepting pupils for boarding and day schools run from their home on Pennsylvania Avenue near President's Square. While Mr. Gardiner taught writing, grammar, arithmetic, and bookkeeping, Mrs. Gardiner taught young ladies needlework and embroidery. The Gardiners also left open the option for girls to split their time between their two schools. And in April 1807, an advertisement in the *National Intelligencer* announced the expansion of an academy for young ladies operated by a Miss Reagan. Already operating a location on F Street, Reagan sought students for a second school on Capitol Hill. Her students learned reading, writing, grammar, geography, and painting, as well as sewing and embroidery.[25]

By spurring on the economy, providing relief for the poor and infirm, and educating the young, the city corporation and elite Washingtonians sought to improve the city by controlling its residents. In the early republic, city governments found themselves newly responsible for the health, safety, and productivity of their residents. Both the poorhouses and the pauper schools represented spatial sorting, a process in which city leaders organized people, activities, or structures within the urban area to promote the culture's dominant notions of good urban form. Through these improvement projects local elites exerted social control over the poor and uneducated residents who might otherwise have threatened the nation's grand experiment in republican government. Taken together, these improvements attempted to address the fears expressed by Jeffersonians about the corrupting and demeaning effects of urban life.[26]

Washingtonians of substantial means began to fill out the spacious city map with new homes. Begun in 1799 and completed in 1802, a house built by John Tayloe is the best-known example of such private construction. Tayloe came from a powerful and wealthy central Virginia family. In 1792, he married Ann Ogle, eldest daughter of a well-to-do and politically powerful Maryland family. When they decided to move to a new city, the choice of Washington represented a gamble. Fast-growing Baltimore or the Virginia state capital, Richmond, offered more obvious opportunities for John, who had considerable economic and political ambitions. Tayloe, however, risked investment in Washington's largely untapped potential.[27]

Tayloe expressed his faith in the new city by making a dramatic architectural statement with his new home. The wealthy Virginian commissioned design proposals from two architects: city commissioner, amateur architect, and designer of the Capitol, William Thornton; and professional architect, Benjamin Henry Latrobe. Tayloe chose Thornton's plan for a three-story hexagonal building fronted by a semicircular tower (fig. 12). Conveniently, this design suited the angular lot at the intersection of New York Avenue and 18th Street West that Tayloe purchased from the commissioners' office for $1,000 in 1797. Although Commissioner Scott handled Tayloe's transaction, Thornton probably guided his client to this unique and valuable piece of property just west of the President's House. In May 1799, construction began under the supervision of an architect,

FIGURE 12. Detail of the exterior of the Octagon House. (Photo taken between 1909 and 1932.) (Library of Congress, Prints and Photographs Division)

William Lovering, because Thornton's busy schedule as a commissioner prevented him from overseeing the project. Begun with an expected budget of $13,000, Tayloe closed the books on the building in April 1802 having spent more than $35,000.[28]

In return for his unexpectedly substantial investment, Tayloe received one of the largest and most architecturally progressive homes in Washington. Now known as the Octagon House, the building represented a departure from the design choices made by other real estate owners and investors in the city. Unlike the speculators who constructed row houses as investment properties, Tayloe erected a single free-standing home. The vertically and horizontally aligned windows and a semicircular fanlight over the front door represented the height of Federal design. But the house's dramatic shape set it apart from other Georgian or Federal-style homes common in American cities. However, Thornton also embellished the Octagon with high-style features, including a dramatic Ionic portico

FIGURE 13. Detail of Duddington Mansion, Daniel Carroll's home in Washington City. (Library of Congress, Prints and Photographs Division)

at the main entrance and marble panels inset between the second- and third-floor windows.[29]

Although not a row house, Tayloe's home was distinctly urban, rising straight and tall above the acutely angled intersection. It stood in contrast, for example, to the large manor house completed by Daniel Carroll in 1793 on square 736 just five blocks south of the Capitol. That building stood two-and-a-half stories high and stretched wide enough to encompass nine vertical sets of windows. With a centered gable resting above a three-window-wide projection at the center of the house and a one-story wooden porch, the home fit the mold of a traditional Chesapeake plantation house (fig. 13). Carroll also surrounded the home's four-acre plot with a six-foot-high brick wall, further reinforcing the home's rural aesthetic.[30]

Tayloe's new urban home also retained features common to Chesapeake plantation homes, including a beautiful and imposing reception hall. Passing through the Iconic columns of the front portico, visitors to the Tayloe home entered a circular hall distinguished by its marble floors and molded plaster cornice. Opposite the front door, an arched opening framed by Corinthian columns offered a glimpse of the winding staircase that led to the second floor. Eighteenth-century Virginia planters had used elegant reception halls as showplaces for their power and status. The Tayloes had no reason to deviate from this tradition for their urban residence.[31]

The Tayloes created distinct spaces within their home for their family, elite guests, and enslaved servants. From the stairway room opposite the entrance, visitors might be led through mahogany doors to either the drawing room or the dining room on the main floor or up the stairs to the only public room on the upper floors, the library. Directly above the entrance hall, this circular room commanded a 180-degree view of the city beyond. Thornton designed each of these rooms to serve and impress guests at both intimate gatherings and grand affairs. John and Ann lavishly decorated each of these rooms. The remaining rooms on the second and third floors included the family bed chambers, dressing rooms, a schoolroom, and possibly a tutor or servant's quarters. The cellar below the main floor contained a kitchen, store rooms, a wine cellar, the housekeeper's room, and a servant's hall. Additional smaller buildings on the grounds housed the laundry, stable, and slave quarters. These careful distinctions between the public, private, and service portions of the home and especially the use of outbuildings to house their slaves connected the Tayloe's Washington home with spatial living patterns common throughout the South. In Charleston's row houses, for example, the placement of the finest rooms on the second floor at the front of the home, and of the functional rooms at the rear of the lower floors reinforced the Southern social order, keeping servants and slaves away from areas of the home designed for the reception and entertainment of guests. Visitors to Tayloe's Richmond County estate would have encountered a similar series of barriers including steps to the main entrance, an interior reception hall, and additional entranceways leading to the main dining area, all of which conveyed Tayloe's high place in the social order and allowed his guests to mark their own social standing as they passed by each successive barrier.[32]

While the Octagon represented the height of private construction during this period, other prominent Washingtonians also promoted city development through construction of fine private homes. Two such homes belonged to a pair of men who both married daughters of wealthy land proprietors and would both serve as mayor of Washington. The first,

FIGURE 14. Detail of *Van Ness Mansion*, undated. (Library of Congress, Prints and Photographs Division)

Robert Brent, began work on a stately Federal-style home at the southeast corner of Maryland Avenue and 12th Street West in 1802. Completed the next year, the building featured a number of stylistic embellishments to the Federal style including a wooden portico, keystone lintels above the windows, and prominent pedimented dormer windows in the roof. In 1813, John P. Van Ness hired Benjamin Henry Latrobe to design a home near the White House. The building exemplified the Greek revival architectural style of which Latrobe was an early adopter. Like Tayloe and Brent before him, Van Ness combined high architectural style and the bravado of a town booster with his new home (fig. 14). Their houses expressed not only their wealth and stature but also their faith in the city.[33]

The builders and owners of such homes employed them as symbols of both self and community. By considering the varied contexts for these buildings, we can better understand the symbolic meanings they carried for early Washingtonians. As three of the largest and finest homes in early Washington, the Tayloe, Brent, and Van Ness buildings each stood out amidst the ramshackle landscape of the city (fig. 15). And all three men

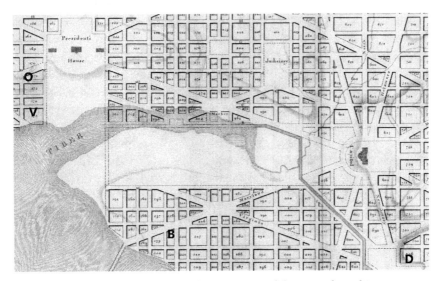

FIGURE 15. The center portion of the 1818 *Map of the City of Washington* by Robert King. Letters superimposed on the map mark the location of Duddington (D), the Brent House (B), the Van Ness Mansion (V), and the Octagon (O). (Library of Congress, Geography and Map Division)

designed their homes to impress not only the small local population but also the many elected officials who made Washington their home during the legislative season. For example, after John and Marcia Van Ness moved into their new home in 1816, it became a social hub for federal politicians. These local efforts drew members of Congress out of their boardinghouses and provided them with a taste of high society and the type of elite social engagement that Washington was often said to lack, especially when compared to cities like New York and Philadelphia.[34]

When it came to large business and infrastructure projects, private citizens in Washington often pooled their limited capital. In 1803, local merchant Benjamin Stoddert explained to Jefferson, "Washington suffers more than any other place, for want of active capital." Men of money, he said, had shown "no disposition" to move to the city and they would not until it was clear that capital could be had without them. He concluded, "The City never can flourish, until active capital, without which there can be no enterprise, shall by some means, be introduced." In this particular instance, Stoddert suggested that the creation of a local insurance company might improve the situation.[35]

District residents also sought congressional charters for organizations designed to improve the physical and economic infrastructure of the city such as banking, bridge, canal, toll road, and manufacturing companies. In response to Jefferson's 1807 embargo against all foreign trade, for example, elite Washingtonians attempted to establish a "cotton manufactory" in the city. In 1809, Seeing an opportunity to combine patriotism and profit, District residents chartered the Columbia Manufacturing Company, which hired an Irishman experienced in this business to erect and supervise a textile factory. Unfortunately, the company's shares sold poorly, and it dissolved by April 1813. Other efforts to bring industry to the federal district met similar fates. As Blodgett had pointed out, a lack of available capital hamstrung city development.[36]

To obtain capital, locals petitioned Congress to charter banks in the District. In 1810, when Congress approved the charters of three new banks for Georgetown, Alexandria, and Washington, William Cranch, Chief Justice of the District of Columbia Circuit Court, predicted that they would "nearly double the commercial capital of the District, and must give activity to commercial enterprise." These new banks brought the District's total to six, with a combined capitalization of $3.5 million. Established by the State of Maryland in 1793 for operation in the District of Columbia, the Bank of Columbia held $1 million of this total, twice as much as any of the other District banks. Seeking to encourage economic development in fast-growing Baltimore, Maryland approved charters for banks in that city from 1790 to 1806 capitalized at $5.8 million, well beyond the capital Congress made available in the District. This disparity speaks to the different ambitions Congress and the State of Maryland had for the District and the city of Baltimore respectively.[37]

Meanwhile, Judge Cranch's involvement with another local enterprise chartered by Congress, the Washington Bridge Company, offers considerable insight into the operation and perception of these projects. In the fall of 1794, twenty-five-year-old William Cranch had come to the District of Columbia bearing a letter of introduction from his uncle, John Adams. The vice president described Cranch as "a Nephew of mine and to me very much like one of my sons" and stated that he was "determined to Settle at least for some years in the Federal City, to the prosperity of which, his Education, Talents, Application and Virtues, may make him very useful." Earlier that year, Cranch had expressed considerable faith in the urban experiment taking shape on the shores of the Potomac, telling his sister that he hoped most of his friends would follow him to "this New Jerusalem." Cranch began work as the principal agent of the Greenleaf, Morris, and Nicholson syndicate, handling all of the speculators' accounts in the city. Like many other employees of these men, Cranch's involvement with their business nearly ruined him. In 1799, faced with the specter of being sent to debtor's prison, Cranch petitioned the Maryland Legislature for discharge of debts in his name, all of which he asserted actually belonged to Morris. Freed from these debts by decree of the legislature in 1800, Cranch established a legal practice.[38]

In January of the following year, his uncle, now the president, appointed him to the Board of Commissioners in charge of the city. And only a few months later, on Adams's very last day in office, the Senate confirmed his nomination of Cranch as an assistant judge on the newly created Circuit Court of the District of Columbia. This made Cranch one of the famed "midnight judges" appointed by Adams in the waning days of his term. This position on the federal court and later his unexpected promotion by President Jefferson to chief judge of that court allowed Cranch to become a well-respected resident of the federal district. Cranch also served as the reporter for the United States Supreme Court from 1801 to 1815.[39]

In 1808, Cranch invested his income from publication of the Supreme Court's rulings and borrowed another $3,000 to buy shares in the Washington Bridge Company. Chartered by Congress earlier that year, the company quickly raised $60,000 for construction of a bridge from the end of Maryland Avenue in Washington across the Potomac to Alexander's Island (now Columbia Island, home of Lady Bird Johnson Memorial Park and the Navy and Marine Memorial), on the Virginia side of the river. The company's charter listed a dozen prominent local residents as its board of directors, including Mayor Brent, Superintendent Munroe, Daniel Carroll, and Samuel Harrison Smith. It authorized them to sell 2,000 shares of stock worth $100 apiece. By the end of the year, they had issued the shares and collected the first three of the ten installments of $10 each on those shares. Cranch wrote to his father in Quincy, Massachusetts, that he expected an additional payment to be called for soon, bringing the total capital of the company to $80,000. In this and subsequent letters, he effusively praised every aspect of the bridge project.[40]

Cranch portrayed the bridge as an engineering marvel. The company's workers sank 1,000 piles into the riverbed to support the nearly mile-long bridge. In the deepest water, crews drove these piles eight feet into the river bottom; in the mudflats by the shores, they sank them as deep as twenty-five feet. Thanks to the Potomac's freshwater and lack of "worms," Cranch felt confident that the piles would not decay. The

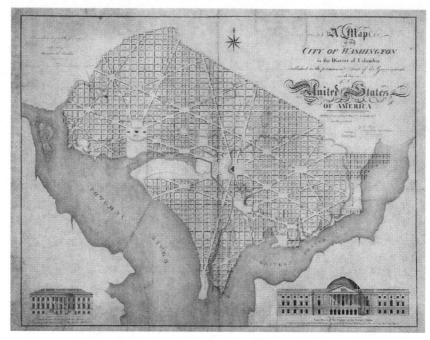

FIGURE 16. The full 1818 *Map of the City of Washington* by Robert King show-ing the Washington Bridge Company's bridge across the Potomac as well as the older bridge across the Eastern Branch. (Library of Congress, Geography and Map Division)

bridge included a pair of draws, one over each of the deep channels in the river. The larger draw over the deeper channel on the Virginia side cre-ated a thirty-five-foot opening that allowed ships to continue upriver to Georgetown. After the judge declared that he believed it to be "the very best stock in which money can now be invested," his father expressed interest in acquiring his own shares.[41]

At this time only two bridges in the area spanned the Potomac or Eastern Branch. One crossed the Eastern Branch connecting the federal city to the eastern parts of Maryland. Cranch dismissed this bridge as merely leading "to the country," although he did complement the 10 percent returns it produced for its investors. The other bridge stretched across the Potomac three miles upriver from Georgetown at Little Falls. Eventually known as Chain Bridge, this structure represented the pri-mary route into the federal city from the south other than ferries, which could be hired to traverse the river. Because the new bridge would link Washington City directly with a turnpike road leading to Alexandria,

Cranch felt confident that it would draw considerable business away from both the ferries and the other bridges (fig. 16).[42]

Cranch laid down fantastic estimates of their expected returns. The Washington Bridge Company planned to turn a profit by charging tolls to cross the bridge. The act incorporating the company spelled out its full schedule of fees in great detail. The span cost $0.0625 to cross on foot and $0.1875 per person to cross on horseback. The fee schedule also covered a wide variety of vehicle types and animals, with the highest charge being $1.00 "for each coach, coachee, stage-wagon, chariot, phaeton or curricle, or other riding carriage" drawn by one or two horses plus an additional $0.125 each for any additional horses. Based on the "lowest estimates" that he had heard of the bridge's projected traffic, Cranch predicted it would produce a return of 10 percent for the first year, and "I believe double that amount the next year."[43]

The judge insisted that ice would not threaten the bridge. In fact, ice on the river posed two types of risk for the bridge. First, winter storms might bring fast-moving chunks downstream, which could break the bridge's piles; and second, broken ice and other debris could potentially collect at the piles, forming a dam in the river that would increase the pressure on the piles or even bring water to the bridge's surface. Cranch dismissed each of these scenarios. Because the river widened considerably just before the bridge, its current lost "nine tenths of its force" before reaching the structure, mitigating the danger posed by any fast-moving objects. At the same time, if ice were to dam at the bridge, water would flood Alexander's Island and dissipate before overtopping it. As proof for his assertions, Cranch noted that, by January 1809, the bridge had already survived two strikes by large pieces of ice.

Unhappy about the bridge because it hindered ships from reaching their port, Georgetown residents gleefully predicted that ice would destroy it. During a storm in the winter of 1809–10, they lined the banks of the Potomac hoping to enjoy a spectacle and a triumph. But, according to Cranch, "they returned disappointed," for the ice caused only minor damage. After a severe storm in January 1810, Cranch reported that the people of Georgetown were again "in high spirits calculating with certainty that when the ice breaks up it will carry away the Bridge." But Cranch had faith in the span and again reported no damage. Finally, in November 1810, a flood greater than residents had seen in forty years washed away the bridge above Georgetown at Little Falls. As a result, thousands of cords of wood lodged against the Washington Bridge and formed a dam across the river. Once again Georgetown residents "came down to witness the destruction of our bridge." But again the span emerged unscathed. In addition to supplying the poor of the city with firewood, the incident reinforced local faith in the bridge's strength and stability.[44]

The bridge opened on May 20, 1809. Cranch reported to his father that toll revenues averaged $35.10 per day for the first week. By his calculation, this represented a 13 percent annual return on the $100,000 invested by stockholders. Cranch remained confident that the returns would remain steady and even grow as new roads were constructed on the Virginia side of the river. Two weeks later, Cranch reported daily receipts of $31.675 but also expressed confidence that they would eventually reach $40.00. Convinced by his son's confidence in the project, the elder Cranch agreed to purchase fifty-four shares of stock in the bridge company for approximately $2,100. After another month, Cranch stated in none-too-confident language that his father "will certainly receive nearly, if not quite 10 per cent per annum." By October, the bridge had earned an average of $22.41 per day since it had opened, representing an annual return of 8 percent for stockholders. But because this was the slower summer season, Cranch continued to predict a 10 percent return for the full year.[45]

At the end of November, the company prepared to pay out its dividend for the bridge's first half-year in operation. Cranch wrote to his father that it would probably amount to 3.5 percent after the company paid the toll taker and the boy stationed at the bridge's draw. Undaunted by the small dividend, he predicted that recent strong toll earnings would continue and would push the next six-month dividend to 5 percent, totaling 8.5 percent for the year. Noting that shares continued sell at below their full invested value, he asserted that if he had the money, he would buy even more. By June 1811, the bridge company's annual dividend had reached 8 percent and maintained that return for two biannual distributions. Having invested $50 in each share of stock, shareholders received $2 per share in both December 1810 and June 1811. The bridge company's 8 percent returns, though considerably lower than the 20 percent Cranch once predicted to his father, nonetheless represented a successful investment.[46]

Like the federal city, the bridge company received its charter but no financial support from Congress. In fact, the company's charter expressly exempted carriers of property or military equipment belonging to the United States from the bridge's toll schedule. Fortunately for the company, the promise of a healthy dividend meant that it had much more success collecting payments due on its shares than the city corporation had collecting property taxes. In the face of lower than expected returns, Cranch focused on the bridge's future prospects, the same choice made by District residents who believed in the vision of a grand national metropolis rising on the Potomac. Believers in Cranch's "New Jerusalem" funded this bridge project, created city infrastructure, built new homes, schools, and social organizations, and strove to boost the city's economy. With little assistance from the federal government, these local elites expended considerable effort and their limited capital to promote development in the capital city.

Between 1801 and 1814, the federal city grew at a dramatic pace. The arrival of the government in 1800 spurred settlement in the city. In that year, federal census takers recorded a total population of 3,210 for Washington City. And by 1810, after the arrival of the government and the passage of ten years, the city housed 8,208 people, an increase of 155 percent. The populations of many other American cities grew rapidly during this decade as well. Baltimore, for instance, grew at about 75 percent, and the population of New York increased at nearly 60 percent. However, Washington City's transition from a nascent, proto-city to an official seat of government spurred its impressive growth.[47]

Along with the government came 116 men from the executive departments, including the cabinet secretaries, officeholders and clerks of all ranks, and even messengers. In addition, the combination of proximity to the halls of political power and the prospect of landing government printing contracts lured newspaper editors to the federal district. For example, Samuel Harrison Smith followed the government from Philadelphia to Washington, where he established the *National Intelligencer*, which served as a mouthpiece for the Democratic-Republicans. Editors also launched at least four new publications in Georgetown and Alexandria. Altogether in December 1800 just after Congress first convened in Washington, readers in the three District cities could choose from four daily newspapers, two triweekly papers, and a magazine.[48]

Washington's free black population increased by more than 600 percent between 1800 and 1810. Other urban areas in the South also experienced expansion of their free black populations during this decade. However, those growth rates were between 50 percent and 200 percent, well below the rate in Washington. As it had for the white population, the arrival of the government in 1800 touched off rapid expansion of the free black population. In addition, laws passed in many Southern states required freed slaves to leave or forfeit their freedom, driving many to cities like Washington.[49]

The District's unique legal code facilitated settlement of free blacks. When Congress determined that the laws in place in Maryland and

Virginia on December 1, 1800, would serve as the legal code for the two halves of the District, it locked in rules for manumission and free black behavior that were comparatively liberal for the nineteenth-century South. During the ensuing decade, both states tightened those rules in response to rumors of slave conspiracies and the overthrow of the French colonial authorities in Haiti by the slave population. Also, both Maryland and Virginia sought to decrease their black populations by requiring the departure of manumitted slaves and restricting additional slaves or free blacks from entering the state. In the District of Columbia, however, the rules remained much as they had been in 1800. Newly freed slaves could remain in the District. Free blacks could legally move there. And, in general, the legal code viewed the enslaved as people who had access to the court system when questions of their status arose. In 1808, the Washington City Council established its first black code, forbidding enslaved people and free blacks from assembling after ten o'clock at night and from "dancing, tippling, quarrelling," or making a public disturbance at any other time. However, the city did not require newly manumitted slaves to leave. This comparatively mild set of regulations contrasted with the restrictive codes put in place by neighboring states during the early nineteenth century.[50]

Contrary to the hopes of the city's planners, the influx of new residents drove only limited sales of government-owned lots. The board of commissioners and Superintendent Munroe moved 1,657.5 lots off of the federal books between 1801 and 1812. This represented only 16 percent of the 10,136 initially placed in the hands of the city commissioners and brought the total percentage sold up to only 52 percent. At the beginning of 1813, 4,781 lots still remained in the hands of the government. The vast majority of sales occurred in 1801, the year the government arrived, and in 1802 as the superintendent sold off lots to pay the city's loans. The 1802 sell-off put nearly 1,000 lots into private hands. However, flooding the market with lots significantly lowered the revenue earned by the superintendent's office. In 1802, the average price per lot sold by the government dropped to $44.84. By comparison, the board of commissioners had earned an average of $185.92 per lot from 1791 to 1800. Although only 106.5 lots sold from 1808 to 1812, their average price of $211.52 per lot reflects a rebound from the lows caused by the 1802 sell-off. However, despite the city's impressive population growth, this average price represented an increase of only 14 percent over the average price earned during the 1790s, suggesting that the market for government lots stagnated during these years.[51]

Other important features of Washington's plan for the city remained unrealized by the end of 1812. By 1802, for example, the Potomac Company had completed the locks and canal around the Great Falls above Georgetown. However, several decades would pass before a canal would connect area residents to the farm and coal country of western Maryland, Virginia, and Pennsylvania. The federal city's internal canal system had also not yet opened. And as Judge Cranch's description of Georgetown residents cheering the prospect of the Washington Bridge's destruction suggests, rivalry between the three District cities limited local support for certain development projects. Congress exacerbated these municipal rivalries by issuing a separate charter for Washington and maintaining the existing charters of Georgetown and Alexandria. Uniting the entire District under a single government might have mitigated local rivalries and promoted local cooperation. And as the failed efforts to bring manufacturing to the city during Jefferson's embargo show, the city remained largely dependent on the few economic opportunities provided by the federal government, such as work on the public buildings and in the newspaper and publishing trades.[52]

As local residents pushed the city toward a grand metropolis, the federal government pulled in the opposite direction, toward a simple town. While the city commissioners had used some of their meager funds to provide infrastructure such as roads and markets for the city prior to the arrival of the government, Congress made no appropriations from 1801 to 1812 for improvements to the city beyond $11,702.66 for a city jail and the funds provided to prevent the city from defaulting on its loans from Maryland. Not surprisingly, these contrary forces produced the mixed picture of growth and development in Washington detailed above. Having thoroughly bested their rivals at the polls, Jefferson and the Democratic-Republicans could not simply have their way with the national capital. They ensured that federal funds flowed only to the government buildings and the central core of the city, but they could not stifle local efforts to improve the city. During the 1790s, Washington residents had coped with George Washington's inability to provide for the city, and now they adapted to Jefferson's unwillingness to do so. Their efforts to improve the capital reflect the strength of their faith in the city and their resolve to harness its potential. In the coming years, that strength and the government's commitment to the District would be tested in the aftermath of the British invasion of the city in 1814.[53]

PART III

Making the Capital National, 1814–1828

As day broke on the morning of August 26, 1814, with smoke rising from the smoldering stone shells of the White House and the Capitol, the city of Washington lay partially in ruins (fig. 17). Over the previous thirty-six hours the city had suffered a cruel combination of military and natural disasters. Two days earlier, British soldiers and marines had routed poorly trained and poorly organized American army and militia forces in battle at the town of Bladensburg, Maryland, four miles northeast of the capital. That evening, the British marched unopposed into the American capital. Shortly after nine o'clock, they set fire to the Capitol. And by midnight, they had put the torch to both the White House and the Treasury Building. After a night's rest, the British completed their assault on the public buildings of Washington by destroying the War and State Department buildings, a rope-making facility, and the city armory, as well as the office and printing press of the *National Intelligencer*, the organ of the Democratic-Republican Party in Washington. The British hoped to deal a psychological blow to the United States and to exact a measure of vengeance for the burning and looting of York, the capital of Upper Canada, the previous year.[1]

Early that afternoon, a powerful storm darkened the skies and broke the deep-summer Washington heat with torrential rains and tornado-like winds. Just nine years old and still enslaved at the time, District resident and diarist Michael Shiner later recorded that none would forget that day's "awful storms which raged for a long time without interruption."

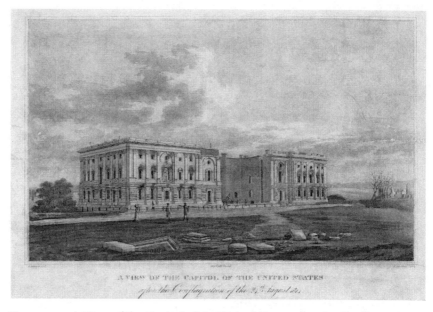

FIGURE 17. *A View of the Capitol of the United States after the Conflagration of the 24th August 1814*, Munger and Strickland, showing the burned-out shell of the Capitol building. (Library of Congress, Prints and Photographs Division)

Amidst the booming thunder and lightning, rain and hail pelted the occupied city. The storm's strong winds added to the damage done by the British troops. Shiner reported that the winds took "some olde houses up from there foundations and [brought] them down." Other buildings in the city lost roofs and chimneys to the storm. Fortunately for city residents, the storm's rains dampened the fires burning at the public buildings, preventing their spread.[2]

In the aftermath of the attack, federal officials faced a choice. They could rebuild the Potomac capital or abandon it, either temporarily or permanently, for another city. After several weeks of debate, Congress chose to stay in Washington and rebuild the public buildings. But the political strength of Democratic-Republicans who disapproved of federal spending in the District meant that the government made few further investments in the city. For their part, local residents rallied to the government's aid, providing quarters for Congress while workers rebuilt the Capitol using funds loaned from District banks. In the same way that surviving the War of 1812 symbolized the permanence of the United States and its break with Great Britain, Congress's decision to remain in Washington finally settled the lingering question of the permanence of the Potomac capital. With the city's place as the seat of government confirmed, elite Washingtonians embarked on the difficult process of transforming the physical and cultural landscape of their city. While striving to achieve the imagined goals set for the capital by George Washington, local elites blurred the lines separating public and private activity in the city, endowing all of their actions with claims to public duty. And through their efforts to beautify the city, support its poorest residents, and create physical and institutional symbols of local authority, they hoped to turn their city into the nation's cultural and intellectual capital.

6 /   Saving and Rebuilding Washington

On June 18, 1812, President Madison signed the first declaration of war passed by the U.S. Congress, bringing the young nation back into military conflict with the British Empire. The president and many of his fellow Democratic-Republicans in Congress hoped that a military invasion of Canada would force Britain to stop arming Native Americans on the American frontier, impressing American sailors on the high seas into the service of the British Navy, and preventing American ships from carrying trade goods to France. For the next two years, American army, navy, and militia forces fought British soldiers, Canadian militia, and their Native American allies along the border region shared by the United States and Canada and in America's western territories. Preoccupied by their battle against Napoleon for control of Europe, the British could initially spare few regular army forces to thwart American invasion attempts and too few warships to enforce a blockade of American ports. But after Napoleon's defeat and subsequent abdication in spring 1814, the British transferred experienced soldiers from the European theater to North America and escalated the naval war along the East Coast. Joined by these reinforcements from Europe, a force of British soldiers and marines sailed up the Patuxent River from Chesapeake Bay in August and began a march through the Maryland countryside toward Washington and Baltimore.[1]

Faced with the war's arrival on their doorstep, federal authorities and local residents offered a belated and inadequate response to the British approach. In 1813, Washington's city council authorized the mayor to borrow $5,000 to aid in any measures adopted by Madison for the defense of the city. However, no such measures came until July 1814, when it was obvious that the addition of troops from Europe would allow the British to advance inland from the coast. The president created a new military district for the Potomac region and ordered his cabinet to place 2,000 to 3,000 armed men between the capital and Chesapeake Bay. He also instructed them to organize 10,000 to 12,000 militia and volunteer troops from the District and neighboring states who could be ready to defend the city.[2]

When the time came to confront the advancing British troops, federal and local authorities mustered about 7,000 men—mostly poorly equipped and poorly organized militia—for the decisive battle at Bladensburg. Secretary of War John Armstrong had refused to consider Washington a likely target of the British. Right up until the moment when British troop movements proved him wrong, he assumed that Baltimore, a larger, richer, commercial city, would draw the attention of the British commanders. Armstrong's miscalculation delayed the muster of militia troops from Maryland and Virginia. And the expiration of a Pennsylvania militia law prevented that state from sending 5,000 additional troops to defend the city. During the two-hour engagement with the British war-hardened regulars, the Americans suffered few casualties but could not hold their position. Their disorganized retreat opened a clear path to the capital for the British. And since nearly everyone with the means to evacuate had already abandoned Washington, the invading army met no resistance upon entering the city.[3]

During their occupation of the capital, William Thornton, now superintendent of the Patent Office, convinced the British to spare that office and its valuable contents. Having already removed most of the office's papers to his farmstead in nearby Bethesda, Maryland, Thornton returned to the city, arriving at Blodgett's Hotel, the building that housed the Patent Office and the Postmaster's Office, just as British troops prepared to set it ablaze. Thornton explained to the officer in charge that the patents and scale models inside represented private, not public, property. In her diary, Anna Maria Brodeau Thornton recorded that her husband portrayed the Patent Office as a "Museum of the Arts" and explained that it would be a "loss to all the world" if the soldiers destroyed it. In his own summary of the events, published two weeks later in the *National Intelligencer*, Thornton recounted telling the British commander that "to burn what would be useful to all mankind would be as barbarous as formerly to burn the Alexandrian Library, for which the Turks have been

FIGURE 18. Detail of *Blodgett's Hotel*, 1793. (Library of Congress, Prints and Photographs Division)

ever since condemned by all enlightened nations." Thornton had therefore placed the intellectual and mechanical inventions of the American populace into a long-held Anglo-American philosophical tradition of respect for private property. And by comparing his office to the Library of Alexandria, Thornton reminded the officer that the protection of such property distinguished civilized societies like theirs from those who lived under the capricious rule of tyrants. Apparently convinced either by Thornton's argument that the building contained little public property or that its destruction would represent a crime against the civilized world, the British commander spared the building. As the largest intact structure remaining in Washington after the attack, it became the meeting place for Congress when President Madison called that body to the capital early for a session beginning that September (fig. 18).[4]

Starting on September 22, Congress debated the recent past and the future of the Potomac capital. Deeply embarrassed by the British conquest of Washington, the House of Representatives created a committee "to inquire into the causes of the success of the enemy in his late enterprise against the Metropolis, and the neighboring town of Alexandria, and into the manner in which the public buildings and property were destroyed, and the amount thereof." A few days later, Democratic-Republican congressman Jonathan Fisk of New York broached the issue of the city's future, proposing the formation of a committee to "inquire into the expediency of removing the Seat of Government." Unlike the

previous proposal, this suggestion met considerable resistance and pro-
voked immediate debate among the members present. The subject of
relocating the capital came to the floor of the House repeatedly over the
next three weeks as a resolution and then a bill for removal made their
way through the legislature's procedures. These debates marked the only
time since 1790 that the full House of Representatives debated the location of the seat of government. Advocates of removal had often raised
the subject. But only in the aftermath of the British attack did they have
sufficient support to bring the issue to the House floor or to come so close
to success.[5]

After the House voted to consider Fisk's resolution, Virginia Federalist Joseph Lewis Jr. defended the local and regional interests that had
invested in the capital city. He suggested that the government could
have protected the District from the British if it had prepared properly
to defend the city. Asserting his firm belief that once departed the seat
of government would never return to the shores of the Potomac, Lewis
reminded the House that both Maryland and Virginia had donated not
only land for the federal district but also substantial sums of money. In
addition, Lewis argued that the "hundreds and thousands of individuals" who had been induced by the permanency of the seat of government
"to expend their all in its improvement" would be "reduced to beggary"
if Congress adopted the resolution. The original proprietors, in particular, had donated much of their land to the federal government with the
understanding that their remaining holdings would increase in value.
And just as William Thornton had leveraged the notion that government
existed to protect private property in order to save the Patent Office,
Lewis now reminded the House that it must protect the investments
made by the local population. This argument highlights the strong links
between, and the unclear lines separating, the public and the private in
the federal city. Because of the symbolic nature of the national capital and
the critical eye with which many Americans viewed the city, the actions
of Washingtonians always bore public meaning. Whether purchasing
land, educating their children, attending social events, or subscribing
for stock in local organizations, Washingtonians, especially those of the
elite ranks, bore the burden of demonstrating the worthiness of their city
to the nation. Lewis exhorted the members to consider the consequences
of removal for the local population. And he hoped that by rejecting this
resolution, the House could finally put an end to attempts to remove the
government from the District. Over the previous ten or twelve years,
he stated, "similar attempts had been made, the effect of which was to

create alarm and paralyze exertion and improvement to the great injury of the public." By confirming the capital's permanence, the House could allow its residents to "continue their improvements here without dread of being sacrificed."[6]

Arguing for removal, Northern representatives repeated long-standing complaints about the city. Fisk asserted that Congress would benefit from sitting in "a place more connected with the moneyed interest of the nation; where they could have better opportunity to call into action the resources of the nation." The suggestion that America's moneyed interests would be more willing to assist the government if it left Washington reflected the federal city's standing outside the elite club of Northern commercial cities that dominated the nation's financial system. Addressing the present accommodations of the government, the Federalist Richard Stockton of New Jersey decried the inconveniences presented by Congress's meeting in the Blodgett's Hotel. Even after displacing the Patent Office and the Post Office Department, the representatives remained tightly packed into the building's main hall, where they lacked seats for every member. He argued that in winter, when the fireplaces would need to be lit, or in the stifling heat of the Washington summer, the health of the members would be at risk. And he suggested that the only alternatives to remaining at this unhealthy site were leaving the city or making costly repairs to the public buildings even while the British threat persisted. Of the latter idea, he asserted that the American people would not be willing to see their tax dollars "squandered only to gratify the false pride of making laws *among ruins*." Such complaints echoed the dissatisfaction often expressed about the capital city's undeveloped appearance, lack of sufficient accommodations, and small social scene.[7]

Southern and Western congressmen rose to defend the Potomac capital during these debates. For example, the North Carolina Federalist Joseph Pearson felt the government's departure would "heap disgrace upon disgrace" and add to the British victory by giving them the satisfaction of knowing that they had driven the government from its home. Pearson also disputed Northern claims that a proper defense of Washington would be more expensive than the defense of Philadelphia or any other city. Since local militias represented the country's primary form of defense, he did not understand those who criticized reliance on militias for the defense of the District. Looking beyond the present conflict with Great Britain, Pearson's fellow North Carolinian, Nathaniel Macon, a Democratic-Republican, echoed the Southern fear that the government would never return to the District. Taking that logic a step further, he predicted that "if the Seat of Government was once set on wheels, there was no saying where it would stop." This warning raised the specter not only of a seat of government set adrift across the American landscape but also of ceaseless congressional conflict over the capital's location.[8]

Catching sight of the forest through the dense thicket of trees that marked the debates, Pearson reduced the entire discussion to an attempt by Northern interests to wrest the seat of government from the South. He warned the Northern members of his own Federalist Party over their sectional alliance with Northern Democratic-Republicans. Reminding them that a wide political gulf remained between the two parties, he suggested that the Federalists who favored removal should consider carefully the motivations of their new allies. During the course of the war, the Federalists had exhibited considerable party unity, voting together, with low levels of dissent against the military measures, trade restrictions, and financial proposals drawn up by the ruling Democratic-Republicans. Concerned about the erosion of their already low voting power, Pearson cautioned against collusion with the majority party. Sarcastically, he congratulated the Northerners "on their first political wedding" and wished them well on their honeymoon. However, he predicted that the marriage would be short-lived and that "perhaps before to-morrow's noon matters of State may demand, and their divorce be pronounced."[9]

As the removal bill advanced through a series of procedural votes, its opponents attempted to thwart permanent loss of the capital by amending the legislation. When the House debated the proper destination for the government, Lewis proposed that the government remove to Georgetown. He reasoned that such a move took the government away from the charred ruins of the public buildings but kept the capital within the federal district. When put to a vote, however, the House chose Philadelphia over Georgetown by "a large majority." Undaunted, Lewis proposed an amendment calling for appropriations of $100,000 per year for the next five years for reconstruction of the public buildings in Washington. Unwilling to rely on text in the removal bill that called for a return to Washington after the war, Lewis wanted to guarantee the government's return by investing $500,000 in the city. Put to a vote, this amendment drew ninety-five ayes, a substantial majority of the House. The speaker then put the question of a third and final reading of the bill before the body.[10]

On October 15, after three weeks of sporadic debate over removal, the federal city finally received a reprieve from the House. Seventy-four members voted in favor of the bill while eighty-three voted against it, ending its chances of passing. Four Democratic-Republicans, Congressmen Findley, Lyle, and Tannehill from Pennsylvania and Congressman Stanford from North Carolina, had switched from voting for the resolution calling for removal to voting against it at the final reading. Of these, Stanford, Lyle, and Tannehill belonged to factions within the party critical of the Madison administration. Since Madison opposed removal and had threatened to veto any removal bill, their initial support for moving the seat of government may have reflected their dissatisfaction with the party leadership. Alternatively, the passage of Fisk's amendment committing $500,000 to reconstruction in Washington may have caused some removal advocates to reconsider their prospects of long-term success. Either way, these four votes did not determine the success of the bill. Members who had not been present for the resolution vote made the difference in defeating the removal bill. A dozen such congressmen arrived in Washington and joined the antiremoval ranks while only eight new votes materialized in favor of the bill.[11]

On this vote, members split along sectional lines. More than 96 percent of the congressmen from Maryland, Virginia, North Carolina, South Carolina, Georgia, and Louisiana voted against removal. Members hailing from Delaware, Pennsylvania, New Jersey, New York, Connecticut, Rhode Island, Massachusetts, New Hampshire, and Vermont, on the other hand, made up only 22 percent of the votes against removal. Congressmen from the western states of Ohio, Tennessee, and Kentucky, meanwhile, mirrored the sectional split seen in the eastern states. However, their line separating North from South seems to have drifted southward. Members from Tennessee voted unanimously with the South against removal, while the Kentucky and Ohio delegations split their votes. Three Ohioans voted in favor of removal and one opposed it, while the Kentuckians divided their ten votes evenly. The prevalence of Federalism in the North gave the vote the appearance of splitting along party lines. In the South, however, sectional interest clearly trumped party identification. The nine Federalists in the House from that region all voted against removal, as did all but two of the forty-six Democratic-Republicans. While Northern Federalists uniformly supported removal, Democratic-Republicans from north of Maryland split their votes fairly evenly: twenty in favor of removal and eighteen against. Recent historical analysis has split the difference between partisan and sectional explanations by suggesting that it hinged on the partisan fidelity of Northern Democratic-Republicans. However, given Pearson's warnings about sectionalism and the near-universal consensus among members from states south of Maryland against the bill, it would appear that the vast majority of Southern representatives perceived the bill as an attempt to remove the capital from the South.[12]

The fact that the two sides fought so intensely over removal suggests that both considered the permanent placement of the seat of government to be at stake. Relying on the same tenet of Anglo-American political philosophy Thornton had wielded in defense of the Patent Office, Southern congressmen decried the ruin that would surely befall the citizens who had invested their time and capital in the federal city. In effect, by remaining in Washington, the government would protect the private property of those Americans. For Washingtonians, therefore, the simple act of buying land or settling in the national capital represented a public political statement. In addition, the arguments made by both sides reflected the growing sense that the federal city stood as an important symbol of the nation. For example, when debating the defensibility of the city or the notion that it would represent a second victory for Great Britain if the government abandoned Washington, House members built their arguments on the basic assumption that the seat of government was the physical embodiment of the United States.

In response to the dire threat of removal, District residents banded together to fight for the survival of the Potomac capital. On October 9, elite Washington gathered at the chambers of the city council to discuss their precarious situation. The group produced a resolution denouncing the House of Representatives' discussion of removal. Published in the following day's issue of the *National Intelligencer*, their statement declared that removal of the government from Washington was "a measure in our opinion repugnant to the constitution and laws, subversive of public faith, injurious to the community at large, and ruinous to our private interests." The citizens formed a committee to draw up a report and a "respectful memorial" to be submitted to Congress. This group consisted of seven of the wealthiest, most respected, and most influential members of Washington society, among them, John P. Van Ness, Daniel Carroll, and Thomas Law.[13]

The following week the *Intelligencer* reported on the committee's plans to save the city. First, the committee offered the volunteer efforts of Washingtonians for "any project or works of defense" that the new secretary of war, James Monroe, might decide on. The man most blamed for the invasion of the city, Secretary of War Armstrong, had resigned just days after the attack when Madison had made it clear to him that the people, especially the soldiers, had lost faith in him and that he held

Armstrong responsible for the failed defense of the city. By providing volunteers, local leaders hoped to undermine the accusation that defense of the city was too costly to be practical. In addition, by offering aid to Monroe in his future defense preparations, the committee implied that a lack of preparation, rather than the city's inherent vulnerability, had allowed for the disastrous British occupation.[14]

The committee also arranged for local banks to offer loans to Congress for reconstructing the public buildings. It had strong ties to the local banks as a number of its members served on the boards of or owned stock in the institutions. These connections no doubt helped ensure the banks' willingness to offer credit to the government while also providing a profit motive to the committee. Given the dire consequences that loss of the government would have wrought on the local economy, however, both the committee and the banks acted simply to avoid financial ruin. With this offer, Washington's business elite pushed back against the notion that the government needed to relocate closer to Northern financial centers. In all, District banks made $500,000 in credit available to the federal government. And although no congressman brought up the loan proposal during the removal debate, we can assume that Washington residents presented this offer to Congress during the week between the plan's announcement and the final vote on the removal bill. After the House rejected removal, a bill that authorized borrowing from District banks made its way through the House and Senate and passed into law in February 1815. Beyond these public attempts to retain the seat of government, each of the local committee members also surely exerted private pressure on the congressmen with whom they often socialized.[15]

Thomas Law showed particular dedication to the cause of his adopted city. In a poem about the aftermath of the British attack written in November 1814 (reproduced below), Law wove together the fate of the capital with that of the nation as a whole. Across twenty-four amateurish couplets, Law described a dream in which he observed Columbia, the goddesslike personification of the American nation, resting dejectedly atop the burned ruins of the Capitol. The personification of Liberty urges Columbia to "mourn not . . . the vandal's savage flame." The attack on the capital, she explains, has inspired Columbia's children to seek a just revenge against the British. And with the help of God, who "shall shield thy chosen land from harm," the Americans will defeat their enemy on land and at sea. About the Capitol Law wrote, "At this, methought a peal of victory rung, / And a new edifice in splendor sprung." The poem concludes with Law waking up to the revelation that "Columbia might be cheered" by the fulfillment of this vision and the erection of a splendid new Capitol for her nation.[16]

A DREAM—Thomas Law, 1814
The scene of conflagration which by day
Excited feelings painful to convey,
Appeared in sleep; and faintly I disclose
The pleasing vision which in dreams arose.
High on the Capitol's smeared, smoky wall,
Midst fractured pillars of the Congress Hall
Columbia sat: full frequent heaved the sigh,
And grief's dull languor floated in her eye.
With wild emotion every feature wrought,
Her air was sorrow, and her look was thought.
Lo! smiling Liberty, with heavenly grace,
And form angelic, gives a warm embrace;
"Mourn not," she said, "the vandal's savage flame,—
A lasting tarnish to the invader's fame;
To just revenge thy children it inspires,
And makes them emulate their sainted sires!
Extend your view o'er lakes, o'er seas, o'er lands,
Triumphant everywhere behold your bands;
Whole fleets are taken and whole armies yield;
Before your sons e'en veterans fly the field.
Even in sight of Albion's cliffs your fleet
Seeks the proud ruler or the waves to meet.
My spirit gives an energy divine,
And makes your sons all former deeds outshine."
Now an effulgent burst of western light,
And gilded clouds, wide spreading struck my sight.
Justice descends! but as she nearer drew
A blaze of glory hid her from my view.
I heard a voice, though solemn, full of love,
Pronounce she came commissioned from above.
"Droop not, Columbia" she exclaimed, "but trust
In power Almighty, and your cause is just;
The machinations of the bad shall fail,
The force of numbers be of no avail.
Our God shall shield thy chosen land from harm,—
Our God protects thee with his outstretched arms!"

At this, methought a peal of victory rung,
And a new edifice in splendor sprung,
Like Phoenix from its ashes, and a sound
Of triumph and rejoicing rose around.
Sudden I woke, all glowing with delight,
And full of faith in all that passed by night.
One dove to Noah in the deluge bore
The welcome tidings of appearing shore:
Two harbingers from heaven methought appeared,
That sorrowful Columbia might be cheered.
O, may it be the Almighty's gracious will,
This welcome vision quickly to fulfill!"

In a letter to President Madison, Law proposed that he take action to improve the capital city. Law asserted that the poor condition of its streets and the lack of social amenities contributed to discord in Congress. And he suggested that the "parsimony and neglect" exhibited by the government toward the capital diminished the nation's reputation in the eyes of foreign dignitaries and visitors. Law also reminded him that George Washington had proposed establishment of a university in the federal city but that the idea had fallen victim to the government's general neglect of the capital. Fortunately, the crisis created an opportunity for Madison to reverse this trend. He stated that "a disposition prevails to re-erect the public buildings and to establish institutions which will be a lasting honor to the government." Given that one month earlier, only a slim majority in the House of Representatives had rejected removal of the government, Law's claim of widespread support for the proliferation of government institutions in the city seems to reflect his own goals for establishing an American metropolis rather than a sentiment widely shared by members of Congress.[17]

However, Law understood that Madison held considerable sway over the plans to rebuild Washington. He told the president that every citizen who saw these new public buildings and national institutions would "feel his bosom swell with exultation and exclaim 'this is ours' and thus identify himself with his nation." As he had in the poem, Law linked development in Washington with a broad nationalist project. Rebuilding the public buildings would secure the city's place as the governmental center of the republic. And creating new national institutions would establish Washington's position as a cultural and intellectual center. Here Law reinforced the symbolic importance of the capital city, a place with which all Americans would identify when government investment made it a showplace for American strength and ingenuity.[18]

Madison probably shared Law's position, but initiated reconstruction efforts focused largely on re-creating the public buildings as they had stood prior to August 1814. Nearly three and a half years later, in his final annual message to Congress, Madison did recommend that that body consider establishing a national university in Washington, calling such a project "worthy of the American nation." Placed in his speech between calls for completing a regular system of weights and measures and for creating a system of national roads, Madison clearly viewed the establishment of a university in Washington part of his efforts to unify the nation. However, even as the Federalist opposition to the Democratic-Republicans all but vanished in the wake of the nation's perceived victory in the War of 1812, disunity within the ruling party stymied Madison's efforts to create a program of national improvements. Members of Congress had heard the call for a national university before, but their interest in such an endeavor remained limited. In response to Madison's call, the House leadership placed Georgia Democratic-Republican Richard Henry Wilde in charge of a committee to review and report on the proposal. In December 1816, Wilde and his committee produced a bill appropriating $200,000 for the erection of a national university in Washington. Three months later, on the last day in session for the Fourteenth Congress, Wilde moved that the House indefinitely postpone any further consideration of the bill. Speaking frankly about the proposal, he suggested that, despite its merits, the idea of a national university ran afoul of the "economical sensibilities" of the House. And he hoped that future politicians might steer clear of "those noble and captivating projects which others heretofore have had the merit of proposing, and the House the odium of rejecting." These projects included the national university and many other efforts to establish national education and internal improvements. Wilde's statement highlights the political divide separating Madison's more nationalist agenda and the priorities of the cost-conscious representatives in the Democratic-Republican rank and file. Forged during its time as an opposition party in the 1790s, orthodox Democratic-Republicanism held fast to a conception of what one historian has called "pure limited government." Facing this type of opposition in Congress, Madison focused on ensuring that the government in Washington would resume its normal operations as quickly as possible. And for that to happen, Congress needed an appropriate place to meet while workers rebuilt the Capitol.[19]

Well aware that removal advocates had complained about the quality of their temporary accommodations, elite Washingtonians formed a stock company to construct a temporary capitol. Selling shares in the company at $100 each, the organizers of the Capitol Hotel Company raised over $17,000 from thirty-eight investors to construct a building at the southeast corner of A and 1st Streets NE. This prime location on Capitol Hill had housed a tavern since 1795. The owners of that property accepted $4,612 in company stock in exchange for the land, and the tavern was razed to make way for a three-story Federal-style brick building known as "the Brick Capitol." Construction began on July 4, 1815, and workers rushed to complete the building. On December 11, Congress held its first session in the Brick Capitol (fig. 19). The company spent $25,000 on the building, and the government paid $5,000 to furnish it. During its four years there, Congress paid the Hotel Company an annual rent equal to 6 percent of the building's cost plus an allowance for insurance that brought the total to $1,650 per year. With only $6,600 in rent received in four years, the company's investors made no profit. However, they accomplished their primary civic goal of keeping the federal government in Washington.[20]

Six weeks after the House of Representatives concluded its discussion of the capital city's future, it returned briefly to the subject of the city's past. On November 29, 1814, the committee that investigated the British invasion of the District submitted its report to the House. Now three months removed from the attack, the representatives showed much less interest in getting to the bottom of the government's failure to protect the capital than it had in mid-September. The resignation of Secretary Armstrong and the lack of British victories since that time may have diminished their zeal for the subject.[21]

The weight of the committee's report may have also crushed their desire for answers. Committee chair Richard Johnson, a Democratic-Republican from Kentucky, presented to the House "a report of very great length, together with a voluminous mass of documents." Largely narrative in nature, the report provided a detailed picture of the invasion based on the testimony of many witnesses and participants. However, the committee drew few conclusions. In particular, it determined that the president and his cabinet had authorized "ample and sufficient" means for the security of the District. But the committee did not evaluate the execution of those orders.[22]

When Johnson moved to print the report and a selection of the documents, Federalist congressman Daniel Webster objected. The freshman

FIGURE 19. The Brick Capitol, also known as the *Old Capitol Prison* since it later held captured Confederates. This 1861 image by William Redish Pywell shows the original building with an addition at the rear. (Library of Congress, Prints and Photographs Division)

congressman from New Hampshire argued that the report did not speak to any of the purposes for which the House had created the committee. Instead, according to the record of the debate, he "thought it was calculated (though not intended) to cover up in a mass of prolixity and detail what he considered a most disgraceful transaction." Webster felt that the Democratic-Republicans had absolved the Madison administration of its failures by burying them in a mountain of detail. Johnson countered that the report had been designed to provide information, rather than conclusions, for the members of Congress. He moved that they print the documents and discuss the report in three weeks' time. These motions passed, and the report and its supporting documents eventually came to occupy 220 pages of the *Debates and Proceedings of Congress*. However, the discussion never occurred, and on February 4, 1815, Johnson moved successfully to have debate on the report postponed indefinitely. Democratic-Republican efforts to stymie discussion of the invasion by producing a massive narrative that drew no conclusions about who to blame for the disaster had succeeded. By this time unofficial rumors had traversed the Atlantic that American and British peace negotiators meeting in Ghent, Belgium, had reached an accord on Christmas Eve, 1814. By February 14, an official copy of the treaty had reached the capital city. News of the treaty's arrival followed closely on the heels of reports from New Orleans of Andrew Jackson's routing of British troops there in early January. Despite failing to evict the British from North America, Americans celebrated the survival of their nation, which stood on the brink of bankruptcy and possible civil war in January 1814. The Senate unanimously ratified the treaty on February 16, bringing the war to an end and dampening congressional desire to dwell upon the mistakes made during the course of the conflict.[23]

On March 13, Madison set rebuilding efforts in motion, establishing a commission to execute the repair and reconstruction of the public buildings. He selected three prominent locals for the commission: John P. Van Ness; Tench Ringgold, a businessman who operated a rope-making facility in the city; and the former U.S. attorney general and northern Virginia congressman, Richard Bland Lee. Two days later, the commissioners received an application from Benjamin Henry Latrobe seeking an appointment to the post of architect of the public buildings. Both the architect and his wife had written to Madison and other government officials hoping to secure a place for him at the head of the reconstruction project. The commissioners responded to Latrobe immediately, proposing that he serve as superintendent of the repairs. Later that month, the commissioners appointed the original designer of the White House, James Hoban, to serve as the architect for that building and the executive offices. With the rehiring of Latrobe and Hoban, the commissioners placed the public buildings back in the hands of two of the men who had been instrumental in their original construction.[24]

Over the next four and a half years, the Capitol, White House, and executive offices rose up from the charred shells left behind by the British invasion. The executive departments moved into their new accommodations within a year, and newly elected president James Monroe and his wife, Elizabeth, moved into the White House in September 1817. Just over two years later, in December 1819, Congress moved back into the Capitol building, although it would not be complete until 1825. This time line is especially impressive when compared to the decade it had taken for George Washington's commissioners and their successors to ready the public buildings for the government. However, the pace of construction should not be seen as an indication that the projects went smoothly. In fact, the men associated with the rebuilding efforts packed a decade's worth of conflict into their accelerated time line.

Only one of the five commissioners and architects chosen for the projects in 1815 saw them through to completion. Congress replaced the three-man reconstruction board with a single commissioner in April 1816. Little record exists detailing the reasons for the change in the board's structure. It appears that Congress and President Madison came to see the three-man commission as top-heavy and inefficient. However, some members of Congress also may have been unsatisfied with the particular members of the board. For example, when Madison nominated Van Ness to serve as the project's single commissioner, the Senate "did not advise and consent to the appointment." The following day, Madison nominated a man previously unaffiliated with the project, Samuel Lane of Maryland, for the post, and the Senate accepted that nomination. Latrobe, meanwhile, chafed under the authority of both the three-man board and the single commissioner. Unlike his previous tenure at the Capitol when he answered directly to Thomas Jefferson, Latrobe disliked answering to nonarchitects and complained to Madison that the board treated him "in a manner more coarse and offensive than I have ever permitted to myself, or felt myself capable to using to my poorest mechanics." During the Madison administration, Latrobe counted on his good relations with the president to ease his service to the nation. However, after President Monroe took office in March 1817, Latrobe's clout within the executive branch evaporated. Making matters worse, Monroe pressured Lane and Latrobe to speed up the pace of work at the Capitol and set up an unofficial committee of advisors to evaluate their progress. Unable to cooperate with Lane and upset about being blamed for cost overruns and delays, Latrobe resigned in November 1817.[25]

In June 1817, before his departure from the project, Latrobe expressed his sense that the reconstruction represented a lost opportunity. Always a critic of William Thornton's original plan for the Capitol, Latrobe wrote to Jefferson that he would have preferred its total destruction by the British. "At a less expense to the U. States," he said, "a much more convenient, and magnificent building could have been erected, than will be made of the ruins of the former." The House briefly considered changing the sites of the public buildings, but a committee that looked into the idea reported back that change would be costly and "inexpedient." Latrobe's disappointment with the decision to rebuild rather than reimagine the Capitol paralleled the feelings of Thomas Law, who had urged Madison to challenge a decade and a half of Democratic-Republican orthodoxy and promote a dynamic national capital in Washington. Although the city's defenders in the federal government had thwarted removal, they made no commensurate attempt to take advantage of the opportunities created by the British attack. Because many Democratic-Republicans remained loyal to the traditional Jeffersonian tenets of fiscal austerity and states' rights, those who hoped to invest in national improvement projects met stiff opposition in Congress. As it had for the previous quarter century, responsibility for the development of Washington would rest on the shoulders of the local residents.[26]

7 /   Striving to Be a National City

Prior to the war with Britain, Washington's social and political leaders kept a leery eye out for those who coveted the seat of government
and sought to extract it from the District of Columbia. During the
war, their attention turned briefly away from plotters in Northern cities and toward encroaching British soldiers. But finally, after enduring
their greatest moment of civic tragedy, Washingtonians helped put an
end to questions about the permanence of the Potomac capital. After
the government's decision to remain in Washington cemented the city's
place as the permanent seat of government, elite Washingtonians rev-
eled in a newfound confidence. After the House vote against removal,
for example, an editorial in Georgetown's *Federal Republican* praised
the decision and hoped that the seat of government would now "be
permitted to remain where nature seems to have fixed, and the founder
of this empire, established it." Freed from the fear of the government's
departure, local residents worked to improve their city and to create an
exemplary American metropolis. To realize this vision, they passed local
ordinances designed to beautify and improve the quality of life in the
city. They used public and private funds to house the city's poor children.
And they established local institutions with bold national goals. Guaranteed the seat of government, they began to strive for supremacy rather
than simply for survival.[1]

The Washington City Council issued regulations and distributed city
funds to improve the function, appearance, and reputation of the capital
city. Between June 1815 and May 1816, for instance, the Thirteenth City

Council approved the paving of footways along portions of many streets throughout the city. Funding for these sidewalks came directly from the owners of lots bounded by the paths. For example, when two-thirds of the lot owners along the south side of D Street between 11th and 12th Streets expressed their desire for a footway, the council required each lot owner on the block to pay a special tax of $2.50 per foot-front of property to cover the cost. Alternatively, they could install a path in front of their property at their own cost. When it came to leveling and graveling streets, the city appropriated tax money collected separately by each ward. This way, each area maintained responsibility for its own streets.[2]

To improve the look of the city, the council provided funding and established regulations for protection, maintenance, and replacement of street trees. New rules prohibited damaging trees planted along city streets as well as tethering horses to city trees or their stakes or protective boxes. The council devoted $200 to the planting and upkeep of street trees. These efforts to promote and maintain tree-lined streets put the council in line with the actions of other city corporations across the nation. After attempting to ban the planting of street trees early in the 1790s, for example, New York began to encourage such plantings in 1806 and by 1810 had established fines for damaging city trees. The planting of street trees by municipalities and private individuals indicates not only an attempt to beautify the city but also a desire to assert control over the urban landscape. Prior to the revolutions that swept Europe and North America in the late eighteenth and early nineteenth century, orderly placement of trees expressed the power and authority held by Europe's monarchs. Spurred by a spirit of growth and civic improvement, America's cities used street trees for their own ends. In Washington those ends included beautification and a desire to improve the city's reputation for being shabby and undeveloped.[3]

During this session, the council also passed resolutions designed to improve the quality of life for residents. In its first act of the term, the council set aside $500 for the "poor, aged and infirm" of the city, continuing the social support network established by the first council in 1802. And throughout the session it provided additional assistance to individuals requesting relief. One curiously vague act appropriated exactly $51.58 to defray expenses incurred in "removing a nuisance" from the east side of 12th Street West. The council also declared it unlawful to keep geese, except in enclosures, in any part of the city south of Massachusetts Avenue. This act allowed Washingtonians to capture geese found in violation of the statute and to turn them in, "for the use of the poor at the infirmary." Each goose thus delivered warranted payment of $0.25. Clearly, the council's vision for the city did not include the presence of large, free-range fowl. Ever concerned with the perceptions of the city held by federal officials and other visitors, the council hoped that such rules might undermine the sprawling city's reputation as a rural backwater. [4]

The council's regulation of geese in the city drew the ire of the Georgetown *Federal Republican*, a Federalist-leaning newspaper. In a long editorial dripping with sarcasm, the paper declared that the public could not account for the "unnatural war waged by the Great Magistrates of Washington" against the geese. The piece concluded with a reader-submitted poem that, in part, warned the geese, "The hungry, half starv'd Corporation / That tyrannizes—like the nation! / Like gluttonous and wicked sinners, / Will cook thee for their Christmas dinners." Partisan posturing aside, the poem shows that some residents clearly chafed at the restriction. By passing regulations like these, the city joined with municipalities all over the nation in an effort to more carefully regulate their public spaces. As growing urban populations demanded cleaner, healthier, and more beautiful cities, local governments responded with a wide range of regulations designed to prevent disease, remove refuse, provide cleaner water sources, and keep free-roaming animals out of public areas. As one historian has put it, the corporations attempted to "confront the varied problems of urban life." However, these efforts often pitted the elite and middling sorts who dominated city governments against the poor, who had no place to keep valuable protein sources like hogs and geese other than on city property. Historian Paul Gilje presents this conflict as a dispute between a nineteenth-century middle-class culture of free market individualism and an eighteenth-century plebian moral economy that placed greater value on service to the community. In Washington, the local elites' ever present goal of improving the status of their city must have exacerbated these tensions because they firmly believed that adherence to such regulations provided an invaluable community service.[5]

In most years, the city borrowed from local banks in order to make up shortfalls in the budget caused by the slow collection of property taxes. In 1814, the city paid $1,300 in interest on the money borrowed up to that point. By 1820, those interest charges had grown to $3,000 as the principal owed jumped from $21,000 to $50,000. In 1818, the corporation stopped borrowing from banks and instead issued stock of its own. In July 1818, the council authorized the mayor to raise $60,000 by selling subscriptions of stock, in amounts no less than $50, on which the city promised to pay 6 percent interest per year. The city used this money to pay its bank debts and to fund city services. However, using this revenue system meant that the corporation now needed to direct income from property taxes to payment of the interest on the city stock.[6]

The corporation also turned to lottery schemes to raise money for major projects. Each year between 1812 and 1821, the city council authorized lotteries designed to raise $10,000 for school buildings, a new city hall, and a new penitentiary. In both 1815 and 1818, the council instructed the mayor to execute lotteries to raise $30,000 and $40,000, respectively. But the lottery system faltered. In part, it suffered because several states taxed or restricted the sale of tickets for the Washington lottery within their borders. And in 1821, a broker who had paid $10,000 for the rights to conduct a city lottery ran off with the proceeds from ticket sales without paying the winner. Making matters worse, in 1827 the Supreme Court ruled that the city was still responsible for payment of that lottery's $100,000 prize to the purchaser of the winning ticket.[7]

The lottery's failure hindered the efforts of city officials to erect a new city hall. In April 1820, the mayor and the city council advertised a $300 prize for the design for a city hall building estimated to cost $100,000. Well beyond the cost of any city project to date, this great sum reflected their faith that the lottery would soon provide an influx of cash. The council selected a plan by George Hadfield, a British architect who had come to Washington in 1795 to superintend construction of the Capitol and had remained after leaving that position in 1798. Subsequently, Hadfield had designed a number of prominent local buildings, including the executive office buildings and a Greek revival mansion for George Washington Parke Custis, a stepgrandson of George Washington, who owned an estate on the Virginia side of the District. Later inherited by Robert E. Lee and subsequently confiscated by the federal government during the Civil War, that building, Arlington House, today serves as the centerpiece of Arlington National Cemetery. Hadfield also proposed a Greek revival building for the city hall. The council initially determined that the plan would cost $750,000 to complete, however, and they asked the architect to alter the design.[8]

Even after scaling down the plan, Hadfield still offered a bold assertion of Washington's civic pride. Mirroring the classical style that defined the White House and the Capitol, the building featured a dramatic Ionic portico set atop a terraced, stepped base at its center. Hadfield flanked this focal point with two parallel wings, also fronted by Ionic columns, connecting them to the center by hyphens with recessed arched windows (fig. 20). A commission appointed by the city council to oversee construction of the building sought permission from President Monroe to place the city hall on the north side of Pennsylvania Avenue in a public reservation just west of 3rd Street. Along with Hadfield's classical design, the request for this location on the primary federal corridor suggests that Washingtonians hoped to co-opt the aesthetic and spatial symbols used to express the power of the federal government in order to elevate the stature and reputation of the city. Standing shoulder to shoulder with the grand edifices of federal authority, Hadfield's bold, classical structure would have allowed city leaders to project a sense of architectural parity in Washington between the federal buildings and the city hall. Despite the desire of some in Congress to develop that part of Pennsylvania Avenue, Monroe rejected the city's request, protecting the federal corridor from local intrusion. On August 14, following a procession of local officials and members of the District's Grand Lodge of Masons, city leaders broke ground for the building at Judiciary Square, two blocks north of the Pennsylvania Avenue location. Today the building houses the District of Columbia Court of Appeals. Speaking at the ground-breaking ceremony, Thomas Law's son John contrasted the penurious congressional attitude toward appropriations for Washington with the generosity of the autocrats who erected capital cities like Byzantium and St. Petersburg. Clearly Law felt comfortable enough about the permanence of the government's residence in the city to so harshly criticize Congress.[9]

As had been the case with the city's street trees and the council's efforts to beautify and regulate Washington's public places, the erection of a grand city hall provided both a reflection of and a direct response to the distinct circumstances facing elite Washingtonians. In recent decades, urban, architectural, and landscape historians have explored the connections between the physical aspects of public and private spaces and the "imaginative structures that all inhabitants of the landscape use in constructing and construing it." In particular, civic structures like city halls speak not only to the goals and desires of the lead architect but also to the beliefs and intentions of the community more broadly. In Washington, where status as the seat of government imbued the entire city with social and political meaning, local elites carried their imagined and idealized vision for the city into their plans to improve the urban landscape. And as Law's complaint about Congress suggests, they did so with a considerable chip on their collective shoulder. Therefore, the grand, classical structure begun on Judiciary Square embodied both the pride

FIGURE 20. *City Hall, Washington,* wood engraving by Van Vranken, 1853. (Library of Congress, Prints and Photographs Division)

and the insecurity of elite Washingtonians. In an attempt to portray and reinforce their own prosperity and social standing, they gambled the city's budget on a project far larger than they had ever attempted.[10]

Within a few years, local funding for the building dried up and city officials needed the assistance of Congress in order to continue the project. In 1822, local officials moved into their new offices at Judiciary Square. But much of the building remained incomplete. Workers had yet to construct the building's defining pillared front portico or the colonnades for each of the wings. And the outer walls remained rough brick without smooth stucco. City officials had planned to pay for the remainder of the project and even replenish the corporation's depleted coffers with income from the lotteries. But the lottery system's troubles undermined that plan.[11]

Fortunately for city officials, their new building represented an opportunity for Congress to establish a permanent home for the Circuit Court of the District of Columbia. Because of the District's peculiar status as a ward of the federal government, this federal court served as the primary civil and criminal court for the District. After the British attack, the circuit court shared facilities in the Brick Capitol with the U.S. Supreme

Court. And after the High Court moved into its new space in the reconstructed Capitol in 1819, the circuit court spent one session there as well. Following that session, however, expansion of Senate offices rendered it homeless.[12]

That December, when the House debated a bill to provide accommodation for the circuit court, many congressmen wondered why the federal government should foot the bill to house a local court. Henry Clay, a Democratic-Republican from Kentucky, asked whether space might be found in one of the existing public buildings so that Congress would not have to rent the Brick Capitol for $800 per year, "a sum which would purchase the fee-simple of very many of the county courthouses in some of the states." Like Clay, the other congressmen who argued against the appropriation ignored the federal nature of the court, choosing instead to consider it a local project properly funded by the local residents. Although the House rejected the bill in question and no other appropriation appears in the records of Congress, federal officials must have found funding for rental of the Brick Capitol, because the circuit court moved into that facility in January 1820. Three years later, Congress took the opportunity to end those rental payments and appropriated $10,000 to construct and furnish apartments in the new city hall building to house the court as well as the offices of the clerk and the marshal of the District. With this infusion of funding, the city completed the central portion and the east wing of the building by 1826. Gradually, the corporation worked toward completion of the west wing, finishing that project in 1849. While it may have come reluctantly, congressional assistance for the city hall project represented one of only a few instances where federal appropriations flowed to the corporation of Washington.[13]

In 1820, Congress approved a new charter for the Washington City government. The new document changed the city's political structure by separating the city into six wards rather than four and providing for the direct election of the mayor by the city's eligible voters instead of allowing the city council to appoint him. These changes put Washington in line with other urban municipalities at this time, many of which expanded councils to accommodate population growth and began direct election of mayors. The new charter also instructed the federal commissioner of public buildings to reimburse the city for "a just proportion of any expense which may hereafter be incurred, in laying open, paving, or otherwise improving any of the streets or avenues in front of, or adjoining to, or which may pass through or between any of the public squares or reservations." With this new willingness to pay for sidewalks and street improvements along federal property, Congress had finally accepted its role as a major landholder in Washington. However, the charter also stated that the commissioner should make such payments from money earned from the sale of government-owned lots in the city, "and from no other fund." And these lots sold very poorly. From 1820 to 1824, for example, the federal government sold only thirty-nine lots for a total of approximately $5,300. At the 1820 cost of $3.00 per foot-front for a city sidewalk, the entire revenue from lot sales for these five years would only have paid for the paving of approximately 1,766 feet, less than the perimeter of the Capitol grounds.[14]

With so little money flowing into the commissioner's office, these two portions of the law clashed. As a result, in March 1823, Congress approved a one-time payment of $5,000 directly from the federal treasury to the city of Washington. Part of a larger appropriations bill, the grant of money to the city included language nearly identical to that used in the city charter. It stated, "For the corporation of the city of Washington to reimburse the said corporation a just portion of the expense of making streets and other improvements adjoining the public property five thousand dollars." The similarity of the texts suggests that Congress intended for this $5,000 to cover the commitments it made in the charter. Together, the appropriation for street improvements and the funding of construction at the city hall define the limits of congressional willingness to assist the District of Columbia in the decade following the British attack. Congress might provide fiscal assistance for local improvements but only if federal institutions or property received a direct benefit as well. And while local officials strove to convince their federal counterparts to support the District, local elites continued to dedicate their own time, attention, and money to the development of the national capital.[15]

During the late 1810s, Washington's most influential women established an asylum for the city's orphaned children. Dolley Madison, Marcia Burns Van Ness, Margaret Bayard Smith (an author and the wife of Samuel Harrison Smith, editor of the *National Intelligencer*), and Elizabeth Brown (wife of the pastor of the First Baptist Church), led the effort. The First Lady also donated $20 and a cow to the asylum. In October 1815, the women advertised a meeting in the *National Intelligencer* calling for the ladies of the city and surrounding county to meet at the Brick Capitol and join an association to provide an asylum for destitute orphans. They raised about $700 and soon accepted additional donations from sources such as the Corporation of Washington and St. Patrick's Catholic Church. By late November, the founders of the asylum announced its readiness to receive female orphans. By concentrating their limited resources on young girls, the founders replicated a choice made by similar women's benevolent associations in the early republic. Because orphaned girls were less likely than their male counterparts to receive an education or learn a marketable skill, the women identified them as the most vulnerable members of society. And they hoped that their assistance would prevent these disadvantages from driving the girls into prostitution later in life.[16]

Serving as "second directress" under Dolley Madison and then as "first directress" after Elizabeth Monroe declined the honorary title, Marcia Van Ness led the "lady managers" who made up the Washington Female Orphan Asylum's board. This group governed almost all aspects of the asylum's affairs, including the initial determination that their funds would only allow for the care of orphaned or severely destitute young white girls. The board members established extensive guidelines for the care, education, and behavior of the girls. The girls were issued a uniform, a bonnet, and a shawl of green and beige. They learned to read and write and studied the Bible. And so that they might earn a living after coming of age and leaving the facility, they also learned needlework and domestic service.[17]

In its first year, the asylum took in eight orphaned or destitute young girls. Van Ness insisted that she and her partners had "snatched from vice and poverty eight little girls, who, sheltered within our humble asylum, have received education, food, and clothing." In 1824, the travel writer Anne Royall called the asylum the "glory of Washington." Seeing fifteen girls between the ages of five and twelve living at the facility, she praised their well-clad and healthy appearance as well as the caring and cultivated mind of their caretaker, Mrs. M'Kenny, who taught them "the rudiments of useful instruction." Royall also noted the asylum's great need for additional space, a problem that the board resolved in 1828 when it broke ground on a large brick building designed as a donation to the asylum by Charles Bulfinch, the architect who had taken over the reconstruction of the Capitol after Latrobe's dismissal.[18]

Only when dealing with the project's finances did the women have male assistance. For money matters, a board of male trustees provided guidance and a connection to the financial marketplace. Both legal and social norms required this male intervention on behalf of the asylum's married female managers. In 1828, Congress granted a charter to the Washington asylum as well as a similar venture operated by the women of Georgetown. The charter listed men, in particular, the husbands of the married women involved, as the directors and board members of the asylums, making them legally and financially responsible for the organizations. At some similar institutions around the country, married women circumvented the legal code of coverture, which subordinated their legal identities to those of their husbands, by having their own names listed on an organization's charter. Through this loophole, married women could act independently of their husbands to engage debts, own stocks, or otherwise participate in the financial markets on behalf of the organization in the ways that only unmarried women, widows, and men could. And while the women at the head of the Washington Female Orphan Asylum did not gain this right via their charter, they participated in a nationwide movement that brought women more clearly into public life. By leveraging the charitable precepts of Christianity and the prevailing gender norms of the period, which regarded white women as the protectors of virtue and morality, the female organizers of benevolent organizations brought the virtues of the household into the public sphere. The historian Cynthia A. Kierner has argued that such forays by Southern women of elite and middling social ranks supported, rather than undermined, the existing patriarchal social hierarchy because their work represented the benevolence of the ruling elite. In Washington, such efforts not only buttressed the existing order; they also showcased the quality of local elite society for the nation's elected officials and for visitors like Royall who were often quite critical of the federal city.[19]

In recent years, several historians have examined the social and political influence wielded by the women of Washington's elite society in the first four decades of the nineteenth century. Their activities show the degree to which the lines between public and private blurred in the early republic, especially in the capital city. Through their social gatherings and events, for instance, the elite women of Washington made a place within the private sphere for the public men of Washington, typically their husbands, to maintain personal connections and negotiate political deals without compromising their public personas. At least in terms of the public's perception, this made possible Jefferson's goal of a political system run by those uninterested in political power. In addition, within this private realm women wielded their own political power, conveying valuable information as well as their own ideas during the dinners, visits, and receptions that made up the Washington social calendar. And even in the most public and political place, the Capitol, the presence women in the galleries forced the men attending to the business of the nation to do so within the rules of what one historian called the "customs of polite society." With women looking on, politicians could not act on the primal, cutthroat calculations of power politics alone. Gentility required that some measure of politeness and restraint color political interactions on the House or Senate floor.[20]

As was the case for women who influenced national politics, the efforts of the women of Washington who operated the asylum blurred the lines between public and private. After all, the asylum applied a mixture of public and private financing to intervene in the private lives of the orphaned girls. And when visitors like Royall praised the girls, their caretaker, and the women of the board, it reflected positively on the city.

Of course, the men of elite Washington society founded several private intuitions of their own. In June 1816, they established the national capital's first learned society, advancing their vision of the city as an intellectual center for the nation. On June 15, eighty-nine District residents signed a plan for what they dubbed the Metropolitan Society. These men planned to collect seeds, vegetation, medicinal plants, and minerals from around the nation and the world. They also hoped congressmen would collect samples of "every thing that will be beneficial to the public" from their districts and return them to the society for identification and storage. They also intended to apply to Congress for an appropriation of about 200 acres of the National Mall. There they planned to cultivate the plants and seeds in their collection to foster their distribution "throughout this extensive continent." The organization followed in the footsteps of several agricultural societies that had operated in Washington prior to the war.[21]

With their inclusion of medical and mineralogical subjects, however, the society's founders intended to pursue a broader range of scientific inquiry. In August, the society adopted a constitution that further expanded the organization's scope and renamed it the Columbian Institute for the Promotion of Arts and Sciences. In addition to plants and minerals, the institute would also seek out information about the location and makeup of "mineral waters" in the United States, invite communication on agricultural subjects such as stock maintenance and disease prevention, and collect "natural curiosities." Setting an impossibly lofty goal for themselves, the drafters of the constitution included an article stating that the institute would "form a topographical and statistical history of the different districts of the United States, noticing particularly the number and extent of streams, how far navigable; agricultural products, the imports and exports; the value of lands; the Climate, the state of the thermometer and barometer; the diseases which prevail during the different seasons; the state of the arts and manufactures; and any other information which may be deemed of general utility." Lacking the resources to carry out most of even its more modest goals, the institute could by no means afford to create a complete encyclopedia of the natural and economic history of the nation, something even the federal government would have had great difficulty accomplishing.[22]

These ambitious designs show that the founders of the institute saw themselves as heirs to the tradition established by the Royal Society in London and Benjamin Franklin's American Philosophical Society (APS) in Philadelphia. Similarities in the founding documents of the APS and the Columbian Institute reflect the former's influence on the founders of the institute. As it was christened in 1769, the full title of the APS included the phrase "for promoting useful knowledge." Similarly, the Columbian Institute's charter made frequent mention of both "general" and "public" utility, suggesting that its members shared the APS's concern for the practical application of knowledge. In addition, Benjamin Franklin and the other founders of the APS divided their membership by subject matter, creating standing committees for groups of related fields, including geography, mathematics, natural philosophy and astronomy; medicine and anatomy; natural history and chemistry; trade and commerce; mechanics and architecture; and husbandry and American improvements. The members of the Columbian Institute adopted similar divisions when they revised their constitution in 1820, establishing five classes for members: mathematical sciences, physical sciences, moral and political sciences, general literature, and the fine arts. For both organizations, such groupings facilitated simultaneous scholarly inquiry into a wide variety of subjects.[23]

Describing his vision for the institute, its first president, Dr. Edward Cutbush, a navy surgeon stationed in Washington, connected the success of the organization with the success of the nation and the capital city. Cutbush suggested that the membership should look forward to a time when their institute "will assume an elevated rank amongst the scientific associations of our country." He also repeated the hope that the representatives of the people would carry seeds, plants, minerals, curiosities, and ideas to Washington from all parts of the continent. The institute would display these items in a botanical garden and museum. He also called on members of Congress to support the institute by providing public land for its activities and by appropriating "a small pecuniary aid" that would enable the organization to more quickly extend its benefits to the entire nation. "Where genius and talents are respected,

rewarded and promoted," he explained, "the arts and sciences will flourish and the wealth and power of the nation increase."[24]

In addition, Cutbush explained that the institute would spur beautification and development of the capital. In particular, its botanical garden
would excite "emulation among the proprietors of the eminences around
our city," inducing them to adorn the city with similar gardens. Chan-
neling the deep-seated sense of untapped potential that Washingtonians
felt for their city, Cutbush suggested that no city in the nation offered
such an array of sublime views and that nothing was wanting there "but
industry, public spirit, and population" to render them "highly advanta-
geous to the District." By promoting art, science, and manufactures, the
institute would spur growth and allow the city to achieve its perceived
full potential.[25]

However, the Columbian Institute proved considerably less effective
and influential than its founders had hoped. In April 1818, the institute
received a twenty-year charter from Congress authorizing procure-
ment of a suitable building for meetings and for the "preservation and
safe-keeping of a library and museum." The institute could also obtain
a tract of land, not to exceed five acres, for a botanical garden. This charter established a far more manageable organization, one appropriately
proportioned for the resources available to the membership without
funding from Congress. It would have to subsist on the $5 annual dues
collected from each member. At the institute's largest, about 150 people
qualified for active membership. However, the number of paid members
in good standing never amounted to even half that number. In 1825, for
example, the treasurer received $218.56 from members and reported
$584.62 worth of unpaid dues. At this level of funding, management of a
200-acre botanical garden on the Mall was hardly possible.[26]

Although it never grew large enough to support extensive activity, the
institute boasted an impressive list of members. To improve the institute's reputation, its founders included a clause in their constitution
stating that the president of the United States could choose to hold the
title "Patron of the Columbian Institute." While James Monroe appears
to have accepted this position, his successors John Quincy Adams and
Andrew Jackson each joined the society as resident members. Other
prominent national figures holding membership included Henry Clay
and John C. Calhoun, along with a number of other cabinet members,
military officers, and congressmen. Of course, locals made up the bulk
of the membership. Dozens of elite Washingtonians participated in the
organization, among them, judges and civilian officeholders such as

Richard Cranch, Richard Bland Lee, and William Thornton; many of the city's doctors; architects such as James Hoban and Benjamin Henry Latrobe; and eleven men who served as mayor of Washington. Despite this impressive membership list, the organization lacked the one thing it needed most to accomplish its goals: scientific experts. By and large, the members of the institute held official or professional jobs that took up most of their time, preventing them from bringing anything more than a gentleman's curiosity to the institute's focus on scientific, technical, and agricultural subjects. The institute's lack of expertise contributed to a corresponding lack of activity. Between 1818 and 1838, when the institute's charter expired, members of the society heard only eighty-five papers read by twenty-six different members, only a few of which were published in any form. However, the institute did accomplish two significant goals: establishment of a botanical garden and a scientific museum.[27]

Although Congress had squashed the notion of turning the entire Mall into a botanical garden by limiting the institute's landholdings to five acres, the institute's members continued to advocate for a national garden. Responding to petitions from the institute, Congress granted five acres of public land for its "use and improvement." The property at the eastern end of the Mall began at the edge of a circular road that surrounded the Capitol. From there it extended west along the borders of Pennsylvania Avenue to the north and Maryland Avenue to the south to about the point where 2nd Street would be if it crossed the Mall. The institute requested an enlargement of their holdings to make more room for "the forest trees and plants of this very extensive republic." In May 1824, Congress extended the grant westward to the Washington Canal, which crossed the Mall at 3rd Street (fig. 21).

The portion of their land lying between 1st and 3rd Streets fell within an area the federal government leased to Mountjoy Bailey in 1812. The institute compensated Bailey and removed two frame houses he had erected there. Unfortunately for the institute, Bailey had not improved the land as Congress had hoped such leaseholders would.[28]

Despite their limited financial resources, the members of the institute turned their trapezoidal corner of the Mall into the capital city's first botanical garden. Located where Tiber Creek began its connection with the Potomac River, the eastern terminus of the Mall often flooded and remained swampy much of the year. By 1823, the institute had cleared and leveled the area. And to manage the excess water, the garden's creators dug an elliptical pond with a large island in its center. They also

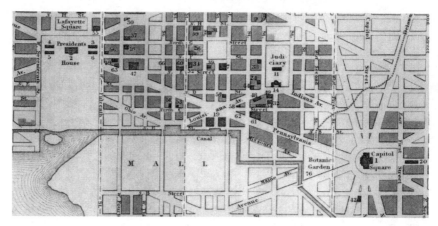

FIGURE 21. A portion of H. S. Tanner's 1836 *City of Washington* map showing the National Mall and the area just west of the Capitol granted by Congress to the Columbian Institute for a Botanical Garden. Item number 14 marks the location of the City Hall building discussed earlier in this chapter. (Library of Congress, Geography and Map Division)

surrounded the garden with a temporary board fence and thorn bushes to protect it from the many wild and domestic animals roaming freely through the city. Finally, the institute graveled a series of walks around the property, each fifteen to twenty feet wide and surrounded by plantings of trees and shrubs. After the garden's enlargement in 1824, members planted samples of plants from around the nation and the world. In 1830, one visitor to Washington called the garden well laid out and noted that "many of the trees and shrubs of other countries have been transplanted and nurtured there."[29]

However, the members struggled to maintain the garden, drawing criticism for the "uncultivated" state of the property in both 1830 and 1832. Critics suggested that the institute's inability to keep up the garden undermined its scientific, educational, and patriotic value. In 1830, an entrepreneur named Francis Barnes proposed turning the property into a for-profit pleasure garden by improving the grounds and constructing ornamental buildings. Barnes's garden would provide "the respectable citizens of Washington and to strangers visiting the seat of government (at a small expense) a cool, comfortable, fashionable and respectable place of innocent recreation." Seeking only the profits from admission and refreshment sales, Barnes proposed that the institute retain ownership of the facilities and continue to make all botanical decisions.

However, the idea met with scorn from many of the institute's members. One member declared that he would rather the garden continue in an uncultivated state due to lack of funds than allow it to become a pleasure garden, "with its usual scenes of debauchery." Having rejected Barnes's idea, the members of the institute allowed the garden to fall into disrepair during the 1830s as the organization slowly faded away. When the Capitol neared completion in 1836, attention turned to the beautification of its surrounding area. As part of that effort, the eastern portion of the garden became part of Capitol Square, signaling the end of the institute's efforts to create a national botanical garden.[30]

Without funding for a building, the institute struggled to establish a permanent museum to house its small collection of minerals, specimens, and oddities. Between 1816 and 1824, the institute moved between a variety of locations throughout the city, including the Blodgett's Hotel building, the Treasury Department, and the new City Hall. In 1821, the institute considered purchasing the contents of Charles Wilson Peale's famous museum in Philadelphia, which he had offered for sale to the United States for $100,000. However, without a suitable home for the items, an appropriation from Congress, permission from that body to hold a lottery, or an unprecedented local fund-raising campaign, the institute could only dream of making the acquisition. Like the founders of the Columbian Institute, Peale had long sought government funding but had encountered Jeffersonian reluctance to apply federal money to such a project. By 1825, Congress allowed the institute to reside in a large room on the ground floor of the Capitol just underneath the Library of Congress. There its members stored and displayed objects holding scientific and cultural significance, including a collection of minerals from around the world; a "herbarium" of dried plants native to the Washington region; fossils and marine shells; clothing and implements from cultures in the American West, the Pacific Islands, China, and Africa; and archaeological items from ancient Greece. In its most popular exhibit case, the institute displayed a "suit of regimentals worn by George Washington," made for him in 1789. A relative of Washington by marriage, founding member of the institute Thomas Law donated the uniform in May 1828.[31]

Although the institute fizzled out of existence less than a decade after Law's donation, the uniform remains on display in Washington today because the Columbian Institute inspired a successor organization. In 1840, Secretary of War Joel R. Poinsett established an heir to the Columbian Institute's vision for a comprehensive, national scientific society in

Washington. Dubbed the National Institution for the Promotion of Science, this new organization invited former members of the Columbian Institute to join and to add their mothballed collections to the new society's holdings. In 1841, the National Institution also took possession of the scientific collections and personal effects of a British scientist named James Smithson. In 1835, Americans had learned that upon his death in 1829 Smithson bequeathed his collections and a fortune worth approximately $500,000 to the United States "to found at Washington, under the name of the Smithsonian Institution," an organization dedicated to the increase and diffusion of knowledge. After receiving the donation in 1838, the Treasury Department invested the funds while Congress debated plans for honoring Smithson's bequest, a process that took eight years. Meanwhile, the Treasury entrusted the collections to the National Institute. Eventually the well-funded Smithsonian Institution took control of the Smithson materials as well as many of those from the Columbian and National Institutes. Although the members of the Columbian Institute failed to achieve their lofty national goals, they had created the first broad scientific society in Washington, lending both credence and physical form to the notion that the national capital should serve as a hub for America's scientific and intellectual culture.[32]

On May 13, 1819, the National Intelligencer published a letter praising the Corporation of Washington and taking to task those who had recently penned criticisms of the city. The author refuted several complaints about the city, including assertions that street paving only occurred on the roads where city council members resided and that the city streets and walkways suffered from an abundance of "fish-garbage." Defending the city government, the author declared that, "since the seat of government has been permanently fixed here beyond all doubt, our corporation, stimulated by a desire to promote the comfort and convenience of the inhabitants, and to render this city what it ought to be, have gone so far, in forwarding the general improvement of the city, as to render themselves nearly bankrupt." The notion of rendering the city "what it ought to be" no matter the cost captures the attitude of local promoters and government officials. Having survived the near-destruction of the city by the British and then by removal advocates in Congress, Washington's social and political leaders came together to ensure that the capital remained along the shores of the Potomac. And despite receiving only limited assistance from the federal government, they embarked on a self-conscious program of civic improvement. By imitating the architectural symbols of federal authority with their grand city hall, taking advantage of the moral power of women acting in public for the good of the less fortunate, and laying down a bold vision for harnessing and disseminating the scientific knowledge and practical expertise in America, Washingtonians strove to meet the expectations for their city laid down during the Washington administration and to establish the capital as the exemplary American city.[33]

PART IV

The Seat of a Continental Empire

On the morning of July 4, 1828, President John Quincy Adams set out from the White House on his way to a celebration of the fifty-second anniversary of the United States' declaration of independence from Great Britain. At the Union Hotel in Georgetown, Adams joined a collection of regional, national, and international political figures, including the mayors and city councils of Washington, Georgetown, and Alexandria, the heads of various executive departments, and foreign ministers. Together these dignitaries marched in procession behind the Marine Corps Band to the Georgetown wharf. Unlike most Independence Day celebrations, however, the participants in this patriotic spectacle had gathered not just to celebrate the past but also to usher in an exciting new future for the Potomac region.[1]

Upon arriving at the wharf, Adams and his companions boarded steamboats that carried them up the Potomac River just outside the boundary of the District of Columbia to the mouth of the Potomac Canal. Originally dug by George Washington's Potomac Company and completed around the turn of the century, this canal provided a water route around the dangerous boulders and rapids that rendered the river impassable just north of Georgetown. Despite their success in circumventing these falls, the company had failed to forge a true connection with the American interior, contrary to Washington's hopes for connecting the Potomac region with the Ohio Valley through a series of canals, portages, and river improvements. But now, more than four decades after the Potomac Company received its charter, local stakeholders came together to make another go of connecting the region to the Ohio country via a canal along the Potomac.[2]

Buoyed by the success of the Erie Canal in New York and by a nationwide fervor for "internal improvements" designed to strengthen the national economy, Washingtonians hoped that the canal would finally bring commercial success to their city. In May 1828, Congress appropriated $1 million for stock in the newly formed Chesapeake and Ohio (C&O) Canal Company and cleared the way for the three District cities to seek loans to purchase company stock totaling another $1.5 million. Along with Maryland, Virginia, and other public and private investors, the leaders of Washington, Georgetown, and Alexandria looked forward to a time when the canal would deliver the agricultural products of the Ohio Valley along with coal and lumber from western Maryland and Pennsylvania to their store shelves and shipping wharves.[3]

Several thousand spectators joined the local, national, and foreign dignitaries on the banks of the Potomac that morning to celebrate the commencement of the canal company's efforts with a groundbreaking ceremony. After some introductory remarks, the company president handed Adams a spade so that he might turn the first shovel of earth for the project. The president raised the spade, drove it downward to the earth, and immediately struck a tree root or stump hidden just below the soil's surface, bringing his effort to a jarring halt. After three or four more attempts, Adams paused and laid down the spade. He removed his coat, set it aside, and once again jabbed the tool into the soil. This time he succeeded. And as he lifted up the spade full of earth the crowd assembled on the nearby hills burst into loud cheers, delighted by their president's perseverance. In his memoirs, Adams noted that his encounter with the stump pleased the crowd far more than the speech he delivered that day. Like most of his work in front of large audiences, he felt that he "got through awkwardly, but without gross and palpable failure."[4]

Adams's political pantomime offered a heartening message about the canal project itself. After all, what better way to kick off a construction project of nearly unprecedented scale than with a symbolic assertion that Americans stood ready to dispatch any obstacle that might impede progress to their lofty goal? One Baltimore newspaper added a political spin to the story in support of Adams's reelection campaign against Andrew Jackson. The *Baltimore Patriot and Mercantile Advertiser* published a small item noting that, on reading about the incident, "a wag" had suggested that Adams had, in fact, encountered a hickory root with his spade and that *"stripping to it and a little manly exertion* very soon conquered even this HICKORY OBSTACLE."* Playing on Jackson's nickname, Old Hickory, the "wag" encouraged all friends of good order, prosperity, and civil rule in the nation to *"strip to it,* and go to work manfully as Mr. Adams did" so that they might triumph over the *"Hickory roots that threaten to obstruct the internal improvements of the country."* However, while spirits may have run high along the shores of the Potomac and among supporters of Adams that morning, another groundbreaking ceremony also took place in the Chesapeake region in commemoration of that Fourth of July, one that would put the region's transportation system on a decidedly different track.[5]

In nearby Baltimore, Washington's larger, more mercantile, and faster growing neighbor to the north, a similar but larger spectacle had unfolded. Thousands of residents and visitors had participated in or watched a two-mile parade featuring marching bands as well as floats constructed by the guilds and trade unions in the city, including a twenty-seven-foot miniature brig fitted out with full rigging, sails, and flags manned by a crew of the city's shipmasters. These festivities culminated just outside of the city with a ceremony marking the laying of the first stone to support tracks for the Baltimore and Ohio Railroad Company. With no sitting president available to lead their delegation of dignitaries, the organizers of this event dug deeper into U.S. history and offered Charles Carroll, the last living signatory of the Declaration of Independence, the opportunity to turn the first spade of earth for the railroad project. Unlike Adams, the ninety-year-old Carroll accomplished his task with little difficulty. And over the next decade, the railroad delivered goods and people to and from Baltimore and the interior of Maryland and Virginia, creating an economic boon for the port city.[6]

Unfortunately for the three cities in the District of Columbia, their substantial investments in the C&O Canal had nearly the opposite effect. Instead of bringing economic prosperity down through its locks to the doorstep of the District, the canal brought Washington, Georgetown, and Alexandria to the brink of bankruptcy. By taking out loans to pay for their shares in the project, the three cities gambled that dividends from the company and increased tax revenue from the expected expansion of their economies would cover the considerable cost of the interest on their loans. But even with tax increases that made Washington residents the most highly taxed citizens in the nation, the city could no longer meet its financial commitments within a decade after the establishment of the canal company. By the mid-1830s, all three cities teetered on the verge of bankruptcy. However, the financial catastrophe brought on by the cities' investment also contributed to a radical change in the relationship between the federal government and the District of Columbia. During the decade and a half between the mid-1820s and the early 1840s, federal officials abandoned the long-held conviction that the federal government should not provide direct assistance to Washington and the federal district.[7]

For the first time since the 1790s, the federal government accepted at least partial responsibility for the maintenance and development of the capital city. During this period, American politics became increasingly tied to the consequences of western expansion and the pitched battle over the abolition of slavery. By expanding the American empire and debating the definition of freedom in federal territories, national politicians lent greater symbolic meaning to the national capital. Coming slowly and sometimes grudgingly from Congress and the executive branch, support for Washington found form in large projects like the C&O canal; financial bailouts that rescued the District cities from their canal debts; smaller infrastructure projects such as bridges across the Potomac; and spending on social and cultural services such as emergency aid for the poor and grants to the District's colleges. Through these efforts the federal government expressed a newfound commitment to the success of the federal city and its District. This commitment also included expansion of the federal government's physical and architectural presence in Washington through the construction of three new large executive office buildings. These buildings matched the grand scale and the neoclassical aesthetic of the White House and the Capitol, making them powerful symbols of the growing American empire.

During the Jacksonian era, national politicians regarded the nation as a powerful empire rapidly expanding across the continent and altered their conception of the capital city to better fit that image. Between the late 1820s and 1840, federal officials finally accepted George Washington's vision for the seat of government as a grand metropolis—a nexus for the commercial, cultural, and political power of the nation. For decades, the District's elites had advocated for just such a capital. And, in part, Jacksonians changed their vision for the city to better meet the needs of the local population. Two powerful national trends spurred this reconsideration of the meaning and value of the federal city: the rapid expansion of the U.S. population and economy and the sectional debate over the existence of slavery and slave trading in the District.

By rebuilding in Washington after the British attack, Congress affirmed the permanence of the city's status as the capital of the nation. After the war, Washington's population continued to grow at significant rates. Each decade between 1800 and 1840 the federal city gained between 4,500 and 5,500 residents. In 1820, this growth pulled the city into ninth position among the most populous cities in the nation, the only time that it would register in the top ten during the nineteenth century. However, without substantial investment from the federal government or the establishment of a dynamic and self-sustaining local economy, the federal city struggled to capitalize on this steady population growth.[1]

Encompassing approximately 10 square miles of the 100-square-mile District, the vast expanse of land covered by the L'Enfant plan promoted

diffusion of the local population. With all areas of the city open for settlement since the publication of the city plan, Washingtonians spread
themselves all over the map. City surveys completed in 1827 and 1830
counted hundreds of private dwellings in each of the city's six wards.
Established by the municipal charter of 1820, the ward system divided
the city into north–south bands of territory roughly along West 15th
Street, West 10th Street, West 1st Street, and East 8th Street, with much
of the peninsula below South E Street reserved as a separate ward. Containing the central core of the city, the Third Ward held 713 dwellings in
1827 and 970 in 1830. This 36 percent rate of growth over the three years
between the surveys marked this ward as not only the largest but also
the fastest growing part of the city. However, these buildings represented
only 26 and 30 percent of the city's housing stock respectively for those
two years. Meanwhile, the First, Second, and Sixth Wards each held
between 15 and 20 percent of the city's homes in 1827. And while they did
not match the rapid growth of the Third Ward during this period, the
First and Second Wards did increase their supply of housing by 18 and
22 percent, respectively. Finally, despite their smaller totals, the Fourth
and Fifth Wards combined still contained roughly 18 to 20 percent of the
city's private dwellings. In cities like Philadelphia or New York, growth
radiated out from a central point, creating a dense urban core. As the
1836 map depicting Washington's ward divisions in figure 22 shows, the
shaded, settled areas of the city stretched all across the map, complicating the lives of the merchants and entrepreneurs attempting to sustain
businesses in the city as well as the local government responsible for its
upkeep.[2]

Lacking a political voice in national politics, the financial and bureaucratic support that states provided to other cities, and even the limited
benefits that their position as the seat of government offered to Washingtonians, some residents of Georgetown and Alexandria sought retrocession back to their original states. Retrocession advocates hoped that
folding their cities back into Maryland and Virginia might free them
from what one petition called "the deprivations and disabilities of the
District of Columbia." In that petition, submitted to the Eighteenth Congress between 1823 and 1825, 426 residents of Alexandria complained of
their subjection to federal taxation without representation, the District's
awkward combination of federal and local courts, the use of an outdated
legal code, congressional unwillingness to attend to the District's problems, and the prospect of an undesired merger with the corporations
of Washington and Georgetown. In the District's two smaller cities,

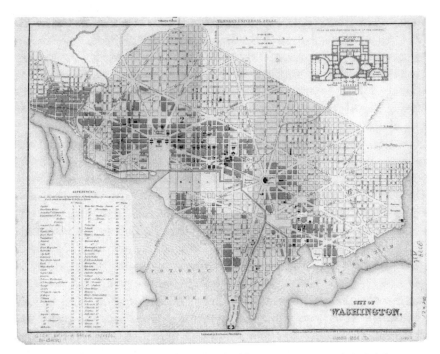

FIGURE 22. City of Washington. Published by H. S. Tanner, Philadelphia, 1836. (Library of Congress, Geography and Map Division)

proximity to the capital had proven insufficient for spurring and sustaining growth. After its population more than doubled from 2,748 in 1790 to 7,227 in 1810, for example, Alexandria experienced only minimal growth over the next four decades, adding only about 1,500 residents by 1850. Georgetown reached a similar population plateau a decade later, rising to a total of 7,360 in 1820, but adding only about a thousand more residents over the next thirty years. The cities' stagnation stands in stark contrast to national growth during this period, when the U.S. population grew at rates of from 32 to 36 percent between each census. In addition, the Alexandria petitioners stated that the national legislature, while "diligently and zealously employed in administering a great and growing empire;—representing free and intelligent millions . . . finds but little time for listening to the wants and demands of a dependent community, which can appeal to your compassion only." From their point of view, the expansion of the American empire meant that their needs would fall further down the long list of congressional priorities. After decades of petitioning both Congress and the Virginia legislature, Alexandrians finally earned congressional approval to hold a vote on retrocession to Virginia in September 1846. And after a vote of 736 to 222 in favor of retrocession, Alexandria and the rest of the District territory south and west of the Potomac returned to Virginia. For their part, supporters of retrocession in Georgetown never mustered similar levels of support. Unlike the Alexandrians, many Georgetown residents hoped that their city might eventually combine with Washington City and Washington County to form a single capital city. However, the city struggled under separate corporate status until 1871, when Congress finally folded it into the Corporation of Washington. The 1820s and 1830s drove home the reality that simply sharing the federal district with the government could not sustain a successful and growing city, let alone three cities.[3]

At the national level, the United States experienced dramatic physical and economic growth in the decades immediately following the War of 1812. Between 1810 and 1830, the nation's population increased by 77 percent, from just over 7 million people to almost 13 million. Also during this period, Americans began a dramatic shift westward, dispossessing Native Americans while taking up their lands through treaty and conquest. While only five new states had joined the union in the first four decades after the Declaration of Independence, six more earned statehood between 1816 and 1821, five of which lay west of the Appalachians. In total, between 1810 and 1830, the population of the western states more than tripled, rising from approximately one million people to over 3.5 million. The proportion of the nation's population living in the West nearly doubled, from 15 percent to 28 percent, during these two decades.[4]

This westward expansion brought an increase in the size and scope of the federal government. With little in the way of revenue, bureaucratic infrastructure, or authority, the U.S. government remained relatively weak during the first two decades after the ratification of the Constitution. Beyond the conduct of international relations and the delivery of mail, the federal government rarely intervened directly in the lives of most Americans. However, the nation emerged from the unsuccessful invasion of Canada and the ultimately successful defense of the country during the War of 1812 with a reinvigorated focus on conquest of the vast continent to its west. And the federal government took up the task of bringing order to the massive migration of Americans into the interior. By providing funding, loans, and charters to many of the companies hoping to profit from infrastructure and development projects in the West, the government exerted some control over western expansion. The government also conducted the military operations and treaty negotiations that left Native American populations in the West confined to small reservations or that forced them onto land beyond the Mississippi. For many Native groups, the U.S. government provided economic assistance and "expertise" as it encouraged them to assimilate into white ways of life. By imposing its will on Native groups, the government asserted its position as the primary authority in the West and the arbiter of American expansion. And as the largest owner of land in the West, it also attempted to orchestrate white settlement of the interior. These organizational activities and the increased federal revenues gained from the sale of western lands imbued the government with considerably more power and authority over the lives of Americans than it had held at any time between the revolution and Jefferson's imposition of a national shipping embargo in 1807.[5]

In Washington, the congressional delegations overseeing this expansion of federal clout also grew larger and more western. Unlike the system used by Congress today, the apportionment formula employed in the early republic period had no fixed upper limit; Congress expanded right along with the nation. Between the Eleventh Congress, elected in 1808 using the apportionment established after the 1800 census, and the Twenty-Third Congress, elected in 1832 and based on the 1830 census, Congress added nearly 100 members to the House, rising from 142 to a total of 240. Further, the admission of seven new states to the union during this period added another fourteen members to the Senate. Because six of the seven new states—Alabama, Illinois, Indiana, Louisiana, Mississippi, and Missouri—lay west of the Appalachians and the three older interior states—Kentucky, Ohio, and Tennessee—had all grown quite rapidly, the proportion of congressmen hailing from states beyond the Eastern Seaboard increased between the Eleventh and Twenty-Third Congresses from 7 to 23 percent. And in the Senate, those states gained even more influence, rising from 18 to 38 percent of its full membership. Given the rise of the West, the interests of Northern merchants and Southern planters alone could no longer dominate the business of Congress. In 1829, for example, when Jackson proposed returning surplus funds to the states based on congressional apportionment, western states cried foul because sale of their lands contributed to the surplus but eastern states had larger populations.[6]

In addition, the extension of the voting franchise to working-class white men also shifted the priorities of the national legislature. During these decades, almost every state in the union substantially decreased or eliminated property requirements that had once prevented many free white men from voting in local and national elections. Therefore, as Americans turned their gaze from the Atlantic coast and toward a western continental empire, their representatives in Congress grew more sensitive not only to the needs of the West but also to those of the ordinary men who propelled continental conquest by moving to the interior. With this reorientation of the nation toward its expanding frontier and the growing role of the federal government in that effort, the symbolic importance of the national capital increased. The power and authority of the American empire emanated from Washington, carried across the continent by its land agents, surveyors, soldiers, and Indian agents.[7]

As Americans migrated into the interior, entrepreneurs improved the nation's river systems with canals and steamboats and laid railroads connecting new settlements with the market towns of the East and South. These advances in transportation became agents of economic growth and integration of the various regions of the nation. For instance, after discovering a cotton variety that grew exceptionally well in the soil and climate of the Deep South, Southern planters had migrated with their workforce of slaves into the region. The federal government supported this process through its efforts to "civilize" the resident Native tribes. By convincing Native Americans to become European-style small farmers, Jefferson and other American leaders hoped that they could be convinced to cede or sell their "surplus" lands to the government. During and after the War of 1812, the United States gained Native land in the South through a number of treaties, some of which resulted from military conflict and some of which simply relied on the threat of military action. As a result, from 1810 to 1820, white and slave migration into the Deep South increased, more than doubling the non-Native population of the region that became Mississippi, Louisiana, and Alabama. Western expansion in the Deep South facilitated greater production of cotton in that region, allowing it to survive a sharp decline in global cotton prices during the 1810s and 1820s. This cotton boom benefited the textile manufacturers in the northeastern states, provided a market for the foodstuffs grown in what is now the Midwest, and offered an outlet for slave owners in the Upper South to sell slaves they no longer wanted as their economy shifted away from tobacco production.[8]

Economic interconnections spurred a sense of nationalism among the American population as the regions became more dependent on one another. In the speech he delivered before attempting to turn the first spade of soil for the C&O Canal, Adams had waxed poetic about the prediction in George Berkeley, Bishop of Cloyne's *Verses on the Prospect of Planting Arts and Learning in America*; as Adams put it, "Time's noblest empire is the last." The president explained that the United States earned its place as history's greatest empire not through conquest as others had done but because it had gained political independence, established a unified republic, and, most important, applied the "physical, moral, and intellectual" powers of the union to subdue its great continent. Bringing the speech back to the reason that he and the crowd had gathered along the banks of the Potomac that morning, Adams asserted that internal improvements like the C&O Canal collectively fostered the success of the American empire. And he concluded by expressing his hope that such improvements might increase and multiply until "every valley shall be exalted, and every mountain and hill shall be made low—the crooked straight, the rough places plain. Thus shall the prediction of the Bishop of Cloyne be converted from prophecy into history, and in the virtues and fortunes of our posterity the last shall prove the noblest empire of time." Delivered at a key moment of potential connection between the national capital and the American interior, Adams's oration exemplifies the logic used by Americans who supported establishing a vast empire and by those who regarded the federal city as the heart of that empire.[9]

Already by the late 1820s, federal officials had placed the national government at the center of efforts to spur American development, primarily through the activities of the Army Corps of Engineers. In 1802, President Jefferson convinced Congress to establish the United States Army Corps of Engineers along with a military academy at West Point. For several decades, the work of the Corps consisted primarily of designing and constructing coastal defenses and fortifications, efforts that were greatly expanded and accelerated by the War of 1812. By the early 1820s, however, the Corps had become much more involved with civil projects. Throughout the nation, the army's engineers performed topographic surveys and drew up engineering plans for internal improvement projects that included roads, canals, mines, and harbors. A nationalist at the time, President Monroe's secretary of war, John C. Calhoun, supported the efforts of the Corps as beneficial not only to the American economy but also to the military since such improvements would assist military operations in a time of war. Use of the Corps for such projects accelerated during the Adams administration. One 1828 report indicated that since 1824 the government had engaged with almost one hundred separate projects in every part of the nation. Under Jackson, the Corps continued to assist with these types of projects, employing as many as fifty engineers working continually on internal improvements during most of the 1830s.[10]

However, integration of the national economy and the growth of nationalism created significant tensions between the regions. As the example of cotton makes clear, slavery played a crucial role in the expansion of the economy in the early republic period. But some Americans in the North rejected the use of enslaved labor in the South and the expansion of slavery into new territories, arguing that slavery had no place in a free republic. The legislative compromise reached when Missouri joined the union in 1820 had restricted expansion of slavery to U.S. territories lying below that state's southern border. However, during the 1820s and 1830s white Americans and their enslaved workers moved into northern Mexico, folding that territory into the American economic orbit. This set the stage for a contentious national discussion of the admission of Texas into the union after those Americans and their Mexican allies rebelled from Mexico in 1836.[11]

This debate over slavery became more contentious during the 1820s. In the early republic only a small minority of Americans had advocated for the abolition of slavery. During the first decades of the nineteenth century, abolitionists, often Quakers, had attempted to convince America's political elite of the need to end slavery. However, as the economic, demographic, and technological changes discussed above swept across the nation during the 1820s and 1830s, the abolition movement broadened. It now drew on the reformist and revivalist spirit of the era, and tapped into the ambition and intellectual energy of the many free blacks, former slaves, and white women who became active abolitionists in this period. The movement also shifted its tactics in favor of forming local abolition societies and putting forward emotional and moral appeals to the public.[12]

During the 1830s, defenders of the slave system twice turned to the federal government for protection from what they viewed as the dangerous message of the abolitionists. By 1835, abolition societies in the North had grown to include tens of thousands of members scattered across hundreds of local branches. They then began a campaign designed to convince Southerners to abandon the slave system by mailing thousands of letters directly to slaveholders. Denouncing the tactic, Southerners demanded that the Postal Service destroy all such material and refuse to deliver any subsequent mailings. They feared that abolitionist material might spark a slave rebellion, asserting that recent rebellions in the Caribbean and failed slave plots in South Carolina and Virginia had been spurred by abolitionist propaganda. Jackson advised his postmaster general to have postmasters in the South hold any suspicious-looking mail until demanded by the recipient and to have those in the North publish the names of the abolitionists doing the mailing. This solution relied on a traditional Southern method of coercion in which the threat of public condemnation deterred undesired behavior. In practice, however, Southern postmasters tended simply to destroy these letters. Thus thwarted in their efforts to reach out personally to slaveholders, abolitionists turned to petitioning Congress. [13]

In 1835 and 1836, petitions signed by thousands of antislavery advocates poured into Congress. Relying on the same fearful logic with which they approached the abolitionist mailings, Southern members of Congress called for the outright rejection of such petitions as dangerous to the peace and safety of their states. Based on a plan offered by Congressman Henry Pinckney of South Carolina, the House created a special committee to receive the petitions but do nothing about them. Because it received fewer abolitionist petitions than the House, the Senate developed a more informal system whereby the petitions would be received but immediately tabled. Both systems allowed Congress to avoid public debate about slavery while nominally protecting the public's constitutional right to petition.[14]

Dubbed the "gag rule" by its opponents, this set of congressional mechanisms for stifling discussion of slavery built on the conceptions of nationhood held by the members of Congress who approved it. The rule reflected white Southerners' insistence that the federal government defend their right to own slaves. After Adams's election in 1824, the Democratic-Republican Party gradually split into two parties, National Republicans (also known variously as Adams Men, Anti-Jacksons, and, eventually, Whigs), who favored internal improvements and an active federal government, and Democrats, who, like their leader, Jackson, generally opposed federal activism and federal funding of improvements that would benefit only one state or region. For Northern Democrats, the rule showcased a desire to maintain national unity in the face of abolitionist attacks on the South. By combining these two goals, Andrew Jackson and Martin Van Buren held together the Northern and Southern wings of the Democratic Party. One historian has recently argued that the debate over internal improvements precipitated the sectional division of that party. Early in the Jackson administration, some Democrats from Northern and free western states supported nationalist improvement projects, while Southerners and those from western slave states advocated an anti-improvement, states' rights point of view. However, the Democrats did show strong party unity in favor of the gag rule, highlighting the ability of party leaders to harness Northern nationalist sentiment in order to overcome sectional divides within the party.[15]

Since the establishment of the federal district, abolitionists had petitioned Congress to end slavery there. Well aware that the Constitution offered Congress no power to alter slavery in the Southern states, abolitionists focused their attention on the two areas over which Congress held such authority, the federal territories and the District of Columbia. In an 1835 petition from female abolitionists in New York, for instance, the authors asked Congress only to act within its authority in the capital but not to "intermeddle" in state rights. However, debate over the abolition of slavery in the District differed from the disputes over slavery in the federal territories, because the District wielded no political power of its own. Behind arguments about slavery in the territories lurked the understanding that when they entered the union new states could alter the balance of power between slave states and free states in Congress. The District's lack of representation in Congress meant that the battle over slavery there held primarily symbolic importance for the two sides. During the late 1820s, abolitionists stepped up their calls for Congress to remove the specter of slavery from its place alongside the institutions that symbolized American liberty. Speaking against the gag rule in 1835, Vermont congressman William Slade caused Southern representatives to storm out of the House chamber when he professed support for petitioners who called for the end of slavery and the trade in human flesh in the District of Columbia "where the flag of freedom floats over [the] Capitol of this great Republic." Arguing that the petitioners regarded themselves as citizens of the republic rather than their individual states, Slade explained that "every thing which concerns this Territory concerns them." For the abolitionists, the District was the nation. And victory there might offer a step toward the eradication of slavery (fig. 23).[16]

Defenders of the slave system also saw the capital as a proxy for the nation. During a long rebuttal to Slade, Virginia Jacksonian James Garland encouraged Congress to protect the liberty and property of slaveholders in the District, protections he no doubt hoped would extend to the rest of the South. By highlighting the symbolic value of the national capital, both opponents and proponents of Southern slavery raised the stature and significance of the federal city.[17]

At the local level, meanwhile, abolitionist sentiment and race relations followed the patterns seen in other areas of the Upper South. In 1816,

FIGURE 23. *Slave Market of America*, an antislavery broadside by William Dorr for the American Anti-Slavery Society depicting various aspects of slavery in the national capital, 1836. (Library of Congress, Prints and Photographs Division)

Speaker of the House Henry Clay and a number of other prominent politicians formed the American Colonization Society in Washington. The society combined the interests of abolitionists with those of whites in Upper South states who could see the dwindling profitability of slavery in their region but did not want to live alongside a substantial population of free blacks. As such, it advocated for the transport of freed slaves to Africa, where there they might build their own republic. Residents of the District made up approximately half of the fifty signatories to the society's constitution, suggesting that this national attempt to bridge the interests of abolitionists and Southerners also had considerable local support. By the 1820s, many local residents also supported abolitionist efforts to rid the District of slavery. In 1828, for example, a thousand District residents signed a petition urging Congress to impose a system of gradual emancipation there.[18]

However, in the aftermath of Nat Turner's bloody, albeit thwarted, slave rebellion in Southampton County, Virginia, in 1831, white District residents soured on the idea of emancipation. Taking the lives of sixty whites, Turner's revolt spurred Southern cities and states to adopt stricter black codes that severely restricted the freedom and mobility of free blacks. Since Southerners blamed the uprising on abolitionist rabble-rousing, they made it much more difficult for antislavery advocates to spread their message in the South. In Washington, the city council passed a set of black codes in summer 1835, just prior to the passage of the gag rule. That year, racial tensions in Washington had come to a head after paranoid rumors connected abolitionist newspapers carried by a visitor to the city with the attempted murder of Anna Maria Brodeau Thornton by one of her slaves one week earlier. This unfortunate coincidence set off a weeklong outburst of violence against the city's free black population. That population had grown steadily with the city and had increased as a percentage of the total with each census. In 1830, the 3,129 free black residents of Washington made up 17 percent of the city population. With 2,330 slaves also living in the city, the combined black population accounted for 29 percent of the total. This percentage roughly equaled Washington's neighbors in the District, Georgetown and Alexandria. It fell below the percentage seen in cities the south of Washington where enslaved people made up larger portions of the population. And it ranked above cities to the north that had free black populations but fewer slaves. Perceiving violent black rebels lurking around every corner, most white District residents lost interest in petitions from outsiders calling for an end to slavery there.[19]

Unfortunately for Southerners and their allies in the North who wanted to ban the subject of slavery from public discussion, the gag rule had the opposite effect. Former president and now Massachusetts congressman John Quincy Adams repeatedly attempted to circumvent it by reading antislavery petitions on the floor of the House and by introducing them at the start of sessions before the rules of debate had been adopted. In addition, the gag rule fueled the abolitionist drive to collect more signatures and submit more petitions to Congress. Before its repeal in 1844, the gag rule had suppressed, or at least diminished, the right to petition of hundreds of thousands, perhaps even millions, of Americans. One 1838 estimate put the number of signatures on petitions received during the third session of the Twenty-Fifth Congress at 500,000, far more than the 23,000 signatures that another source estimated came to Congress in the year prior to the gag rule's passage. When defenders of the slave system attempted to stifle national debate, advocates of abolition and emancipation redoubled their efforts in response. However, all parties to this national controversy agreed on the importance of the District of Columbia. With exclusive jurisdiction over the District, Congress could abolish slavery there or step in to protect it, a decisive authority it did not have over any state. In the course of arguing about these possibilities, both sides acknowledged that the city's place as the national capital would add significance to any congressional action. As the subject of many of these petitions and not simply the place to which they were delivered, the federal city had transcended its once-minor role as a mere meeting place for the government and had become a powerful symbol of the American nation.[20]

After Jackson's election in 1828, District residents had every reason to expect that their relationship with the federal government would soon worsen. After all, as a candidate, Jackson promised to reassert Thomas Jefferson's antiurban, agrarian republicanism. Three key tenets of his platform threatened the growth and development of the capital. First, Jackson advocated a spoils system in which positions in the federal bureaucracy would transfer to the loyal partisans of the victor in a presidential election. By undermining the livelihoods of the hundreds of Washingtonians who held federal posts, this proposal threatened to replace a stable and permanent segment of Washington society with temporary officeholders unlikely to put down meaningful roots in the city. Second, District residents feared that Jackson's crusade against the Bank of the United States might extend to local banks that had also received their charters from Congress. Finally, the Jacksonians' contempt for federally financed internal improvements suggested to Washingtonians that federal support for the development of their city might evaporate completely, including the funding provided for the C&O Canal project.[1]

Fortunately for Washingtonians, their worst fears went unrealized. Two years into the Jackson administration, two-thirds of officeholders who had served under John Quincy Adams remained on the government payroll. The Jacksonians had not attempted a complete purge of the federal workforce. Likewise, District banks survived Jackson's war on banking interests. But, on the subject of internal improvements, the Jacksonian Democrats in Congress initially fulfilled the negative expectations of local residents. In time, however, the Jacksonians would radically alter the federal government's relationship with the District.[2]

Just seven months before Jackson's 1828 election, Congress decided to purchase $1 million worth of stock in the C&O Canal Company, an unprecedented federal investment in the development of the District. Backers and promoters of the project had spent five years seeking financial support from Congress. Their efforts began in November 1823, when representatives from the three District cities as well as counties along the Potomac in Maryland, Virginia, and Pennsylvania gathered in Washington to discuss the idea of creating a canal along the river. After President Monroe recommended the project to Congress the following month, that body appropriated $30,000 for the United States Board of Engineers to conduct a detailed survey of the proposed route. When the board confirmed the feasibility of linking the Chesapeake to the Ohio country in February 1825, Congress approved a charter for the company. However, that company could not issue stock and raise funds until it had an estimate for the cost of the project. And when the final report of the Board of Engineers estimated that the canal would cost a staggering $22.3 million, hopes quickly faded that sufficient funding could be obtained.[3]

Supporters presented the canal to Congress as a national project aimed at linking the eastern and western portions of the nation. Such internal improvement projects became particularly volatile political issues during the 1820s and 1830s because federal funding for projects directly benefiting only some states ran counter to the traditional Jeffersonian preference for a small and inexpensive federal government. Opponents of these projects feared that they might increase the power of the government, add to the tax burden of the citizenry, promote the interests of some Americans at the expense of others, and commit the government to unexpected future costs. During the two decades prior to this period, Jeffersonians in Congress had generally rejected national improvement projects as beyond the scope of the federal government. In 1811, for example, Congress rebuffed requests from New Yorkers seeking financial support for a canal connecting Lake Erie with the Hudson River. When fund-raising for that project resumed after the War of 1812, New York augmented state spending with loans funded by subscriptions purchased by private citizens. Some scholars have pointed out that both Jefferson and Madison at one time or another supported amending the Constitution in order to clear the way for certain internal improvements. However, neither man pressed hard for such an amendment, even when backed by large congressional majorities.[4]

After 1815, a new generation of nationalist-minded politicians pushed for federal support of economic development projects designed to strengthen and unify the national economy. This faction included such figures as John Quincy Adams and Henry Clay. However, their efforts awakened a localist reaction that built on a states' rights argument against this type of federal spending. For example, one extreme states' rights advocate, Virginia Democratic-Republican Archibald Austin, argued that sovereignty lay with the states as if they were independent countries and that the national government represented merely a "league or confederation between them." For decades to come, the question of federal authority over the states would loom over all aspects of national politics. Spreading beyond the debate over internal improvements, this divide dominated discussion of issues such as the nation's tariff policy and the spread of slavery into the western territories. Because the states' rights position was most popular among Southerners, Jackson adopted it to compete with Southern rivals, and to set himself apart from Clay and Adams. Carefully crafting his message vetoing part of a national road in 1830, for example, Jackson praised the value of the transportation revolution while warning against increasing the nation's debt or, worse, its taxes, by funding local improvement projects with federal dollars. Likewise, his willingness to allow the Army Corps of Engineers to assist with improvement projects around the nation reflected his desire to promote national development while minimizing federal spending. By appealing to the traditional Jeffersonian logic of small government, Jackson satisfied many Democrats, especially in the South. However, he had come into office too late to stop a substantial federal investment in the C&O Canal.[5]

With the backing of Virginia, Maryland, Pennsylvania, and Ohio, canal supporters had a fighting chance of securing federal funding. However, the canal's projected $22.3 million price tag represented a sum nearly $8 million over the total outlays of the federal government in 1825. At that price, even the most ardent supporter of internal improvements could not support the canal.[6]

Proponents of the canal overcame the lofty cost estimate by working up a more palatable projection. Convinced that the board overestimated or overstated costs, the project's main stakeholders encouraged Adams to present their criticism of the report to an independent third party that might reach a more convenient conclusion. Adams agreed to their request. In 1827, the civil engineers he selected projected a cost of only $4.5 million because they relied more closely on the labor and construction costs incurred during the construction of canals in New York and Pennsylvania. By May 1828, Congress had pledged its $1 million for stock in the canal company and authorized the District cities to seek loans and subscriptions for a total of $1.5 million, $250,000 each for Georgetown and Alexandria and $1 million for Washington.[7]

Spurred on by their anticipation of an economic windfall, the District's leaders quickly set aside the spirit of cooperation that had helped secure federal support and returned to the old rivalries that had long defined their relationships. Residents in both Washington and Alexandria disliked the planned termination point of the canal, just upriver from Georgetown. Washingtonians used the clout within the canal company that their million-dollar investment provided to push for an extension of the canal down to the Georgetown-Washington border at Rock Creek. There it would join with the existing Washington Canal so that goods could make their way across the city to its deepwater wharves on the Eastern Branch. This extension added $500,000 to the cost of the project and required that the city increase its own debts to purchase the Washington Canal, widen and deepen it, and create a basin where the two canals connected. Seeking equal footing with the other two cities, Alexandria officials put forth an even bolder—and costlier—plan to connect the canal with their city. In 1828, the newly chartered Alexandria Canal Company began work on a canal along the south bank of the Potomac between Georgetown and Alexandria. And in order to get goods across the river, they erected a 1,500-foot aqueduct. Thirty feet wide and five feet deep, this structure rested on eight stone piers set into the riverbed and stone abutments on each shore (fig. 24). When completed in 1843, the Alexandria Canal had cost $1.25 million, almost $1 million more than had been originally projected. As had been the case with the Washington Canal, the canal companies, the city corporation, and Congress shared financial responsibility for the project. Federal investment in these local additions to a national improvement project signaled a partial shift in the federal government's attitude toward development in the District. That change, however, did not happen overnight.[8]

During the Adams administration, the House and Senate Committees on the District of Columbia both advocated for substantial federal spending in Washington. Unhappy with the poor condition of Pennsylvania Avenue, members of Congress and executive officers had urged the local government to pave it. Already burdened with responsibility for the sprawling city and hamstrung by their limited tax revenues, Washington officials balked at the request. They insisted that Congress bear the cost

FIGURE 24. View of Aqueduct Bridge, with the Chesapeake and Ohio Canal in the foreground, undated. (Library of Congress, Prints and Photographs Division)

of improving the primary artery connecting the White House and the Capitol, as it had during the Jefferson and Madison administrations. The sympathetic congressmen and senators on Committees on the District of Columbia agreed with this interpretation. In 1827, the Senate's Committee on the District recommended an appropriation of $37,000 to provide a crushed-rock road surface for Pennsylvania Avenue from the Capitol all the way to Georgetown. By extending this paving project beyond the federal core of the city, the committee signaled the willingness of some in Congress to establish a new relationship between the federal government and the city. However, the full Senate did not vote on the bill and the road remained unpaved. [9]

Three years later, in 1830, the House Committee on the District of Columbia accepted partial federal responsibility for improvements in Washington and for the miserable fiscal condition of the city government. Instructed to investigate the "expediency" of paving Pennsylvania Avenue between the White House and the Capitol, the committee estimated that the roadwork would cost over $48,000. They also concluded that the city government would be unable to afford such an expense because it earned no tax revenue from the federal government's extensive landholdings yet bore almost exclusive responsibility for city improvements. The committee also recognized that the city's grand scale and wide avenues added to its burden. Finally, they attempted to dispel the widely held notion that federal spending in Washington had far outstripped the revenues gained from sales of government-owned lots. By setting aside the expenditures for the public buildings, the committee calculated that the federal government had spent only about $187,000 in the District, while the combined income from government lots sold and the value of those still held represented nearly $1.8 million. With this report, the House committee cast aside the long-standing Jeffersonian notion that Washington was an ordinary municipality that should be responsible for its own physical and economic development.[10]

The report marked a turning point for federal willingness to fund development in the District. In 1832, for example, Congress appropriated $62,000 for the Pennsylvania Avenue project. And between 1830 and 1836, Congress authorized funding to repair and improve various local bridges and canals. These appropriations included funds for reconstructing the "Long Bridge" built by the Washington Bridge Company in 1809 after ice, debris, and floodwaters from a late winter freshet washed away portions of it in 1831, just as its Georgetown opponents had hoped would happen two decades earlier. Finally, each of the local municipalities received large appropriations from Congress for local improvement projects. Washington and Alexandria received $150,000 and $400,000 respectively for their extensions of the C&O Canal. And Georgetown accepted $150,000 for clearing obstructions from the Potomac and removing the tolls from the upper Potomac Bridge. For three decades, leaders from the District cities had requested appropriations for projects like these and been flatly rebuffed by Congress. Up to this point, local bridge, road, and canal projects had received federal charters but no federal funds.[11]

During this period, the Jacksonians also funded some of the District's social and cultural institutions. In the early 1830s, both Georgetown College and Columbian College, the future George Washington University, received grants of government-owned lots in the city valued at $25,000. Congress also donated land worth $10,000 to two of the District's orphanages. However, such gifts proved to be of little use to the institutions because the commissioner of public buildings overestimated the value of the difficult to sell city lots. Finally, after decades of requests from local residents, Congress approved an overhaul of the District's legal code. The peculiar decision to borrow the legal codes from Maryland and Virginia when the District was established had not only resulted in a cumbersome dual legal system, but it also saddled the cities with outdated eighteenth-century laws. Under the new system, petty thieves no longer faced capital punishment but instead received more humane sentences. [12]

Even this unprecedented level of support could not stave off the looming threat of bankruptcy for the District's cities. In fact, congressional support for internal improvements in Washington, Georgetown, and Alexandria hastened the cities' financial decline because Congress had also authorized the District cities to borrow funds for their substantial subscriptions of canal company stock. The debts incurred by the cities during this period proved too large for them to handle. For instance, between 1822 and 1828, Washington's city council made appropriations for an average of about $42,000 in city spending each year. After the city's purchase of $1 million worth of canal company stock in 1828, the average for the next six years ballooned to over $265,000 per year, a 530 percent increase. For each of the three cities, the addition of the canal debts either doubled or tripled their existing debt load. Because of delays in the construction of the canal, the municipalities could not rely on increased tax revenue and canal fees to pay the interest on their debts. Clearly reeling from a fiscal year in which the city council appropriated more than $508,000 in spending, approximately $400,000 of which went to payments on the C&O Canal or for work on the Washington Canal, in 1834 Washington's city council introduced a special tax of $0.60 per $100 of assessed real and personal property. This assessment more than doubled the city's property tax rate, bringing it to $1.10 per $100 of assessed property, the highest such rate for any city in the nation at the time. Having bitten off far more than they could chew, the District municipalities very nearly choked to death on their canal debts. In 1835, agents arrived in Washington representing the Dutch creditors from whom the cities had secured their canal stock loans. Unable to make their payments, the cities faced the prospect of a forced sale or transfer of property to satisfy their creditors. Responding to pleas for assistance from the city governments, the Senate Committee on the District of Columbia proposed congressional relief of the debts held by Washington, Georgetown, and Alexandria. [13]

That committee also acknowledged federal responsibility for the entire District of Columbia because of its special status as the national capital. Authored by New Jersey senator Samuel Southard, the committee's report lamented the "well known pecuniary embarrassments" of the city of Washington. However, he carefully avoided placing complete blame on the city leaders. Instead, the senator suggested that while the city's investments in the C&O Canal were imprudent, local officials made those choices with the advice and support of the federal government. Southard also criticized Congress's refusal to fund city projects, stating that it "was bound by every principle of equal right and justice" to pay for improvements proportionate to the amount of federal land in the city. Looking back across three decades of federal spending there, the committee found only one instance of funding for a project that did not directly benefit the federal government, the recent appropriation of $150,000 for improvements to the Washington Canal. Declaring that they had "been unable to separate the interests of the District from the interests of the United States," the committee countered the decades-old states' rights ideology that opposed federal support of one local population over any other. During this Congress, which served between 1833 and 1835, Jackson's opponents controlled the Senate and each of its committees. As a supporter of internal improvements and an active federal government, Southard had made his own politics clear in the report. However, this fleeting moment of opposition power cannot explain the wider congressional acceptance of federal intervention in the District during the Jacksonian era. After all, those two years marked the only time during the Jackson or Van Buren administration that the Jacksonians did not control both houses of Congress.[14]

By the 1830s, a majority of national politicians had come to see the capital as an object of national rather than local interest. As a result, Congress began acting to improve the physical and cultural infrastructure of the city. For four decades, local elites had pressured presidents and congressmen to adopt this nationalist vision for the District. While their arguments had not changed, their circumstances had worsened. Southard's report described the prospect of foreign bankers owning "a great proportion of the property within the capital of the union" as "little creditable to the nation" and "abhorrent to the feelings of the committee." However common this sentiment might have been, it only explains willingness to support a debt bailout for the cities. The District did not become a subject of national interest more broadly until the republic expanded into a continental empire and sectional pressures strained the bonds holding that empire together. When defending the proposal to assist the cities with their debts, for instance, Maryland Jacksonian congressman John Stoddert made all of the usual arguments about local donation of land for the city and the government's tax-free ownership of land there. In addition, he concluded his remarks by stating, "Every state in the Union had an interest in the prosperity of this common city." This idea of a common city differed greatly from the notion that the District was simply the seat of government, a place where Congress happened to reside but which bore no additional national significance. Now acting as a powerful empire orchestrating western expansion with military and bureaucratic force, the American government needed a symbolic national capital that properly portrayed the strength of the nation. The District gained additional symbolic importance as the sectional argument over slavery in the American republic focused on the existence of slavery in the capital. It is no coincidence that later in 1835 Congressman Slade would repeat Southard's suggestion that the interests of the District and the nation were inherently interwoven as he railed against the presence of slavery in the District. For many Americans on both sides of the sectional divide, the federal city had come to represent the nation.[15]

Even when faced with the financial collapse of the District cities, some Jacksonians held firm to the traditional Jeffersonian vision for the government and the federal city. In 1834, for example, New Jersey Jacksonian congressman James Parker denounced an appropriation of $200 to have the mud and dust removed from Pennsylvania Avenue, which had recently been paved using federal funds. Parker argued that the District should manage its own affairs. Quite bluntly, he suggested that the people of Washington should "do as the people of other cities did, namely: keep their own streets in repair, and keep the dust out of their own eyes." Later in that debate when the subject of providing debt assistance to the city came up, New York Jacksonian congressman Abijah Mann stated that he considered the debt of the city the result of a private transaction. While the city might be insolvent and the taxes on its residents intolerable, he did not see how or why Congress should engage in an act of charity by assuming "the debts which a corporate body had improvidently contracted."[16]

These objections, however, could not stem the rising tide of congressional opinion in favor of federal support for the District of Columbia. In May 1836, with Jacksonians once again in control of both houses, Congress voted to assume the C&O Canal debts of all three cities. In the House, 102 members voted in favor of the final bill for relief of the cities and 69 voted against it. A breakdown of the votes by both party and region suggests that both factors affected the voting. For instance, members of parties desiring a weak central government, Jacksonians,

Democrats, and Nullifiers, split their votes almost evenly, with fifty-three voting in favor of the bill and forty-eight voting against it. Members of parties favoring a stronger government, including National Republicans, Anti-Masons, and Whigs, leaned much more heavily toward approval of the bailout, amassing forty-nine votes in favor of and twenty-one votes opposed to the bill. But even among these smaller parties none exhibited a strict party line vote for either side of the issue. Sectional influence explains some of these breaks from strict party ideology. For example, Jacksonians and Democrats in the North voted in favor of the bailout by a wide margin, 70 percent to 30 percent. And the few supporters of a strong central government in the South split their votes, seven voting against the bill and six voting for it. In the Midwest, Jacksonians and their opponents split their votes fairly evenly. These voting patterns suggest that a slim majority of the Jacksonians in the House turned away from their states' rights ideology in order to save the District cities from financial ruin. Largely from the North and the Midwest, Jacksonian dissenters from Jeffersonian orthodoxy joined with 70 percent of the members of opposition parties to affirm the importance of the city to the national government.[17]

By the mid-1830s, despite their rhetoric portraying themselves as defenders of Jeffersonian ideals and as enemies of internal improvements, a majority of Jacksonians embraced federal action in favor of development and improvement in the District of Columbia. They had not changed their overall stance on these broad issues. Jacksonians held firm to their states' rights ideology. They had simply come to accept the District as a necessary exception to their preference for a weak and inactive government. Despite their many differences, both parties promoted American nationalism. For those who supported a strong federal government, the social and economic linkages provided by internal improvement projects would carry a nationalist message of American strength, and the capital would both reflect and project that vision for the nation. For the Jacksonians, their preference for a weak federal government made it even more important to have a well-developed federal district. In the absence of active government effort to bind the nation together, the country would need powerful symbols of American nationalism to stave off disintegration. Already during Jackson's administration, South Carolina's assertion that states could nullify federal laws had forced the president to defend the federal government's power and authority over the states. Although he supported a relatively small and weak federal government, Jackson had always retained a strong sense of nationalism and of the importance of keeping the union together under federal control. The nullification crisis showed very clearly how politicians could extend the states' rights ideology to the point where it threatened the very fabric of the union. Jacksonians who voted in favor of development and improvement in the District, therefore, revived George Washington's vision for a grand metropolis on the Potomac and promoted a symbolic nationalist agenda in the capital. In the long term, however, this attempt to foster national unity proved insufficient, as sectional tensions continued to mount over the next three decades.[18]

Driven by this increased federal acceptance of Washington's vision for a national metropolis, Jacksonians began construction of three grand public buildings during the 1830s. Together, the Treasury Building, the Patent Office, and the General Post Office embodied both the Jacksonian shift away from the traditional Jeffersonian reluctance to fund development in the city and also the emerging consensus that Washington represented a powerful symbol of the nation. In July 1836, President Jackson approved a plan for the Treasury Building drafted by the architect Robert Mills, who also designed the General Post Office and had a significant influence on the Patent Office. To all of these projects Mills applied his conviction that "the character of a nation is judged by the character of its public buildings." Each of these structures featured the Greek and Roman design principles Mills had learned as an apprentice to Benjamin Henry Latrobe. These characteristics connected the buildings to the republican imagery used at the White House and the Capitol. And by building on an imposing scale Mills hoped to remind viewers of the strength and power of the rapidly expanding American empire.[19]

Unrelated fires in 1833 and 1836 provided the impetus for this federal construction binge. At around 2:00 a.m. on March 31, 1833, witnesses noticed smoke and flames pouring out of the Treasury Building, a two-and-a-half-story brick federal-style office building located one block east of the White House. Presumably to save time and money during the building's reconstruction after the War of 1812, the commissioner of public buildings did not render the building fireproof through the addition of stone or brick interior walls. Two decades later, that decision played to the advantage of a pair of arsonists hired to torch the building in order to cover up evidence of a fraudulent Revolutionary War pension claim lodged with the Treasury. While local residents and federal workers saved many important Treasury files—including those the arsonists had hoped to destroy—local fire response efforts failed to save the structure. In July 1836, Congress approved replacement of the Treasury

Building and a new home for the Patent Office, which had outgrown its home in the Blodgett's Hotel building. Having lost the Treasury to fire and learned of the damage caused by a fire that destroyed nearly seven hundred buildings in New York City the previous year, Congress called for fireproof construction of the new buildings. Unfortunately for America's inventors, in December 1836 a fire tore through the Patent Office after a servant placed hot fireplace ashes in a wooden refuse box. That fire destroyed 26,000 patent specifications, drawings, and scale models. The building had also housed the local and federal post offices. Their loss required the construction of another new federal office building to house the General Post Office.[20]

To replace the Treasury Building, Mills envisioned an E-shaped structure reversed so that its spine ran along 15th Street with three shorter, porticoed wings facing the White House. The 466-foot unbroken line of Ionic columns along the east side of the building provided its most prominent architectural feature (fig. 25). Still imposing today, the columned eastern facade of the Treasury Building dominates the full city block. Mills called the colonnade the "only ornament to the building." And he asserted with pride, "We have no Colonnade in this country by which we can draw a comparison, and there is none in Europe, not even that of the Louvre, that will exceed it in extent." In order to fit a building large enough to accommodate the number of rooms demanded by the treasury secretary without encroaching on the White House gardens to the west, Mills pushed his design to the limits of the Treasury lot. To the north, his building came within feet of the existing State Department building; to the east, he set back his grand colonnade only far enough to allow for a sidewalk along the road; to the south, his plan brought the building close to Pennsylvania Avenue.[21]

The building's placement, design, and high cost contributed to political controversy that rapidly engulfed the project. Standing so close to Pennsylvania Avenue, the main thoroughfare of government business and the symbolic connection between the executive and legislative branches, the building disrupted the sightlines between the Capitol and the White House. When members of Congress realized that the building might diminish the aesthetic power of L'Enfant's city plan, many demanded that Mills alter the plans to preserve the original sightlines. Not all congressmen accepted this logic, however. Speaking against a bill that called for an abrupt end to the project, Arkansas Democrat Archibald Yell mocked the motives of congressmen seeking to protect their view of the White House, stating that the Treasury "impedes their

FIGURE 25. *Washington—U.S. Treasury*, E. Sachse & Co., undated. (Library of Congress, Prints and Photographs Division)

vision, and, forsooth, they cannot see that building, for the occupancy of which their hearts palpitate, and all their aspirations are breathed by midday, and on which their dreams are based at the midnight hour." For his part, Mills argued that the number of rooms demanded by the Treasury secretary necessitated full use of the lot available.[22]

Opponents also argued that its design and implementation failed to meet the standards required by the Treasury Department. Complaints from the Treasury about dampness in the basement and lack of light in the third floor offices prompted the House Committee on Public Buildings to solicit reports from three outside architects between 1837 and 1838, each of whom criticized Mills's work to varying degrees. Within the politically charged halls of Congress, however, none of these assessments had much impact on the opinions of those congressmen who had already dedicated themselves to one opinion or another about the building.[23]

For Congress, the issue of the project's cost attracted more attention than the comfort of the Treasury Department's clerks and officers. Approved during an economic boom enjoyed by Americans during the first half of the 1830s, cost overruns for the project drew scrutiny from Congress in the aftermath of the financial Panic of 1837. Using Mills's estimates in 1838, New York Democrat Zadoc Pratt projected that the total cost for the Treasury, including the southern wing and the adaptation of the State Department building as a northern wing, would be $900,000—nine times the amount originally appropriated in 1836. Because he worried that the cost could rise to as much as $3 million, Pratt favored cutting the nation's losses by dismantling the partial building. Defending the building, Congressman Yell likened dismantling it to the profligate ways of Adams and other promoters of internal improvements. He questioned how any friend of the current administration could, "with retrenchment and economy on their lips, consent to an act so opposite the sincerity of their professions." With all eyes on the nation's bottom line, the building became a large sandstone pawn in the political games playing out in Congress.[24]

In spring 1838, President Van Buren stepped in to settle the matter, naming the secretaries of state, treasury, and war to serve as a board of commissioners to oversee work on the public buildings. Hearing praise of Mills's ability to design fireproof structures from the District's commissioner of public buildings, the new commission chose to ignore the congressional report calling for the dismantling of the Treasury. Like his mentor, Benjamin Henry Latrobe, Mills learned on the job that creating federal architecture in Washington was inherently political. Influenced by complaints about the building from Treasury officials and rival architects, congressmen on both sides of the aisle sought to score political points by painting their rivals as wasteful, no matter what side of the Treasury argument they supported.[25]

The architectural historian Dell Upton has argued that Mills's difficulty pleasing Treasury Department officials stemmed from their divergent visions of the purpose and meaning of the spaces inside the building. Both sides conceived of the Treasury Building as an architectural extension of the mercantile countinghouses that dotted the cities of the Atlantic world rather than as an inheritor of the British imperial architectural system. However, each sought to reproduce a different aspect of the merchants' business model. Mills filled the building with many small, identical offices designed to facilitate the public's access to department clerks. Treasury officials, on the other hand, wanted to replicate the type of precise record keeping used by countinghouses. Mills's small rooms, damp basements, and dim attic worked against that ideal. These officials demanded larger, better-lit workspaces and plenty of storage room for their files. Such complaints drove calls for demolition or radical remodeling of the building for the next several decades. This analysis helps us understand the disagreement between Mills and the Treasury officials over the merits of the building. It also highlights the direct connection between this building's design and the empires and economies of the Atlantic world. However, this approach does not explain the ferocity of the congressional arguments over the structure. [26]

Only acknowledgment of the inherent symbolic significance of government buildings in Washington explains Congress's reaction to this architectural debate. When members of Congress painted either the construction or the destruction of the building as a foolish boondoggle, they accepted the symbolic value of an executive office building standing at the center of the national capital. During a speech in which he railed against Mills's work, Massachusetts Whig Levi Lincoln asserted that it should be redone "in a style consistent with economy, and not dishonoring the good taste and architectural skill of the nation." He concluded by warning that future generations would look upon the building, compare it to the Capitol and the White House, and judge their generation harshly for their poor work during a time of peace and prosperity when their predecessors had erected those great buildings amidst "debt, insecurity, and public embarrassment." A simple dispute over the size of the rooms in the building would not have turned into such a pitched congressional battle. As a part of the Washington landscape, the Treasury Building represented both the aspirations and the abilities of the nation. Since he disliked the building very much, that fact greatly disturbed Representative Lincoln. He worried that Mills's Treasury Building would fail to showcase the nation's best attributes in the same way that the White House and Capitol did. This line of reasoning shows us that although they disagreed over the Treasury, Mills and his opponents all accepted as a given the idea that federal architecture in Washington should represent the expanding American empire while also inspiring faith in it.[27]

On July 4, 1836, the same day that Jackson chose the Mills design for the Treasury, he also chose the design for a new United States Patent Office. Passing on a submission turned in by Mills, Jackson instead selected a plan designed by William P. Elliot and based at least in part on work done by Alexander Jackson Davis whose New York firm employed Elliot as a commission agent for federal projects. Elliot proposed a rectangular building with a central courtyard that could be constructed one side at a time as funding and space demands dictated. Despite losing the design competition, Mills still had considerable influence over the Patent Office because Jackson placed him in charge of its construction. A composite of ideas from all the architects involved, the final Patent Office structure totaled 333,000 square feet, making it the nation's largest

FIGURE 26. *Washington—Patent Office*, E. Sachse & Co., printed between 1865 and 1869. (Library of Congress, Prints and Photographs Division)

office building on its completion in 1868. It encompasses two full city blocks between F and G Streets and 7th and 9th Streets NW (fig. 26). On the original plan for the city, L'Enfant reserved this position for a non-denominational church that would also house monuments to national heroes. The building erected has more in common with a Greek temple than a Christian church. Enormous porticoes replicating the dimensions and Doric columns of the Athenian Parthenon dominate each facade. It was only too fitting then that in this era of industrialization the official repository of America's faith in its own ingenuity, the Patent Office, should come to occupy a building and a city square steeped in religious symbolism.[28]

Finally, in 1839, a few years after construction began on the Patent Office and the Treasury Building, Mills received a commission for the General Post Office. Rising on the block just across F Street to the south of the Patent Office between 7th and 8th Streets, Mills's General Post Office struck a decidedly less imposing tone than its neighbor. Originally a U-shaped building fronted along E Street, a later addition extended and connected the building's wings with a new section along F Street, creating an enclosed rectangle. Mills modeled this building after a traditional Italian Renaissance palace. Unlike the previous two buildings, a collection of features and fine details rather than one dominant characteristic defined the look of the General Post Office. For example, the front facade facing E Street included a single four-columned central portico. Its fluted Corinthian columns gave way to the left and right

FIGURE 27. *Washington—General Post Office*, 1850. (Library of Congress, Prints and Photographs Division)

to narrow pilasters, or flattened columns, between each of the windows along the facade. And the east and west sides of the building both included smaller, double-columned porticoes (fig. 27).[29]

Mills also incorporated marble, a building material previously unused in Washington. Just decades after their reconstruction, the White House and the Capitol had already begun to discolor and show signs of weathering. The porous nature of the Aquia, Virginia, sandstone used on those buildings as well as Mills's two existing projects required frequent and costly painting in order to ensure color stability and weatherization. Mills argued to the commissioner of public buildings and to members of Congress that they could avoid the high cost of repair and maintenance of the sandstone by employing granite or marble for the exterior of the General Post Office. Of course, some members of Congress disagreed with this logic, one going so far during the debate as to ask about the "necessity of building these Departments on the scale of Palaces." But a report issued by the House Committee on Public Buildings described the available sandstone as "perhaps the worst material for building in the world." Mills's logic that greater up-front costs would save the public money in the future won the day. The architect then set to work on the city's first marble building, tweaking the design so that his pilasters matched those of the Temple of Jupiter Stator, which was said to have been Rome's first marble building.[30]

Considered together, these buildings give a physical form to the Jacksonian break with Jefferson's vision for the federal city. Already, by providing funding for development and infrastructure projects in the District, Congress had signaled the Jacksonians' intention to raise the stature of the nation's capital. By approving these grand public buildings, they took the process a step further. Previous iterations of the executive office buildings had adhered to the understated and economical precedents set during the 1790s. But during the 1830s, the Jacksonians in the White House and Congress elected to build on a scale rivaled only by the Capitol. In an 1835 report of the House Committee on Public Buildings, Congressman Leonard Jarvis of Maine stated, "The public edifices in the capital of our confederated republic ought not to be inferior to those erected for federal or State purposes in our large commercial cities; and if not in advance of public opinion, they ought at least to keep pace with it." In other cities, the federal government had also erected imposing public buildings. In Philadelphia, for instance, the First and Second Banks of the United States each occupied classical structures with prominent columned porticoes. In addition, before coming to Washington to work on the Treasury Building, Mills had designed several federal customhouses, all in the same dramatic Greek revival style, the great columns and heavy stones of which conveyed the power, authority, and permanence of the federal government. By insisting that Washington architecture match, if not best, the products of other cities, Jarvis suggested that cutting-edge architectural superiority would mark the city's primacy among America's urban places.[31]

In all, despite coming to power with the avowed intention of continuing Jefferson's policy in support of an agrarian republic, the Jacksonian politicians who controlled the presidency and Congress during the 1830s instead accepted the local elites' vision for the capital as a grand metropolis at the head of a powerful American empire. By 1840, congressmen from twenty-six states stretching beyond the Mississippi River came to Washington each year to attend to the business of the nation. And for the first time, a citizen from a state beyond the Appalachians, Jackson, had won the presidency. In an era defined by broadening of the electorate, rapid growth of the capitalist market, western expansion, and national political debate over slavery in the national capital, Jacksonians had finally resurrected President Washington's grand vision for the city. Along the Potomac, a dynamic federal metropolis would now lead the expanding American empire by its powerful aesthetic example.

Epilogue

In the fifteen years after the federal government began to accept responsibility for the District of Columbia, the three District cities stepped back
from the brink of financial ruin. After retrocession, Alexandria experienced steady business growth and connection to the growing regional
network of railroads. In addition, as a part of Virginia, its profitable
trade in slaves continued without any external interference. In Georgetown, meanwhile, industrial output rose during the 1840s when the flow
of grain from western Maryland and Virginia prompted several firms
to construct flour mills along the C&O Canal and a cotton mill opened
in the city. The addition of these industrial enterprises at least partially
alleviated the local economy's dependence on the federal government.
By the 1850 census, when census takers gathered occupation information for the first time, approximately 55 percent of free males over the
age of fifteen in the District fell into the category that included commerce, trade, and manufacturing, while nonagricultural laborers and
domestic servants made up only 27 percent of the male workforce. That
census also revealed that Washington had added nearly 17,000 residents
since 1840 to reach a total population of 40,001, a growth rate of over 70
percent for the decade. In Georgetown, the population grew at a more
modest 14 percent. But that growth had followed a decade in which the
city had experienced a 13 percent loss in its population. By the 1840s, the
growth of the District's population and the greater availability of goods
and services encouraged dozens of representatives and senators to bring

their families with them for the congressional seasons, further fueling and stabilizing the District's economy.[1]

Although no major manufacturing facilities opened in Washington, local residents continued to seek a place for their city at the heart of the American economy and culture. In 1846, for example, when Congress finally approved the creation of the Smithsonian Institution and the construction of its iconic castle on the National Mall, Washington mayor William Winston Seaton took a seat on the institution's Board of Regents. For the next two decades, Seaton served the board and the institution tirelessly, contributing, as another longtime regent put it after Seaton's death in 1866, "to the popularity as well as to the true interests of the Institution." Through his efforts on the board, Seaton connected the Smithsonian to the local elites who had long desired a national scientific society for the capital.[2]

Also in 1846, Washington hosted the First National Fair for the Exhibition of American Manufactures. The committee selected by Congress to put on the fair consisted largely of Washington residents, including Mayor Seaton. That group put out a bold national call for "specimens of every kind of manufacture and handicraft known to the artizans of the United States." Since no single room in the city could house such a collection, they constructed a tentlike building 60 feet wide and 500 feet long. The fair ran from May 21 to June 3, serving an estimated sixty thousand visitors, who admired textiles, manufactured goods, tools, farm implements, and a variety of other products from around the nation. Although the fair failed to spur industrial investment in the city, as some local organizers had hoped, its placement in Washington reaffirmed the city's role as a showplace for American learning and ingenuity.[3]

For more than half a century, local elites had nurtured the notion that the federal city and its District should stand as powerful symbols of the nation. After working for decades to realize President Washington's vision for a grand federal metropolis, many local leaders had left public office or died by the late Jacksonian era. The city's first mayor, Robert Brent, served for a time as the army's paymaster general before dying in 1819. William Thornton, original architect of the Capitol, city commissioner, and savior of the Patent Office, died in 1828. After his death, the Columbian Institute passed a resolution that a "discourse be delivered . . . on the character of the late Doctor Thornton" and that the members would wear mourning crepe for a month "as a mark of respect for his memory." Four years later, in 1832, First Directress of the Washington Female Orphan Asylum, Marcia Burns Van Ness, was laid to rest in a ceremony that included orphan girls in the green outfits of the asylum and was witnessed by many members of Congress, that body having for the first time in its history adjourned to attend the funeral of a woman. At the time, her husband, John P. Van Ness, was serving as mayor of Washington. In 1834, Thomas Law, who had come from England via India to become one of the city's earliest investors and most prominent boosters, also lived his last day in the city. The most influential married pair of writers in the capital, Samuel Harrison Smith and Margaret Bayard Smith, he with his early work on the *National Intelligencer* and she with her novels describing elite Washington society, died in 1845 and 1844, respectively. Finally, Judge William Cranch lived until 1855; he had remained on the Circuit Court of the District of Columbia for fifty-four years, nearly fifty of which as its chief justice.[4]

Their departures left the city in the hands of a new generation of local elites whose influence on national politicians diminished as the number of congressmen and senators coming to Washington each season rose from 174 in 1800 to 284 by 1840. With fewer opportunities to establish personal connections and influence with federal officials, this new generation of elite Washingtonians relied even more heavily on the idea that the city deserved federal support specifically because it represented the American nation.[5]

Within two decades, the Civil War would further magnify the symbolic importance of the capital. Perched across the Potomac from Confederate Virginia, the Union capital offered an alluring target for Confederate generals. For Abraham Lincoln, the city represented the Union. And he made defense against Southern invasion a top military priority. In addition to transforming the city into a military garrison, Lincoln and the Republicans who controlled Congress also set in motion dramatic social and political changes in the city by emancipating slaves in the District and repealing local black codes. In all, the militarization of the city, the substantial growth of the scope and size of the federal government during the war, and the arrival of tens of thousands of escaped and newly freed slaves from surrounding states resulted in a near-doubling of the city's population, from 61,112 in 1860 to 109,199 in 1870. These changes also increased the city's black population from 25 percent of the total in 1860 to 32 percent in 1870. The rapid growth and wartime importance of the capital brought it even closer to George Washington's vision of a grand federal city on the Potomac at the head of a powerful and united American empire.[6]

In the aftermath of the war, the national capital gained further stature as the center of the newly strengthened union. Over the next 150 years, with the symbolic status of the capital well established, the District continued to serve as a laboratory for federal policy as the nation began to seek fulfillment of the revolutionary generation's promises of freedom and equality. It also became a destination for Americans who wanted their voices heard when local and national politicians refused to listen. Their efforts transformed the capital from a place of governance and symbolic meaning into a place of actual public engagement. Although the founders had purposefully separated the seat of government from the people, pilgrimage to and protest in the city William Cranch called a "New Jerusalem" became a defining feature not only of America's empire but also of its democracy. In this way, the city has both lived up to and evolved well beyond Washington's vision of a grand federal metropolis on the Potomac.[7]

NOTES

Introduction

1. Robert Fortenbaugh, *The Nine Capitals of the United States* (York, PA: Maple Press, 1948), 9.; U.S. Constitution, Art. 1, sec. 8.

2. Kenneth R. Bowling, *The Creation of Washington, D.C.* (Fairfax: George Mason University Press, 1991), 18–20, 30–32.

3. Bowling, *The Creation of Washington, D.C.*, 32–34.

4. Antifederalist views of the federal district are described and quoted in Bowling, *The Creation of Washington, D.C.*, 80–82; Madison quoted from "Federalist No. 43," in Alexander Hamilton, James Madison, and John Jay, *The Federalist Papers* (New York: Penguin Books, 1961), 271–73.

5. For details on the compromise and discussion of Thomas Jefferson's possible role in making it happen, see Jacob E. Cooke, "The Compromise of 1790," *William and Mary Quarterly*, 3rd ser., 27, no. 4 (Oct. 1, 1970): 524–45; and Kenneth R. Bowling, "Dinner at Jefferson's: A Note on Jacob E. Cooke's 'The Compromise of 1790,'" *William and Mary Quarterly*, 3rd ser., 28, no. 4 (Oct. 1, 1971): 629–48.

6. "An Act for Establishing the Temporary and Permanent Seat of the Government of the United States," July 16, 1790, in *The Public Statutes at Large of the United States of America*, vol. 1, ed. Richard Peters (Boston: Charles C. Little and James Brown, 1850), 130; hereafter *Public Statutes*.

7. Exceptional general histories of the nation's capital include W. B. Bryan, *A History of the National Capital from Its Foundation through the Period of the Adoption of the Organic Act*, vols. 1 and 2 (New York: Macmillan, 1914 and 1916); Constance McLaughlin Green, *Washington: Village and Capital, 1800–1878* (Princeton: Princeton University Press, 1962); Bowling, *The Creation of Washington, D.C.*; Bob Arnebeck, *Through a Fiery Trial: Building Washington, 1790–1800* (New York: Madison Books, 1994). Each of these authors has penned numerous other books and articles on the District of Columbia. Quality histories of Washington extending well beyond the period covered by this volume include Constance McLaughlin Green, *Washington,*

Capital City, 1879–1950 (Princeton: Princeton University Press, 1963); Howard Gillette Jr., *Between Justice and Beauty: Race, Planning, and the Failure of Urban Policy in Washington, D.C.* (Baltimore: Johns Hopkins University Press, 1995); and Lucy G. Barber, *Marching on Washington: The Forging of an American Political Tradition* (Berkeley: University of California Press, 2002).

8. The importance of taking the local population into consideration in the history of Washington has been particularly underscored by Gillette, who suggested in his study of race and development in Washington, "Washington should not viewed as a passive victim of federal control. Its development has been thoroughly contested ." Gillette, *Between Justice and Beauty*, xi.

9. Alan Lessoff, *The Nation and Its City: Politics, "Corruption," and Progress in Washington, D.C., 1861–1902* (Baltimore: Johns Hopkins University Press, 1994), 2–8; Kirk Savage, *Monument Wars: Washington, D.C., the National Mall, and the Transformation of the Memorial Landscape* (Berkeley: University of California Press, 2011), 10.

10. Catherine Allgor, *Parlor Politics: In Which the Ladies of Washington Help Build a City and a Government*, Jeffersonian America (Charlottesville: University Press of Virginia, 2000); Fredrika J. Teute, "Roman Matron on the Banks of Tiber Creek: Margaret Bayard Smith and the Politicization of Spheres in the Nation's Capital," in *A Republic for the Ages: The United States Capitol and the Political Culture of the Early Republic*, ed. Donald R. Kennon (Charlottesville: Published for the United States Capitol Historical Society by the University Press of Virginia, 1999), 89–121; Jan Lewis, "Politics and the Ambivalence of the Private Sphere: Women in Early Washington, D.C.," in Kennon, *A Republic for the Ages*, 122–54.

11. Anthony Sutcliffe, Foreword to *Planning Twentieth Century Capital Cities*, ed. David L. A. Gordon (New York: Routledge, 2006), vii.; Carl Abbott, *Political Terrain: Washington, D.C. from Tidewater Town to Global Metropolis* (Chapel Hill: University of North Carolina Press, 199), 5. Excellent work on architecture, planning, and monument building in Washington not cited elsewhere in this introduction includes Pamela Scott and Antoinette J. Lee, *Buildings of the District of Columbia* (New York: Oxford University Press, 1993); James M. Goode, *Capital Losses: A Cultural History of Washington's Destroyed Buildings* (Washington: Smithsonian Books, 2003); Daniel Reiff, *Washington Architecture, 1791–1861: Problems in Development* (Washington: U.S. Commission of Fine Arts, 1971); John Reps, *Monumental Washington: The Planning and Development of the Capital Center* (Princeton: Princeton University Press, 1967); Jeffrey F. Meyer, *Myths in Stone: Religious Dimensions of Washington, D.C.* (Berkeley: University of California Press, 2001). And for a more explicitly theoretical discussion of the development of the capital, demonstrating, for example, the "recursive relationship between ideational and material spaces" there, see Margaret E. Farrar, *Building the Body Politic: Power and Urban Space in Washington, D.C.* (Urbana: University of Illinois Press, 2008).

12. Dell Upton, *Another City: Urban Life and Urban Spaces in the New American Republic* (New Haven: Yale University Press, 2008), 1–15. Similar efforts to blend insights from social and political history with material culture and the built environment include Maurie Dee McInnis, *The Politics of Taste in Antebellum Charleston* (Chapel Hill: University of North Carolina Press, 2005), 7–13; and Bernard L. Herman, *Town House: Architecture and Material Life in the Early American City, 1780–1830* (Chapel Hill: University of North Carolina Press, 2005), 2–6.

Part I: Grand Visions and Financial Disasters

1. Washington's Diary, Mar. 28–30, 1791, in George Washington, "The Writings of George Washington Relating to the National Capital," *Records of the Columbia Historical Society, Washington, D.C.* 17 (1914): 15–17; William Tindall, *Origin and Government of the District of Columbia* (Washington: U.S. Government Printing Office, 1908), 89–91; Laurence Schmeckebier, *The District of Columbia, Its Government and Administration* (Baltimore: Johns Hopkins University Press, 1928), 6, 21; William C. di Giacomantonio, "All the President's Men: George Washington's Federal City Commissioners," *Washington History* 3, no. 1 (Spring–Summer 1991): 59–64.

2. Don Alexander Hawkins, "The Landscape of the Federal City: A 1792 Walking Tour," *Washington History* 3, no. 1 (Spring–Summer, 1991): 17–21.

1 / Dreams of Metropolis

1. Di Giacomantonio, "All the President's Men," 59–64; Priscilla W. McNeil, "Rock Creek Hundred: Land Conveyed for the Federal City," *Washington History* 3, no. 1 (Spring–Summer 1991): 35; Arnebeck, *Through a Fiery Trial*, 3.

2. Hawkins, "The Landscape of the Federal City," 25, 33, 36; H. Paul Caemmerer, *A Manual on the Origin and Development of Washington* (Washington: U.S. Government Printing Office, 1939), 37; Arnebeck, *Through a Fiery Trial*, 3, 42, 131–32; Bryan, *A History of the National Capital*, vol. 1 (New York: Macmillan, 1914), 498; Allen C. Clark, *Life and Letters of Dolly Madison* (Washington: Press of W. F. Roberts, 1914), 42.

3. Kenneth R. Bowling, *Creating the Federal City, 1774–1800: Potomac Fever* (Washington: American Institute of Architects Press, 1988), 39–42; Bryan, *A History of the National Capital*, vol. 1, 64; Ada Hope Hixon, "George Washington Land Speculator," *Journal of the Illinois State Historical Society* (1908–84) 11, no. 4 (1919): 566–75.

4. Washington's Diary, Mar. 28, 1791; and Washington to Mr. S. Fairfax, May 16, 1798, in Washington, "The Writings of George Washington," 16, 202.

5. Woody Holton, *Forced Founders: Indians, Debtors, Slaves, and the Making of the American Revolution in Virginia* (Chapel Hill: University of North Carolina Press, 1999), 5–7; Richard White, *The Middle Ground: Indians, Empires, and Republics in the Great Lakes Region, 1650–1815* (New York: Cambridge University Press, 1991), 256–71.

6. Joel Achenbach, *The Grand Idea: George Washington's Potomac and the Race to the West* (New York: Simon and Schuster, 2004), 121–25; Philander D. Chase, "A Stake in the West: George Washington as a Backcountry Surveyor and Landholder," in *George Washington and the Virginia Backcountry*, by Warren R. Hofstra (Madison, WI: Madison House, 1998), 183.

7. Bowling, *The Creation of Washington, D.C.*, 116–21; Bryan, *A History of the National Capital*, vol. 1, 69; Douglas R. Littlefield, "The Potomac Company: A Misadventure in Financing an Early American Internal Improvement Project," *Business History Review* 58, no. 4 (Winter 1984): 567–70; Washington to Marquis de Lafayette, Feb. 15, 1785, in *The Papers of George Washington, Confederation Series*, vol. 2, *18 July 1784–18 May 1785*, ed. W. W. Abbot (Charlottesville: University Press of Virginia, 1992), 363–67; James K. Searcy and Luther C. Davis Jr., *Time of Travel of Water in the Potomac River Cumberland to Washington*, Geological Survey Circular 438 (Washington: U.S. Department of the Interior, U.S. Geological Survey, 1961).

8. Merritt Roe Smith, "George Washington and the Establishment of the Harpers Ferry Armory," *Virginia Magazine of History and Biography* 81, no. 4 (1973): 418–30.

9. Bowling, *The Creation of Washington, D.C.*, 114.

10. Thomas Johnson to George Washington, Dec. 11, 1787, GWP; George Washington to the Marquis de Lafayette, July 25, 1785, GWP.

11. Washington's Diary, Mar. 28–30, 1791, in Washington, "The Writings of George Washington," 16–17.

12. Kenneth R. Bowling, "The Other G. W.: George Walker and the Creation of the National Capital," *Washington History* 3, no. 2 (Fall–Winter 1991–92): 5–9, 17–18.

13. Bowling, "The Other G. W.," 18–19.

14. Reiff, *Washington Architecture*, 8–9; L'Enfant's explanation of the plan, in Elizabeth Kite, *L'Enfant and Washington, 1791–1792 Published and Unpublished Documents Now Brought Together for the First Time* (Baltimore: Johns Hopkins University Press, 1929), 62–67.

15. Kite, *L'Enfant and Washington*, 34.

16. L'Enfant to Washington, June 10, 1783, GWP; Kenneth Bowling, *Peter Charles L'Enfant: Vision, Honor and Male Friendship in the Early American Republic* (Washington: Friends of the George Washington University Libraries, 2002), 4–5; H. Paul Caemmerer, "The Life of Pierre Charles L'Enfant," *Records of the Columbia Historical Society, Washington, D.C.* 50 (1948): 326–32; Kite, *L'Enfant and Washington*, 9–10.

17. For an examination of the use of symbolic images as ornaments that add meaning to an architectural structure, see Egon Verheyen, "On Meaning in Architecture," in *The Emblem and Architecture: Studies in Applied Emblematics from the Sixteenth to the Eighteenth Centuries*, ed. Hans J. Böker and Peter M. Daly, Imago Figurata (Turnhout: Brepols, 1999), 17–30. For analysis of indigenous and classical imagery in early America, see E. McClung Fleming, "From Indian Princess to Greek Goddess: The American Image, 1783–1815," *Winterthur Portfolio* 3 (Jan. 1, 1967): 37–66; and Caroline Winterer, "From Royal to Republican: The Classical Image in Early America," *Journal of American History* 91, no. 4 (Mar. 1, 2005): 1264–90; American Academy of Arts and Sciences, "The Early History of the American Academy of Arts and Sciences," *Bulletin of the American Academy of Arts and Sciences* 24, no. 4 (Jan. 1, 1971): 7; Jefferson quote, from Thomas Jefferson, *The Papers of Thomas Jefferson*, ed. Julian P. Boyd and Ruth W. Lester (Princeton: Princeton University Press, 1982), 13:269, as quoted in Egon Verheyen, "'Unenlightened by a Single Ray from Antiquity': John Quincy Adams and the Design of the Pediment for the United States Capitol," *International Journal of the Classical Tradition* 3, no. 2 (October 1, 1996): 216 n.

18. Jefferson to L'Enfant, Mar. 1791, and Washington to Jefferson, Mar. 31, 1971, in Saul K. Padover, *Thomas Jefferson and the National Capital* (Washington: U.S. Government Printing Office, 1946), 42 and 54. Ellicott's team included a free black named Benjamin Banneker who took astronomical observations for the project. Stories that place Banneker at the heart of the city design process are apocryphal. For details about Ellicott's and Banneker's work together, see Silvio A. Bedini, "The Survey of the Federal Territory: Andrew Ellicott and Benjamin Banneker," *Washington History* 3, no. 1 (Spring–Summer 1991): 76–95.

19. Jefferson to L'Enfant, Apr. 10, 1971, in Padover, *Thomas Jefferson and the National Capital*, 58; Washington to L'Enfant, Apr. 3, 1791, in Washington, "The Writings of George Washington," 22; Caemmerer, *A Manual on the Origin and Development of*

Washington, 139; Kite, *L'Enfant and Washington*, 17; Bowling, *Peter Charles L'Enfant*, 25–26; Reps, *Monumental Washington*, 15.

20. J. P. Dougherty, "Baroque and Picturesque Motifs in L'Enfant's Design for the Federal Capital," *American Quarterly* 26, no. 1 (Mar. 1974): 34–36.

21. Washington to Alexander White, Mar. 25, 1798, GWP; U. S. Grant III "The L'Enfant Plan and Its Evolution," *Records of the Columbia Historical Society, Washington, D.C.* 33–34 (1932): 5–6; Washington's Diary, Mar. 28–30, 1791, in Washington, "The Writings of George Washington," 15–17; Michael Bednar, *L'Enfant's Legacy: Public Open Spaces in Washington, D.C.* (Baltimore: Johns Hopkins University Press, 2006), 30–31. Both Benjamin Stoddert and William Thornton confirmed President Washington's reasoning for separating the public buildings in 1805 in response to suggestions that Washington intended to place them together. Stoddert to Thornton, Jan. 18, 1805, William Thornton Papers, 1741–1865, Library of Congress, Manuscript Division, Washington, DC, roll 2, vol. 3, 454.

22. L'Enfant to Hamilton, Apr. 8, 1791, as quoted in Kite, *L'Enfant and Washington*, 16, 64–66; L'Enfant to Hamilton, Apr. 8, 1791, as quoted in Bednar, *L'Enfant's Legacy*, 2; Gillette, *Between Justice and Beauty*, 6–7; Pamela Scott, "L'Enfant's Washington Described: The City in the Public Press, 1791–1795," *Washington History* 3, no. 1 (Spring–Summer 1991): 99.

23. John Reps, *Washington on View: The Nation's Capital since 1790* (Chapel Hill: University of North Carolina Press, 1991), 20; L'Enfant to Washington, June 22, 1791, in Peter Charles L'Enfant, "L'Enfant's Reports to President Washington, Bearing Dates of March 26, June 22, and August 19, 1791," *Records of the Columbia Historical Society, Washington, D.C.* 2 (1899): 35; Grant, "The L'Enfant Plan and Its Evolution," 7.

24. L'Enfant to Tobias Lear, Oct. 6, 1791, in Kite, *L'Enfant and Washington*; Washington to the Commissioners, Nov. 20, 1791, in Washington, "The Writings of George Washington," 30–34.

25. It is important to distinguish between Daniel Carroll of Duddington, the city's largest landowner, and his uncle Daniel Carroll, the city commissioner. In order to avoid continued reference to "Carroll of Duddington," a phrase that sounds awkward in contemporary prose, the landowner will be referred to simply as Carroll, and the commissioner will be referred to as Commissioner Carroll. L'Enfant to the Commissioners, Dec. 6, 1791, *Letters Received by the Commissioners for the District of Columbia*, vol. 1 (National Archives Microfilm Publication M371, reels 8–27), Correspondence, 1791–1931, General Records, 1790–1931, Records of the Office of Public Buildings and Public Parks of the National Capital, Record Group 42, National Archives Building, Washington, DC; hereafter *Commissioners' Letters Received*.

26. Bednar, *L'Enfant's Legacy*, 9–10. For discussion of L'Enfant's resignation as well as the anglicization and francization of L'Enfant's first name, see Bowling, *Peter Charles L'Enfant*, 31, 63–67.

27. L'Enfant to Washington, Aug. 19, 1791, in L'Enfant, "L'Enfant's Reports," 48.

2 / Speculating in Failure

1. Carroll Davidson Wright, "The Economic Development of the District of Columbia," *Proceedings of the Washington Academy of Sciences* 1 (Dec. 29, 1899): 161–87; Malcolm J. Rohrbough, *The Land Office Business: The Settlement and Administration*

of American Public Lands, 1789–1837 (New York: Oxford University Press, 1968), 5–18; Bowling, *The Creation of Washington, D.C.*, 190–93, 222.

2. Robert D. Arbuckle, *Pennsylvania Speculator and Patriot: The Entrepreneurial John Nicholson, 1757–1800* (University Park: Pennsylvania State University Press, 1975), 16–17, 20–38; Sakolski, *The Great American Land Bubble: The Amazing Story of Land-Grabbing, Speculations, and Booms from the Colonial Days to the Present Time* (New York: Harper & Brothers, 1932), 32, 36.

3. Chase, "A Stake in the West," 167–84; Sakolski, *The Great American Land Bubble*, 46–47.

4. Chase, "A Stake in the West," 183. For a summary of the scholarship pointing to the Constitution's defense of American moneyed interests as well as a description of the many American voices calling for the opposite action, see Woody Holton, "An 'Excess of Democracy'—Or a Shortage? The Federalists' Earliest Adversaries," *Journal of the Early Republic* 25, no. 3 (2005): 347–51. For a comparison of the speculation-based system of land development common in the United States and British Canada's efforts to lure settlers with nearly free land, see Alan Taylor, "The Late Loyalists: Northern Reflections of the Early American Republic," *Journal of the Early Republic* 27, no. 1 (2007): 4–8.

5. Bruce H. Mann, *Republic of Debtors: Bankruptcy in the Age of American Independence* (Cambridge, MA: Harvard University Press, 2002), 201–6; Sakolski, *The Great American Land Bubble*, 53; Alexander White to the Commissioners, Feb. 4, 1796, *Commissioner's Letters Received*, vol. 8.

6. U.S. Bureau of the Census, *Historical Statistics of the United States: Colonial Times to 1970: Bicentennial Edition, Part 2* (Washington: U.S. Government Printing Office, 1975), 1104, 1115; L'Enfant to Washington, Jan. 17, 1792, in Kite, *L'Enfant and Washington*, 110–32.

7. Jefferson to Thomas Johnson, Mar. 8, 1792, in Padover, *Thomas Jefferson and the National Capital*, 109–12; Arnebeck, *Through a Fiery Trial*, 129.

8. Arnebeck, *Through a Fiery Trial*, 44–45; Bowling, *Creating the Federal City*, 91; Caemmerer, *A Manual on the Origin and Development of Washington*, 15; U.S. Congress, Senate, 1901, *List of Squares and Lots Assigned to Original Proprietors of Land in Washington, D.C.*, 57th Cong., 1st sess., S. Doc. No. 18 (hereafter *Proprietor's List*).

9. Sakolski, *The Great American Land Bubble*, 29–34.

10. Proprietors Peters, J. Davidson, S. Davidson, Lingan, Young, King, Stoddert, Forrest, Prout, Carr, Burnes, and Douglas to Walker, Mar. 9, 1792, in Padover, *Thomas Jefferson and the National Capital*, 113–15; Walker to the Commissioners, Jan. 21, 1792, and Davidson to the Commissioners, June 1, 1792, *Commissioners' Letters Received*, vol. 1.

11. Di Giacomantonio, "All the President's Men," 53–59.

12. Arnebeck, *Through a Fiery Trial*, 34–35; di Giacomantonio, "All the President's Men," 59–64.

13. Stuart and Carroll to Secretary of State Edmund Randolph, July 31, 1794, *Letters Sent by the Commissioners for the District of Columbia*, vol. 2, 110–11, Proceedings and Letters Sent, 1791–1802 (National Archives Microfilm Publication M371, reels 3–4), Records of the Commissioners for the District of Columbia, 1791–1925, Records of the Office of Public Buildings and Public Parks of the National Capital, Record Group 42, National Archives Building, Washington, D.C. (hereafter *Commissioners'*

Letters Sent); Arnebeck, *Through a Fiery Trial*, 186–87, 273; di Giacomantonio, "All the President's Men," 64.

14. Di Giacomantonio, "All the President's Men," 65–70, 75.

15. Bryan, *A History of the National Capital*, vol. 1, 237–38; Arnebeck, *Through a Fiery Trial*, 415; Dec. 26, 1800, *Proceedings of the Commissioners for the District of Columbia, 1791–1802*, vol. 6, 73, Proceedings and Letters Sent, 1791–1802 (National Archives Microfilm Publication M371, roll 1), Records of the Commissioners for the District of Columbia, 1791–1925, Records of the Office of Public Buildings and Public Parks of the National Capital, Record Group 42, National Archives Building, Washington, D.C. (hereafter *Commissioners' Proceedings*); di Giacomantonio, "All the President's Men," 74–75.

16. Oct. 17, 1791, *Commissioners' Proceedings*, vol. 1, 33–34; Notes on Commissioners' Meeting, Sept. 8, 1971, in Padover, *Thomas Jefferson and the National Capital*, 70–73.

17. On the historiography of recent urban history, see Timothy J. Gilfoyle, "White Cities, Linguistic Turns, and Disneylands: The New Paradigms of Urban History," *Reviews in American History* 26, no. 1 (1998): 175–93. On the efforts of early republic cities to regulate economic and social relations, see Jon Teaford, *The Municipal Revolution in America: Origins of Modern Urban Government, 1650–1825* (Chicago: University of Chicago Press, 1975), 91–110; David Schuyler, *The New Urban Landscape: The Redefinition of City Form in Nineteenth-Century America* (Baltimore: Johns Hopkins University Press, 1986), 11–17; and Hendrik Hartog, *Public Property and Private Power: The Corporation of the City of New York in American Law, 1730–1870* (Chapel Hill: University of North Carolina Press, 1983), 143–45. And on the aesthetic and symbolic means of control used by cities, see Katharine Tehranian, *Modernity, Space, and Power: The American City in Discourse and Practice* (Cresskill, NY: Hampton Press, 1995), 2–5; and Upton, *Another City*, 1–15.

18. Upton, *Another City*, 19–26; Jefferson to L'Enfant, Apr. 10, 1971, in Padover, *Thomas Jefferson and the National Capital*, 58–59.

19. Commissioners to Washington, June 22, 1796, *Commissioners' Letters Sent*, vol. 3, 151; Bryan, *A History of the National Capital*, vol. 1, 278.

20. Dec. 11, 1794, *Commissioners' Proceedings*, vol. 1, 305; Commissioner White to Mr. Hartshorne and Son, Sept. 7, 1799, *Commissioners' Letters Sent*, vol. 5, 293–94.

21. Mar. 26, 1792, and Jan. 9, 1795, *Commissioners' Proceedings*, vol. 1, 84–86, 332–33; Commissioners to Peter, Aug. 2, 1791, *Commissioners' Letters Sent*, vol. 1, 119; White to the Commissioners, Jan. 21, 1796, *Commissioner's Letters Received*, vol. 8.

22. Thomas Law to the Commissioners, July 15, 1796, and Aug. 5, 1796, *Commissioners' Letters Received*, vol. 9; Morris and Nicholson to the Commissioners, Sept. 28 and 29, 1796, *Commissioners' Letters Received*, vol. 9.

23. July 31, 1801, *Commissioners' Proceedings*, vol. 6, 190; Commissioners to John Tayloe, Jan. 29, 1802, *Commissioners' Letters Sent*, vol. 6, 125.

24. Commissioners to Jefferson, Dec. 5, 1801, *Commissioners' Proceedings*, vol. 6, 238–47; Commissioner White to Mr. Hartshorne and Son, Sept. 7, 1799, *Commissioners' Letters Sent*, vol. 5, 293–94; Commissioners Scott and Thornton to Joshua Dawson Esq., Sept. 23, 1800, *Commissioners' Letters Sent*, vol. 6, 12.

25. Dec. 24–25, 1793, *Commissioners' Proceedings*, vol. 1, 211–21; Jan. 28, 1801, *Commissioners' Proceedings*, vol. 6, 88–101.

26. *Journals of the Commissioners for the District of Columbia*, vol. 1, 50, Financial Records 1791–1924, Records of the Commissioners for the District of Columbia, 1791–1925, Records of the Office of Public Buildings and Public Parks of the National Capital, Record Group 42, National Archives Building, Washington, D.C. (hereafter *Commissioners' Journals*); Jan. 28, 1801, *Commissioners' Proceedings*, vol. 6, 88–101.

27. Commissioners to Randolph, June 10, 1795, *Commissioners' Letters Sent*, vol. 3, 6–8.

28. Mann, *Republic of Debtors*, 199–204; Greenleaf to Nicholson, Dec. 26, 1794, General Correspondence, 1772–1819 (series #96m1), Manuscript Group 96, *Sequestered John Nicholson Papers*, Pennsylvania State Archives, Harrisburg, PA (as viewed on National Historical Publications Commission microfilm of the John Nicholson Papers, roll 9) (hereafter *Nicholson Papers*).

29. Commissioners to Morris, Sept. 28, 1795, and July 15, 1796, *Commissioners' Letters Sent*, vol. 3, 112–14, 162–64.

30. Tindall, *Origin and Government of the District of Columbia*, 114–15; Jan. 28, 1801, *Commissioners' Proceedings*, vol. 6, 88–101; Commissioners to Morris, July 15, 1796, *Commissioners' Letters Sent*, vol. 3, 162–64; Commissioners to Morris and Nicholson, May 4, 1797, and Commissioners to William Cranch Esquire agent of Greenleaf, Jan. 15, 1798, *Commissioners' Letters Sent*, vol. 4, 47–49, 215.

31. Commissioners to Morris and Nicholson, July 17, 1797, *Commissioners' Letters Sent*, vol. 4, 90–91; Commissioners to Henry Pratt and other creditors of Morris and Nicholson, Nov. 22, 1799, *Commissioners' Letters Sent*, vol. 5, 343–44; Jan. 28, 1801, *Commissioners' Proceedings*, vol. 6, 88–101.

32. Bob Arnebeck, "Tracking the Speculators: Greenleaf and Nicholson in the Federal City," *Washington History* 3, no. 1 (Spring–Summer 1991): 120; Commissioners Scott and Thornton to Maryland Assembly Members Thomas G. Addison, James Magruder, George Calvert, and Allen B Duckett, Dec. 4, 1798, and Commissioners to Maryland Assembly Members Charles Carroll of Carrolton, Philip B. Key, and Thomas Buchanan, Jan. 21, 1799, *Commissioners' Letters Sent*, vol. 5, 182–85, 201–2; Commissioners to Uriah Forrest, Jan. 19, 1797, *Commissioners' Letters Sent*, vol. 3, 245; Commissioners to President Adams, Sept. 25, 1799, *Commissioners' Letters Sent*, vol. 5, 303–5.

33. Jefferson to the Commissioners, Mar. 6, 1792, *Commissioners' Letters Sent*, vol. 1, 74–76; Washington to the Commissioners, Feb. 17, 1797, *Photostatic Copies of Letters from Presidents of the United States to the Commissioners for the District of Columbia and Their Successors, 1791–1869*, Correspondence, 1791–1931, General Records, 1790–1931, Records of the Office of Public Buildings and Public Parks of the National Capital, Record Group 42, National Archives Building, Washington, D.C. (hereafter *President's Letters Sent*).

34. Attorney General Charles Lee to the Commissioners, Mar. 20, 1796, *Commissioners' Letters Received*, vol. 8; Commissioners to Washington, Oct. 31, 1796, *Commissioners' Letters Sent*, vol. 3, 213–15; Arnebeck, *Through a Fiery Trial*, 410; Scott and Thornton to Washington, Dec. 25, 1796, *Commissioners' Letters Sent*, vol. 3, 237–38; Commissioners to Adams, Jan. 3, 1798, *Commissioners' Letters Sent*, vol. 4, 224–25; Scott and Thornton to Secretary of the Navy Benjamin Stoddert, Dec. 30, 1799, and Scott and Thornton to James M. Lingan, Feb. 24, 1800, *Commissioners' Letters Sent*, vol. 5, 357–58, 383; Dec. 9, 1799, *Commissioners' Proceedings*, vol. 5, 274–76.

35. Scott and Thornton to Thomas G. Addison, James Magruder, George Calvert, and Allen B. Duckett representatives in the Maryland Assembly from Prince Georges County, Dec. 4, 1798, *Commissioners' Letters Sent*, vol. 5, 182–85.

36. Commissioners to Pickering, June 6, 1799, and Aug. 9, 1799, *Commissioners 'Letters Sent*, vol. 5, 257–58 and 281.

37. Commissioners to Adams, Sept. 25, 1799, and Oct. 25, 1799, *Commissioners' Letters Sent*, vol. 5, 303–5 and 320.

38. As quoted in Bryan, *History of the National Capital*, 377–78; On Adams's health, see John Ferling and Lewis E. Braverman, "John Adams's Health Reconsidered," *William and Mary Quarterly* 55, no. 1 (1998): 97–98.

39. White to the Commissioners, Mar. 7, 1796, May 6, 1796, and Mar. 16, 1796, *Commissioners' Letters Received*, vol. 8.

40. Lot sales data and calculations are based on three reports compiled by the War Department at the request of the Senate in 1899 and 1900. U.S. Congress, Senate, 1899, *Partial List of Lots in the District of Columbia Sold by the United States*, 55th Cong., 3rd sess., S. Doc. No. 47; U.S. Congress, Senate, 1899, *Partial List of Lots in the District of Columbia Sold by the United States*, 56th Cong., 1st sess., S. Doc. No. 47; U.S. Congress, Senate, 1900, *Additional and Final, List of Lots in the District of Columbia Sold by the United States*, 56th Cong., 2nd sess. S. Doc. No. 32.

41. Commissioners to Washington, Oct. 10, 1796, and Scott and Thornton to Washington, Dec. 25, 1796, *Commissioners Letters Sent*, vol. 3, 213–15 and 237–38; Commissioners to Jefferson, Dec. 5, 1801, *Commissioners' Proceedings*, vol. 6, 237–48; *An Act to Abolish the Board of Commissioners in the City of Washington*, May 1, 1802, in Peters, *Public Statutes*, vol. 2, 175–78.

3 / A Boomtown without a Boom

1. Bryan, *A History of the National Capital*, vol. 1, 415–17; Adams to Mrs. Smith, Nov. 21, 1800, in Abigail Adams and John Quincy Adams, *Letters of Mrs. Adams, the Wife of John Adams*, 4th ed. (Boston: Wilkins, Carter, and Co., 1848), 381–82; John Cotton Smith, *The Correspondence and Miscellanies of the Hon. John Cotton Smith, LL.D., Formerly Governor of Connecticut* (New York: Harper & Brothers, 1847), 204–6.

2. The commissioners submitted a report to President Jefferson detailing the number of brick and wooden houses completed in 1800 and 1801. Commissioners to Jefferson, Dec 5, 1801, *Commissioners' Proceedings*, vol. 6, 238–47. That report was submitted by Jefferson to Congress whereupon it entered the Congressional Record. "City of Washington: Communicated to Congress, January 11, 1802," *American State Papers, Miscellaneous* 1:254–57; Smith, *Correspondence*, 204–7.

3. Bowling, *The Creation of Washington, D.C.*, 191–97; Green, *Washington: Village and Capital*, 39.

4. Campbell Gibson, *Population of the 100 Largest Cities and Other Urban Places in the United States: 1790 to 1990* (Washington: U.S. Bureau of the Census, Population Division, June 1998), http://www.census.gov/population/www/documentation/twps0027/twps0027.html; District of Columbia Returns, roll 5, *Second Census of the United States*, 1800 (NARA microfilm publication M32, 32 reels); Records of the Bureau of the Census, Record Group 29, National Archives, Washington, DC (hereafter *Second Census*).

5. Georgetown had a sex ratio of 1:22 and a children's population percentage of 43.8. *Second Census.*

6. Population data from Gibson, *Population of the 100 Largest Cities.* Settled area sizes for Boston, Philadelphia, New York, and Baltimore as listed in Carole Shammas, "The Space Problem in Early United States Cities," *William and Mary Quarterly*, 3rd ser., 57, no. 3 (July 1, 2000): 509. The settled areas of Washington City south and west of Massachusetts Avenue, Georgetown, Alexandra, Charleston, and Savannah were calculated using Draft Logic's Google Maps Area Calculator Tool (https://www.daftlogic.com/projects-google-maps-area-calculator-tool.htm) in conjunction with historical maps of each city. Areas for Washington and Georgetown are based on H. S. Tanner's 1836 map of the District, Library of Congress. The area for Charleston is based on the 1788 "Ichnography of Charleston" map, Library of Congress. The area for Savannah is based on an 1812 "Map of the City of Savannah" hosted online by the University of Georgia Library at http://www.libs.uga.edu/darchive/hargrett/maps/1812h6.jpg; Jan. 28, 1801, *Commissioners' Proceedings*, vol. 6, 88–101.

7. David R. Goldfield, "Antebellum Washington in Context: The Pursuit of Prosperity and Identity," in *Southern City, National Ambition: The Growth of Early Washington, D.C., 1800–1860*, ed. Howard Gillette (Washington: Published by George Washington University Center for Washington Area Studies in conjunction with the American Architectural Foundation, 1995), 9–10; Carl Abbott, *Political Terrain*, 45–58; James Burns to the Commissioners, Aug. 29, 1792, *Commissioners' Letters Received*, vol. 2; Commissioners to David Burns, Feb. 19, 1796, *Commissioners' Letters Sent*, vol. 3, 93; Commissioners to Carroll, Aug. 21, 1799, *Commissioners' Letters Sent*, vol. 5, 284.

8. *Second Census*; Campbell Gibson and Kay Jung, *Historical Census Statistics on Population Totals by Race, 1790 to 1990, and by Hispanic Origin, 1970 to 1990, for Large Cities and Other Urban Places in the United States*, U.S. Census Bureau, Population Division, Feb. 2005, http://www.census.gov/population/www/documentation/twps0076/twps0076.html; Gibson, *Population of the 100 Largest Cities*. For a detailed analysis of free black society in the national capital, see Letitia Woods Brown, *Free Negroes in the District of Columbia, 1790–1846*, Urban Life in America (New York: Oxford University Press, 1972), 9–16.

9. Thomas Dwight to Mrs. Hannah Dwight, Dec. 28, 1803, Dwight-Howard Papers, Box 2 of 4, 1803–1815, folder 1803 Dec., Massachusetts Historical Society (Boston); Goldfield, "Antebellum Washington in Context," 3–20; On "hiring out" and the urban slave economy, see Claudia Goldin, *Urban Slavery in the American South, 1820–1860: A Quantitative History* (Chicago: University of Chicago Press, 1976), 11–27; and Wade, *Slavery in the Cities*, 38–40. On the mixture of labor types in the urban market, see Brown, *Free Negroes*, 38–40. Because of this mixing, one prominent historian of the early American city includes laborers of all races and degrees of freedom in his definition of the "laboring classes"; see Gary B. Nash, *Urban Crucible: Social Change, Political Consciousness, and the Origins of the American Revolution* (Cambridge, MA: Harvard University Press, 1979), x–xii.

10. Much of this name-by-name examination of householders appears in Green, *Village and Capital*, 19–22; *Second Census*.

11. Robert S. Starobin, "The Economics of Industrial Slavery in the Old South," *Business History Review* 44, no. 2 (Summer 1970): 139–46. Starobin's analysis of

industrial labor costs in the antebellum South show that slave labor may have been 25 to 40 percent less expensive than free labor. Nov. 3, 1794, *Commissioners' Proceedings*, vol. 1, 292; Thornton to Commissioners, July 18, 1795, *Commissioners' Letters Received*, vol. 6. For a detailed breakdown of all types of work done by enslaved laborers in Washington, see Bob Arnebeck, *Slave Labor in the Capital: Building Washington's Iconic Federal Landmarks* (Charleston, SC: History Press, 2014).

12. Arnebeck, *Through a Fiery Trial*, 431–32; Commissioners to John McDonaugh and other stone cutters, May 7, 1795, *Commissioners' Letters Sent*, vol. 5, 35; Mar. 17 and 23, 1798, *Commissioners' Proceedings*, vol. 5, 109–10.

13. On state and local enforcement of labor contracts, see Richard B. Morris, "Labor Controls in Maryland in the Nineteenth Century," *Journal of Southern History* 14, no. 3 (1948): 385–97. On the colonial rights of municipalities to manage their poor, see Gary B. Nash, "Urban Wealth and Poverty in Pre-Revolutionary America," *Journal of Interdisciplinary History* 6, no. 4 (Apr. 1, 1976): 562–65. For a review of scholarship on labor in the colonial period, see Seth Rockman, "Work in the Cities of Colonial British North America," *Journal of Urban History* 33, no. 6 (Sept. 2007): 1021–32. And on the varying degrees of unfreedom experienced by American workers and women, see Seth Rockman, *Scraping By: Wage Labor, Slavery, and Survival in Early Baltimore* (Baltimore: Johns Hopkins University Press, 2008), 7–8; and Ellen Hartigan-O'Connor, *The Ties That Buy: Women and Commerce in Revolutionary America* (Philadelphia: University of Pennsylvania Press, 2009), 3–7.

14. July 5, 1792, and Jan 3, 1793, *Commissioners' Proceedings*, vol. 1, 120–22 and 160–61. Conversions from British currency to Maryland dollars is based on an exchange rate of 4 shillings 6 pence per dollar.

15. Van Staphorst and Hubbard to the Commissioners, Sept. 8, 1792, and John Laird to the Commissioners, Nov. 15, 1972, *Commissioners' Letters Received*, vol. 2; Joseph Fenwick to the Commissioners, Apr. 4, 1793, *Commissioners' Letters Received*, vol. 3; Commissioners to Seth Barton, June 20, 1796, *Commissioners' Letters Sent*, vol. 3, 149.

16. Jefferson to Commissioners, Apr. 20, 1792, in Padover, *Thomas Jefferson and the National Capital*, 137–38; John Joseph Walsh, *Early Banks in the District of Columbia, 1792–1818* (Washington: Catholic University of America Press, 1940), 59–65; Green, *Village and Capital*, 33; Peter Miller to Nicholson, Feb. 17, 1797, *Nicholson Papers*, roll 13.

17. Deblois to Nicholson, Mar. 9, 1795, Nicholson Papers, roll 6; Mrs. Deblois to Nicholson, Mar. 25 and 31, 1795, *Nicholson Papers*, roll 6.

18. Arbuckle, *Pennsylvania Speculator and Patriot*, 124–27; Deblois to Nicholson, Oct. 16, 1795, July 25, 1795, and June 7, 1797, *Nicholson Papers*, roll 6.

Part II: A "Federal Town" on the Potomac

1. Frederick Nichols, *Thomas Jefferson, Landscape Architect* (Charlottesville: University Press of Virginia, 1978), 68; Jefferson to Thomas Munroe, Mar. 21, 1803, in Padover, *Thomas Jefferson and the National Capital*, 300–301; Bryan, *A History of the National*, vol. 1, 456–57; Munroe to Jefferson, Mar. 14, 1803, *Letters Received and Draft Letters Sent by the Superintendent of the City of Washington*, vol. 20, item 2085 (National Archives Microfilm Publication M371, reel 18), Correspondence, 1791–1931, General Records, 1790–1931, Records of the Office of Public Buildings and Public Parks of the National Capital, Record Group 42, National Archives Building, Washington, DC (hereafter *Superintendent's Letters*).

2. Nichols, *Thomas Jefferson, Landscape Architect*, 139–41; Pamela Scott, "'The City of Living Green': An Introduction to Washington's Street Trees," *Washington History* 18, no. 1–2 (Jan. 1, 2006): 22.

3. Today Washington, D.C., officials sometimes attempt similar visual obfuscation using billboards. The one-block walk down Half St. SE from the Metro station to Nationals Park was lined with large billboards that obstructed views of nearby construction sites or less picturesque neighborhoods when the park opened in 2008.

4. Jefferson to Washington, Nov. 6, 1791, in Padover, *Thomas Jefferson and the National Capital*, 75.

5. Thomas Jefferson, *Notes on the State of Virginia* (Boston: Lilly and Wait, 1832), 172–73.; Jefferson to Benjamin Rush, Sept. 23, 1800, in Thomas Jefferson, *The Writings of Thomas Jefferson: Volume VII, 1795–1801*, ed. Paul Leicester Ford (New York: G. P. Putnam's Sons, 1896), 458–59; Francis E. Rourke, "Urbanism and American Democracy," *Ethics* 74, no. 4 (July 1, 1964): 255–58.

4 / Jeffersonians and the Federal City

1. Melvin Yazawa, "Republican Expectations: Revolutionary Ideology and the Compromise of 1790," in *A Republic for the Ages: The United States Capitol and the Political Culture of the Early Republic*, ed. Donald R. Kennon (Charlottesville: Published for the United States Capitol Historical Society by the University Press of Virginia, 1999), 3–5, 35; Jefferson Note on Residence Bill, listed as ca. May 1790, actually penned in 1818, in Padover, *Thomas Jefferson and the National Capital*, 11–12. A spirited exchange between historians on this point can be found in Cooke, "The Compromise of 1790," 523–45; and Bowling, "Dinner at Jefferson's," 629–48.

2. Washington to L'Enfant, Dec. 13, 1791, Jefferson to L'Enfant, Feb. 22, 1792, L'Enfant to Jefferson, Feb. 26, 1792, and Jefferson to L'Enfant, Feb. 27, 1792, in Kite, *L'Enfant and Washington*, 92–93, 144–55.

3. Washington to Jefferson, Aug. 29, 1791 (two letters), Jefferson to Washington, Sept. 8, 1791, and Jefferson's Notes, Sept. 8. 1791, in Padover, *Thomas Jefferson and the National Capital*, 11–12; and Sept. 8, 1791, *Commissioners' Proceedings*, vol. 61, 181–83.

4. Washington to David Stuart, Feb. 1, 1793, in George Washington, "The Writings of George Washington," 72; Jefferson to Commissioner Carroll, Feb. 1, 1793, as quoted in Gordon Brown, *Incidental Architect: William Thornton and the Cultural Life of Early Washington, D.C., 1794–1828* (Athens: Published for the U.S. Capitol Historical Society by Ohio University Press, 2009), 1–3; Washington to Jefferson, June 30, 1793, and Jefferson to Washington, July 17, 1793, in Padover, *Thomas Jefferson and the National Capital*, 181–86.

5. Commissioners to Jefferson, June 1, 1801, and Jefferson to the Commissioners June 1, 1801, in *Commissioners' Letters Sent*, vol. 6, 84; "An Act Additional to, and Amendatory of, an Act Entitled 'An Act Concerning the District of Columbia,'" in Peters, *Public Statutes*, vol. 2, 193–95; Daniel Brent to Jefferson, Aug. 3, 1802, in Padover, *Thomas Jefferson and the National Capital*, 279–80.

6. Latrobe to Jefferson, Dec. 1, 1804, in Padover, *Thomas Jefferson and the National Capital*, 347–55; Talbot Hamlin, *Benjamin Henry Latrobe* (New York: Oxford University Press, 1955), 300–301.

7. Anna Maria Brodeau Thornton's Diary, Mar. 20, 1800, in Abby Gunn Baker, "The Erection of the White House," *Records of the Columbia Historical Society, Washington, D.C.* 16 (1913): 145; Hamlin, *Benjamin Henry Latrobe*, 300–301.

8. "An Act Concerning the City of Washington," in Peters, *Public Statutes*, vol. 2, 235–36; Jefferson to Latrobe, Mar. 6, 1803, in John C. Van Horne and Lee W. Formwalt, eds., *The Correspondence and Miscellaneous Papers of Benjamin Henry Latrobe*, vol. 1, 1784–1804, Correspondence and Miscellaneous Papers, vol. 4 (New Haven: Published for the Maryland Historical Society by Yale University Press, 1984), 263.

9. Latrobe to Jefferson, Dec. 1, 1804, Feb. 20, 1804, and May 25, 1808, in Padover, *Thomas Jefferson and the National Capital*, 335–40, 347–55, 428; Latrobe to Jefferson, May 23, 1808, in John C. Van Horne, ed., *The Correspondence and Miscellaneous Papers of Benjamin Henry Latrobe*, vol. 2, 1805–10, Correspondence and Miscellaneous Papers, vol. 4, 621–27; Hamlin, *Benjamin Henry Latrobe*, 257–59.

10. Bob Arnebeck, *Through a Fiery Trial*, 475–78. U.S. Congress. Senate. 1878. *Statement of Appropriations and Expenditures from the National Treasury for Public and Private Purposes in the District of Columbia from July 16, 1790 to June 30, 1876: 45th Cong., 2nd sess., Ex. Doc. No. 84.*

11. Jefferson to Latrobe, Feb. 28, 1804, in Padover, *Thomas Jefferson and the National Capital*, 342–43. Jefferson's statement on public buildings appears in Caroline Winterer, *The Culture of Classicism: Ancient Greece and Rome in American Intellectual Life, 1780–1910* (Baltimore: Johns Hopkins University Press, 2002), 29.

12. Jefferson to Latrobe, Apr. 22, 1807, and Latrobe to Jefferson, May 21, 1807, in Van Horne, *Papers of Latrobe*, 2, 1805–10: 410–11, 427–29.

13. On the shifting views of the classics' influence on the founders, see Carl J. Richard, *The Founders and the Classics: Greece, Rome, and the American Enlightenment* (Cambridge, MA: Harvard University Press, 1995), 2–5. On Jefferson's ideology, see Drew R. McCoy, *The Elusive Republic: Political Economy in Jeffersonian America* (Chapel Hill: Published for the Institute of Early American History and Culture, Williamsburg, Va., by the University of North Carolina Press, 1980), 9–10, 67–75; Mark R. Wenger, "Thomas Jefferson and the Virginia State Capitol," *Virginia Magazine of History and Biography* 101, no. 1 (Jan. 1, 1993): 77–88.

14. Latrobe to Jefferson, Aug. 13, 1807, in Padover, *Thomas Jefferson and the National Capital*, 394–96.

15. Henry B. Hibben, *Navy-Yard, Washington: History from Organization, 1799, to Present Date* (Washington: U.S. Government Printing Office, 1890), 21.

16. "An Act Providing for a Naval Peace Establishment, and for Other Purposes, March 3, 1801," in Peters, *Public Statutes*, vol. 2, 110–11; Jefferson to Latrobe, Nov. 2, 1802, in Van Horne and Formwalt, *Papers of Latrobe*, 1, 1784–1804: 221–22.

17. Jefferson Proclamations, Nov. 10, 1802, and Oct. 28, 1805, *President's Letters Sent.*

18. Jefferson to Munroe, Feb. 23, 1806, and Jefferson to Davidson, Mar. 30, 1806, in Padover, *Thomas Jefferson and the National Capital*, 364–65.

19. On the use of commons in colonial cities, see John W. Reps, *The Making of Urban America: A History of City Planning in the United States* (Princeton: Princeton University Press, 1992), 117–25, 187; and John W. Reps, "Town Planning in Colonial Georgia," *Town Planning Review* 30, no. 4 (Jan. 1, 1960): 278; J. R. Wordie, "The Chronology of English Enclosure, 1500–1914," *Economic History Review*, n.s., 36, no. 4 (Nov. 1, 1983): 483–84, doi:10.2307/2597236. On the use of urban commons in Great Britain, see H. R. French, "Urban Agriculture, Commons and Commoners in the Seventeenth and Eighteenth Centuries: The Case of Sudbury, Suffolk," *Agricultural History Review* 48, no. 2 (Jan. 1, 2000): 171–74.

20. Brent to Jefferson, Mar. 9, 1807, in Padover, *Thomas Jefferson and the National Capital*, 384.

21. Jefferson to Brent, Mar. 10, 1807, in Padover, *Thomas Jefferson and the National Capital*, 385–86.

22. Upton, *Another City*, 3–9, 114–23, 165–66.

23. Diane Shaw, *City Building on the Eastern Frontier: Sorting the New Nineteenth-Century City* (Baltimore: Johns Hopkins University Press, 2004), 10–14.

24. "An Act Concerning the District of Columbia," Feb. 27, 1801, and "An Act Supplementary to the Act Entitled 'An Act Concerning the District of Columbia,'" Mar. 3, 1801, in *Public Statutes*, vol. 2, 103–8 and 115–16; Green, *Washington: Village and Capital*, 24–27.

25. Green, *Village and Capital*, 29–30. White's encounter with Goodhue is described in Arnebeck, *Through a Fiery Trial*, 475; *Annals of Congress*, 7th Cong., 2nd sess., 493–94; and 13th Cong., 3rd sess., 312–13, 394–96.

26. "An Act to Abolish the Board of Commissioners in the City of Washington; and for Other Purposes," May 1, 1802, in *Public Statutes*, vol. 2, 175–76.

27. "An Act to Abolish the Board of Commissioners in the City of Washington; and for Other Purposes," May 1, 1802, in *Public Statutes*, vol. 2, 175–76; Munroe to Jefferson, Dec. 20, 1802, *Superintendent's Letters*, vol. 20, #2088. The number of lots sold is based on three reports compiled by the War Department at the request of the Senate in 1899 and 1900. See chapter 2, n. 40.

28. "An Act to Incorporate the Inhabitants of the City of Washington, in the District of Columbia," May 3, 1802, in *Public Statutes*, vol. 2, 195–98; Green, *Village and Capital*, 31; Allen C. Clark, "The Mayoralty of Robert Brent," *Records of the Columbia Historical Society, Washington, D.C.* 33–34 (1932): 267–69. Congress received a petition from the city council requesting alterations to the city's charter in December 1803, as mentioned in *Annals of Congress*, 7th Cong., 2nd sess., 16; mention of the later petitions begins with 11th Cong., 2nd sess., 1445, and 3rd sess., 19–20.

29. Teaford, *The Municipal Revolution*, 3–4, 26–34, 64–78.

30. "An Act to Incorporate the Inhabitants of the City of Washington, in the District of Columbia," May 3, 1802. "An Act Supplementary to 'An Act to Incorporate the Inhabitants of the City of Washington, in the District of Columbia,'" Feb. 24, 1804, and "An Act Further to Amend the Charter of the City of Washington," May 4, 1812, in *Public Statutes*, vol. 2, 195–98, 254–55, 721–27; Schmeckebier, *The District of Columbia*, 24; Green, *Village and Capital*, 31; W. B. Bryan, "The Beginnings of Government in the District," *Records of the Columbia Historical Society, Washington, D.C.* 6 (Jan. 1, 1903): 90–91; Teaford, *The Municipal Revolution*, 64–78.

31. Acts passed by Congress granting charters and authority for private infrastructure projects in the District of Columbia during this period included "An Act Concerning the Insurance of Buildings, Goods and Furniture, in the County of Alexandria, in the Territory of Columbia," Mar. 3, 1803; "An Act Authorizing the Erection of a Bridge over the River Potomac," Feb. 5, 1808; and "An Act to Authorize and Empower the president and Managers of the Washington Turnpike Company of the State of Maryland when Organized to Extend and Make Their Turnpike Road to or from Georgetown in the District of Columbia through the said District to the Line thereof," Feb. 27, 1813, in *Public Statutes*, vol. 2, 227, 465–61, 808. Potomac Bridge discussion and vote results appear in *Annals of Congress*, 9th Cong., 1st sess., 413–28. Acts

passed appropriating funds for the public buildings in this period included "An Act Making an Appropriation for Completing the South Wing of the Capitol at the City of Washington and for Other Purposes," Jan. 25, 1805; "An Act to Make Good a Deficit in the Appropriation of Eighteen Hundred and Seven for Completing the Public Buildings and for Other Purposes," Apr. 25, 1808; "An Act Making a Further Appropriation towards Completing the Two Wings of the Capitol at the City of Washington and for Other Purposes," Mar. 3, 1809; "An Act to Make Public a Road in Washington County in the District of Columbia," Mar. 30, 1810; "An Act Making Further Appropriations for Completing the Capitol and for Other Purposes," May 1, 1810; "Act Making an Appropriation for the Purpose of Discharging All the Outstanding Claims for the Construction and Repair of the Capitol and the presidents House; for the Compensation of the Late Surveyor of the Public Buildings, and for furniture for the different apartment of the Capitol, and for Other Purposes," July 5, 1812; and "An Act Making an Appropriation for Alterations and Repairs in the Capitol," Mar. 3, 1813, in *Public Statutes*, vol. 2, 311, 499, 537, 569–70, 607, 776, 822.

32. The enduring notion that the White House earned its name in the aftermath of the War of 1812 when white paint was applied in order to cover the scars from its burning at the hands of the British is, like many stories told to today's tourists, apocryphal. W. B. Bryan references several instances of the name's use prior to the war in W. B. Bryan, "Correspondence: The Name White House," *Records of the Columbia Historical Society, Washington, D.C.* 33–34 (Jan. 1, 1932): 306–8; Robert Benedetto, Jane Donovan, and Kathleen DuVall, *Historical Dictionary of Washington, D.C.* (Lanham, MD: Scarecrow Press, 2003), 242–43; Catherine Allgor, *Parlor Politics*, 58–64.

33. "An Act Authorizing the President of the United State to Lease for a Term of Years Any Part of the Reservation of Public Ground in the City of Washington," July 5, 1812, in *Public Statutes*, vol. 2, 775; Van Ness to Munroe, Aug. 18, 1812, and Middleton to Munroe, Aug. 24, 1812, *Superintendent's Letters*, vol. 21, #2155 and #2159; Frances Carpenter Huntington, "The Heiress of Washington City: Marcia Burnes Van Ness, 1782–1832," *Records of the Columbia Historical Society, Washington, D.C.* 69–70 (Jan. 1, 1969): 81–90; Benedetto, Donovan, and DuVall, *Historical Dictionary of Washington, D.C.*, 45–46, 226–27.

34. Paperwork Prepared for Mountjoy Bailey (here spelled Bayly), Mar. 26, 1813, *Superintendent's Letters*, vol. 21, #2160.

5 / The Limits of Local Control

1. "An Act for Establishing the Temporary and Permanent Seat of the Government of the United States," July 16, 1790, in *Public Statutes*, vol. 1, 130; "An Act to Incorporate the Inhabitants of the City of Washington, in the District of Columbia," May 3, 1802, in *Public Statutes*, vol. 2, 195–98; *Annals of Congress*, 8th Cong., 1st sess., 282–88.

2. W. B. Bryan, *Forms of Local Government in the District of Columbia, with List of Washington City Officials Appended* (Washington: McGill & Wallace, 1903), 30–32; Bryan, *A History of the National Capital*, vol. 1, 292.

3. James Dudley Morgan, "Robert Brent, First Mayor of Washington City," *Records of the Columbia Historical Society, Washington, D.C.* 2 (1899): 236–39.

4. "An Act to Establish a Direct Tax," Oct. 6, 1802, in *Acts of the Corporation of the City of Washington Passed by the First Council to Which Is Prefixed the Act of Incorporation* (Washington: A. and G. Way, 1803), 13–17; "An Act Imposing Certain Taxes,

and Providing for Their Collection," Sept. 12, 1803, in *Acts of the Corporation of the City of Washington Passed by the Second Council to Which Is Prefixed A Supplement to the Act of Incorporation* (Washington: A. and G. Way, 1804), 13–17; "An Act Imposing Certain Taxes and Providing for Their Collection," Sept. 5, 1804, in *Acts of the Corporation of the City of Washington Passed by the Third Council* (Washington: A. and G. Way, 1805), 13–17; Bryan, *A History of the National Capital*, vol. 1, 478.

5. "An Act Imposing Certain Taxes, Providing for Their Collection, and for Other Purposes," Nov. 11, 1808, in *Acts of the Corporation of the City of Washington Passed by the Seventh Council* (Washington: A. and G. Way, 1809), 16–20; "An Act Amendatory to the Act, Entitled 'An Act for Laying and Collecting an Annual Tax on Dogs,'" Aug. 4, 1809, in *Acts of the Corporation of the City of Washington Passed by the Eighth Council* (Washington: A. and G. Way, 1810), 3–4; "An Act Imposing Taxes for the Year 1810," Dec. 15, 1810, in *Acts of the Corporation of the City of Washington Passed by the Tenth Council* (Washington: A. and G. Way, 1813), 26–28.

6. Leonard P. Curry, *The Corporate City: The American City as a Political Entity, 1800–1850* (Westport, CT: Greenwood Publishing Group, 1997), 33–44.

7. U.S. Constitution, art. 1, sec. 8; McCulloch v. Maryland, 17 U.S. 316 (1819).

8. Bryan, *A History of the National Capital*, vol. 1, 468–70; Annual Council Budget Reports, *National Intelligencer,* June 1, 1803; May 30, 1804; May 29, 1805; June 2, 1806; May 29, 1807; June 6, 1811.

9. "An Act Concerning Roads and Bridges," June 23, 1804; "An Act making an Appropriation for Defraying the Expense of Re-building the Bridge in New Jersey Avenue," Aug. 6, 1804; "An Act for Repairing the Main Road that Leads through the City to Bladensburgh," Oct. 9, 1804; An Act Making Appropriations for the Repairs of Certain Streets," Oct. 17, 1804; and "An Act Making an Appropriation for Bridges and Streets," Dec. 20, 1804, in *Acts of the Third Council*, 3, 11, 18, 19–21, and 28–29.

10. Annual Council Budget Reports, *National Intelligencer,* June 1, 1803, May 30, 1804, May 29, 1805, June 2, 1806, May 29, 1807, and June 6, 1811; "An Act for the Erection of Pumps and Sinking of Wells and for Conveying Water in Pipes on the Pennsylvania Avenue," Dec. 31, 1808, in *Acts of the Seventh Council*, 26; "An Act Making Appropriations for sinking wells, and the Erection and Repairs of Pumps," Oct. 9, 1809, in *Acts of the Eighth Council*, 11; "An Act for the Erection of Pumps, Sinking of Wells and Conveyance of Water in Pipes," Nov. 16, 1810, in *Acts of the Corporation of the City of Washington Passed by the Ninth Council* (Washington: A. and G. Way, 1811), 23–24;" An Act for the Sinking of Wells, and Erecting of Pumps, Conveying of Water in Pipes and Fixing of Hydrants, for the Improvement of Springs and for Other Purposes," Aug. 5, 1812, in *Acts of the Tenth Council*, 8–10; "An Act Making an Appropriation for the Preservation and Clearing of Springs," Sept. 23, 1806, in *Acts of the Corporation of the City of Washington Passed by the Fifth Council* (Washington: A. and G. Way, 1807), 4; "An Act Making Appropriations for Opening the Gutter and Draining the Water off the East side of First Street, and for Other Purposes," Nov. 5, 1807, in *Acts of the Corporation of the City of Washington Passed by the Sixth Council* (Washington: A. and G. Way, 1808), 8.

11. "An Act providing for the Erection of Wharf on the Tiber," July 24, 1804, and "An Act Making an Appropriation for the Completion of the Wharf on the Tyber," Dec. 1, 1804, in *Acts of the Third Council*, 8 and 22.

12. Hartog, *Public Property*, 44–64, 132–44; Upton, *Another City*, 282–84.

13. "An Act for the Erection of a Tobacco Warehouse, on Lots Number 13 and 14, in Square No. 801, and a Wharf at the South End of Seventeenth Street West," Nov. 10, 1806, in *Acts of the Fifth Council*, 9–10. The act does not list the name of the proprietor. However, the original land division maps list Carroll as the owner of Square 801. *Record of Squares, Squares 650–975*, vol. 3, 801–2, Cartographic Files Vol. 3, Records of the Government of the District of Columbia, Record Group 351, National Archives and Records Administration Cartographic and Architectural Section, College Park, MD.

14. "An Act Authorizing the Mayor to Contract for a Lot of Ground and Wharf thereon, for the Use of the Corporation," Dec. 1, 1804, in *Acts of the Third Council*, 21–22; Munroe to Brent, Dec. 15, 1804, *Superintendent's Letters*, vol. 21, item 2103; *National Intelligencer*, June 2, 1806; U.S. Congress, Senate, 1899, *Partial List of Lots in the District of Columbia Sold by the United States*, 55th Cong., 3rd sess., S. Doc. No. 47.

15. "An Act to Establish and Regulate Markets," Oct. 6, 1802, and "An Act to Regulate Weights and Measures," Nov. 19, 1802, in *Acts of the First Council*, 17–21, 33–34; "An Act Regulating the Weight and Quality of Bread," Apr. 17, 1806, in *Acts of the Corporation of the City of Washington Passed by the Fourth Council* (Washington: A. and G. Way, 1806), 30–32; Teaford, *The Municipal Revolution*, 91.

16. Latrobe's Journal, Aug. 12, 1806, in Edward C. Carter II, John C. Van Horne, and Lee W. Formwalt, eds., *The Journals of Benjamin Henry Latrobe 1799–1820 From Philadelphia to New Orleans*, vol. 3, Journals, I (New Haven: Published for the Maryland Historical Society by Yale University Press, 1984), 69–74.

17. "An Act for the Relief of Poor, Infirm and Diseased Persons," Oct. 28, 1802, in *Acts of the First Council*, 26–29.

18. *National Intelligencer*, June 1, 1803, May 30, 1804; "An Act to Establish an Infirmary," Oct. 31, 1806, in *Acts of the Fifth Council*, 5–8; "An Act for the Improvement of the Washington Infirmary," May 23, 1809, in *Acts of the Seventh Council*, 38; Green, *Washington: Village and Capital*, 41–42; Bryan, *A History of the National Capital*, vol. 1, 482n.

19. Seth Rockman, *Welfare Reform in the Early Republic: A Brief History with Documents* (Boston: Bedford/St. Martin's Press, 2003), 12–24. On the Southern experience with poor relief, see James W. Ely, "'There Are Few Subjects in Political Economy of Greater Difficulty': The Poor Laws of the Antebellum South," *American Bar Foundation Research Journal* 10, no. 4 (Oct. 1, 1985): 851–78.

20. "An Act Supplementary to an Act Intitled 'An Act to Incorporate the Inhabitants of the City of Washington, in the District of Columbia,'" Feb. 24, 1804, in Peters, *Public Statutes*, vol. 2, 254–55; Bryan, *A History of the National Capital*, vol. 1, 475; *National Intelligencer*, Aug. 17, 1804.

21. Allen C. Clark, "The Mayoralty of Robert Brent," 86–90; Bryan, *A History of the National Capital*, vol. 1, 478–81; "An Act to Establish and Endow a Permanent Institution for the Education of Youth in the City of Washington," Dec. 5, 1804, in *Acts of the First Council*, 24–27; Emmett D. Preston, "The Development of Negro Education in the District of Columbia, 1800–1860," *Journal of Negro Education* 12, no. 2 (Apr. 1, 1943): 189–90, doi:10.2307/2292971; Board Meeting Minutes, Feb. 2, May 5, and June 9, 1806, *District of Columbia Board of Education Trustees' Minutes Aug. 5, 1805–July 11, 1818*, 57–65, Library of Congress, Washington, D.C.

22. "An Act to Establish and Endow a Permanent Institution for the Education of Youth in the City of Washington," Dec. 5, 1804, in *Acts of the First Council*, 24–27; Bryan, *A History of the National Capital*, vol. 1, 481–84.

23. Board, quoted in Bryan, *A History of the National Capital*, vol. 1, 483–85; Resolution to Raise, by Lottery, the Sum of Ten Thousand Dollars for the Purpose of Building Two Public School Houses on the Lancastrian System, Nov. 19, 1812, in *Acts of the Tenth Council*, 51–52; J. Ormond Wilson, "Eighty Years of the Public Schools of Washington: 1805 to 1885," *Records of the Columbia Historical Society, Washington, D.C.* 1 (Jan. 1, 1897): 8–9; *Second Census*.

24. M. B. Goodwin, "Schools and Education of the Colored Population," in *Special Report of the Commissioner of Education on the Condition and Improvement of Public Schools in the District of Columbia*, by Henry Barnard (Washington: U.S. Government Printing Office, 1871), 195–98; Lillian Gertrude Dabney, *The History of Schools for Negroes in the District of Columbia, 1807–1947* (Washington: Catholic University of America Press, 1949), 1–15.

25. *National Intelligencer*, June 22, 1803, and Apr. 17, 1807; Clark, "The Mayoralty of Robert Brent," 273.

26. Teaford, *The Municipal Revolution*, 91–92; Upton, *Another City*, 242–43; Shaw, *City Building*, 1 and 28–29; M. J. Heale, "Humanitarianism in the Early Republic: The Moral Reformers of New York, 1776–1825," *Journal of American Studies* 2, no. 2 (Oct. 1, 1968): 165–66.

27. Scott and Lee, *Buildings of the District*, 216–17; Orlando Ridout V, *Building the Octagon*, Octagon Research Series (Washington: American Institute of Architects Press, 1989), 1–5, 35–37.

28. Ridout, *Building the Octagon*, 35–37, 71–75, 94–95.

29. James M. Goode, with photography by Bruce White, *Capital Houses: Historic Residences of Washington, D.C. and Its Environs, 1735–1965* (New York: Acanthus Press, 2015), 93–98; Scott and Lee, *Buildings of the District*, 216–17; Virginia McAlester and Arcie Lee McAlester, *A Field Guide to American Houses* (New York: Knopf, 1984), 138–58.

30. Ridout V, *Building the Octagon*, 23–24; Goode, *Capital Losses*, 5.

31. Dell Upton, "Vernacular Domestic Architecture in Eighteenth-Century Virginia," *Winterthur Portfolio* 17, no. 2–3 (July 1, 1982): 102–3; Ridout, *Building the Octagon*, 107–9.

32. For analysis of eighteenth-century Virginians' propensity to fold new architectural styles into their vernacular tradition while retaining the traditional social meanings of their spaces, see Upton, "Vernacular Domestic Architecture," 107–19; Ridout, *Building the Octagon*, 108–17. On the links between urban architecture in Washington and Charleston, see Herman, "Southern City, National Ambition," 33–35. On Tayloe's country estate, see Dell Upton, "White and Black Landscapes in Eighteenth-Century Virginia," in *Material Life in America, 1600–1860*, ed. Robert Blair St George (Boston: Northeastern University Press, 1988), 362–64.

33. Goode, *Capital Losses*, 9, 34–35; McAlester and McAlester, *Guide to American Houses*, 179–83; Bryan, *A History of the National Capital*, vol. 1, 571–72.

34. Herman, *Town House*, 1–6; Upton, *Another City*, 1–6.

35. Stoddert to Jefferson, Georgetown, Oct. 12, 1803, in Padover, *Thomas Jefferson and the National Capital*, 321–22.

36. *Washington Federalist*, July 23, 1808; Clark, "The Mayoralty of Robert Brent," 274–78; Bryan, *A History of the National Capital*, vol. 1, 528–30.

37. Congressional acts establishing companies in the District included "An Act Concerning the Insurance of Buildings, Goods and Furniture, in the County of Alexandria, in the Territory of Columbia," Mar. 3, 1803, "An Act Authorizing the Erection of a Bridge over the River Potomac within the District of Columbia," Feb. 5, 1808, and "Act to Incorporate a Company for Opening the Canal in the City of Washington," Feb. 16, 1809, in Peters, *Public Statutes*, vol. 2, 227, 457–61, 517–20.; Walsh, *Early Banks*, 106–10, 166–72; Alfred Cookman Bryan, *History of State Banking in Maryland* (Baltimore: Johns Hopkins University Press, 1899), 19–25. Other petitions to Congress from district residents appear in "Transcribed Reports of the Committee on the District of Columbia, 10th Cong., 1st sess., through 27th Congress, 1st sess. (1807–1841)," 1–10, *Transcribed Reports of the Committees of the U.S. House of Representatives, 1789–1841* (National Archives Microfilm Publication M1267, reel 5), Records of the U.S. House of Representatives at the National Archives, 1789–1989, Record Group 233, National Archives Building, Washington, DC (hereafter *Transcribed Reports of the Committee on the District of Columbia*); and William Cranch to Richard Cranch, Jan. 11, 1810, Christopher P. Cranch Papers, Box 2 of 5, 1797–1811, Folder 1810 (Jan.–Sept.), Massachusetts Historical Society (Boston).

38. John Adams to Daniel Carroll, Dec. 10, 1794, and Richard Cranch to Lucy Cranch, Mar. 30, 1794, Cranch Family Papers, Bound Volume, Papers of William Cranch, Library of Congress, Manuscript Division, Washington, D.C.; Christopher Pearse Cranch, "William Cranch," in *Memorial Biographies of the New England Historic Genealogical Society: Volume II 1853–1855* (Boston: New England Historic Genealogical Society, 1882), 446–55; William F. Carne, "Life and Times of William Cranch, Judge of the District Circuit Court, 1801–1855," *Records of the Columbia Historical Society, Washington, D.C.* 5 (1902): 296; William Cranch to Richard Cranch, Oct. 3, 1794, Christopher P. Cranch Papers, Box 1 of 5, n.d., 1782–1796, Folder 1794.; Declaration signed by President Adams making Cranch Assistant Judge for the District of Columbia, Christopher P. Cranch Papers, Box 2 of 5, 1797–1811, Folder 1801 (Jan.–Apr.).

39. Declaration signed by President Adams making Cranch Assistant Judge for the District of Columbia, Christopher P. Cranch Papers, Box 2 of 5, 1797–1811, Folder 1801 (Jan.–Apr.).

40. William Cranch to Richard Cranch, Dec. 18, 1808, Christopher P. Cranch Papers, Box 2 of 5, 1797–1811, Folder 1808; "An Act Authorizing the Erection of a Bridge over the River Potomac, within the District of Columbia," Feb. 5, 1808, in Peters, *Public Statutes*, vol. 2, 457–61; Fred A. Emery, "Washington's Historic Bridges," *Records of the Columbia Historical Society, Washington, D.C.* 39 (1938): 58–59.

41. William Cranch to Richard Cranch, Dec. 18, 1808, and Jan. 21, 1809, Christopher P. Cranch Papers, Box 2 of 5, 1797–1811, Folders 1808 and 1809.

42. William Cranch to Richard Cranch, Dec. 18, 1808, Christopher P. Cranch Papers, Box 2 of 5, 1797–1811, Folder 1808; Emery, "Washington's Historic Bridges," 51–54, 66–67.

43. "An Act Authorizing the Erection of a Bridge over the River Potomac, within the District of Columbia," Feb. 5, 1808, in Peters, *Public Statutes*, vol. 2, 457–61; William Cranch to Richard Cranch, Dec. 18, 1808, and Jan. 21, 1809, Christopher P. Cranch Papers, Box 2 of 5, 1797–1811, Folders 1808 and 1809.

44. William Cranch to Richard Cranch, Dec. 18, 1808, Jan. 21, 1809, Jan. 22, 1809, Jan. 11, 1810, and Dec. 22, 1810, Christopher P. Cranch Papers, Box 2 of 5, 1797–1811, Folders 1808, 1809, 1810 (Jan.–Sept.), and 1810 (Oct.–Dec.).

45. William Cranch to Richard Cranch, May 28, 1809, and June 11, 1809, and Richard Cranch to William Cranch, June 30, 1809, Christopher P. Cranch Papers, Box 2 of 5, 1797–1811, Folder 1809 (Jan.–June); Richard Cranch to William Cranch, June 26, 1809, Cranch Family Papers, Massachusetts Historical Society (Boston); William Cranch to Richard Cranch, July 17, 1809, Christopher P. Cranch Papers, Box 2 of 5, 1797–1811, Folder 1809 (July–Sept.); William Cranch to Richard Cranch, Oct. 12, 1809, Christopher P. Cranch Papers, Box 2 of 5, 1797–1811, Folder 1809 (Oct.–Dec.).

46. William Cranch to Richard Cranch, Nov. 24, 1809, Box 2 of 5, 1797–1811, Folder 1809 (Oct.–Dec.); William Cranch to Richard Cranch, Dec. 2, 1810, Box 2 of 5, 1797–1811, Folder 1810 (Oct.–Dec.); William Cranch to Richard Cranch, June 12, 1811, Box 2 of 5, 1797–1811, Folder 1811 (May–June).

47. Campbell Gibson, *Population of the 100 Largest Cities*; Green, *Village and Capital*, 21.

48. Elaine C. Everly and Howard H. Wehmann, "'Then Let Us to the Woods Repair:' Moving the Federal Government and Its Records to Washington in 1800," in *Establishing Congress: The Removal to Washington, D.C., and the Election of 1800*, ed. Kenneth R. Bowling and Donald R. Kennon (Athens: Published for the United States Capitol Historical Society by Ohio University Press, 2005), 57; Bryan, *A History of the National Capital*, vol. 1, 364–70.

49. Gibson, *Population of the 100 Largest Cities*; Brown, *Free Negroes*, 41–63.

50. Brown, *Free Negroes*, 41–63, 142; "An Act to Appoint Two Officers of Police, and for Other Purposes," Dec. 6, 1808, in *Acts of the Seventh Council*, 23–26.

51. Lot sales data and calculations are based on three reports complied by the War Department at the request of the Senate in 1899 and 1900. See chapter 2, n. 40.

52. Green, *Village and Capital*, 28–29, 128.

53. Commissioners Thornton and Dalton to Jefferson, Aug. 24, 1801, in *Letters Sent by the Commissioners for the District of Columbia*, vol. 6, 97–99; *Statement of Appropriations and Expenditures from the National Treasury for Public and Private Purposes in the District of Columbia From July 16, 1790 to June 30, 1876: Senate Ex. Doc. No. 84* (Washington: U.S. Government Printing Office, 1878).

Part III: Making the Capital National, 1814–1828

1. Anthony S. Pitch, *The Burning of Washington: The British Invasion of 1814* (Annapolis: Naval Institute Press, 1998), 98–144.

2. Pitch, *The Burning of Washington*, 139–40; Michael Shiner, "The Diary of Michael Shiner Relating to the History of the Washington Navy Yard, 1813–1869," Oct. 2007, 8, http://www.history.navy.mil/library/online/shinerdiary.html.

6 / Saving and Rebuilding Washington

1. Pitch, *The Burning of Washington*, 17–19.

2. "An Act Making an Appropriation in Aid of the Defense of the City of Washington," in *Acts of the Corporation of the City of Washington Passed by the Tenth Council* (Washington: A. and G. Way, 1813), 48; Pitch, *The Burning of Washington*, 17–18.

3. Linda Arnold, "Congressional Government of the District of Columbia, 1800–1846" (PhD diss., Georgetown University, 1975), 87–93; Pitch, *The*

Burning of Washington, 71–85; Bryan, *A History of the National Capital*, vol. 1, 618–26.

4. Brown, *Incidental Architect*, 78–79; John Nelson, *Liberty and Property: Political Economy and Policymaking in the New Nation, 1789–1812* (Baltimore: Johns Hopkins University Press, 1987), 1–8; Anna Maria Brodeau Thornton, quoted from her diary, Aug. 25, 1814, Anna Maria Brodeau Thornton Papers, 1793–1861, Diaries of Mrs. William Thornton, 1793–1863, vol. 3, 1807–1818, Microfilm Reel 1, Library of Congress, Washington, DC; transcription published in Anna Maria Brodeau Thornton, "Diary of Mrs. William Thornton: Capture of Washington by the British," ed. W. B. Bryan, *Records of the Columbia Historical Society, Washington, D.C.* 19 (1916): 175–76; William Thornton, quoted from *National Intelligencer*, Sept. 7, 1814; Allgor, *Parlor Politics*, 96.

5. *Annals of Congress*, 13th Cong., 3rd sess., 305–12.

6. *Annals of Congress*, 13th Cong., 3rd sess., 312–13.

7. *Annals of Congress*, 13th Cong., 3rd sess., 312–22, 345–56.

8. *Annals of Congress*, 13th Cong., 3rd sess., 313–16, 356–76.

9. For detail on Federalist vote cohesion during the War of 1812, see Donald R. Hickey, "Federalist Party Unity and the War of 1812," *Journal of American Studies* 12, no. 1 (Apr. 1, 1978): 26–34; *Annals of Congress*, 13th Cong., 3rd sess., 356–76.

10. Green, *Washington: Village and Capital*, 64–65; *Annals of Congress*, 13th Cong., 3rd sess., 394–96.

11. Richard C. Rohrs, "Sectionalism, Political Parties, and the Attempt to Relocate the National Capital in 1814," *Historian* 62, no. 3 (2000): 538–55, doi:10.1111/j.1540–6563.2000. tb01996.x; *Annals of Congress*, 13th Cong., 3rd sess., 376, 394–96.

12. *Annals of Congress*, 13th Cong., 3rd sess., 394–96; Rohrs, "Sectionalism," 638–55.

13. Bryan, *A History of the National Capital*, vol. 1, 635; Catherine Allgor, *Parlor Politics*, 96–97; memorial quoted from the *National Intelligencer*, Oct. 10, 1814.

14. Pitch, *The Burning of Washington*, 167–69; *National Intelligencer*, Oct. 15, 1814.

15. *National Intelligencer*, Oct. 15, 1814. Involvement of individual Washingtonians with local banks can be traced through the documents and descriptions in Walsh, *Early Banks*, 18–165; "An Act Making Appropriations for Repairing or Rebuilding the Public Buildings within the City of Washington," Feb. 13, 1815, in Richard Peters, ed., *Public Statutes*, vol. 3, 205; Green, *Village and Capital*, 64–65; Allgor, *Parlor Politics*, 97.

16. Law's poem, "A Dream," in Allen Culling Clark, *Greenleaf and Law in the Federal City* (Washington: W. F. Roberts Company, 1901), 294–95. On the personification of Liberty and Columbia in American imagery, see Fleming, "From Indian Princess," 37–66.

17. Law to Madison, Nov. 26, 1814, as printed in Clark, *Greenleaf and Law in the Federal City*, 291–93.

18. Law to Madison, Nov. 26, 1814, as printed in Clark, *Greenleaf and Law in the Federal City*, 291–93.

19. Madison's Eighth Annual Message to Congress appears in James Madison, *The Writings of James Madison: Volume VIII 1808–1819*, ed. Gaillard Hunt (New York: G. P. Putnam's Sons, 1908), 375–85. The phrase "pure limited government" appears in Daniel Walker Howe, *What Hath God Wrought: The Transformation of America, 1815–1848* (New York: Oxford University Press, 2007), 158–59. For a description of the divisions within the Democratic-Republican Party, see John Lauritz Larson, *Internal Improvement: National Public Works and the Promise of Popular Government in the Early United States* (Chapel Hill: University of North Carolina Press, 2001), 50–67;

and Steven Watts, *The Republic Reborn: War and the Making of Liberal America, 1790–1820* (Baltimore: Johns Hopkins University Press, 1989), 16–28; *Annals of Congress*, 14th Cong., 2nd sess., 257–60, 1063–64.

20. Bryan, *A History of the National Capital*, vol. 1, 636–37; Goode, *Capital Losses*, 328–30.

21. *Annals of Congress*, 13th Cong., 3rd sess., 689–91, and for the full report, see 1518–1738; Arnold, "Congressional Government," 109–12.

22. *Annals of Congress*, 13th Cong., 3rd sess., 689–91, 1518–1738. "Ample and sufficient" quote as printed in Arnold, "Congressional Government," 109–12. The *National Intelligencer* printed a summary of the report on Dec. 12, 1814.

23. *Annals of Congress*, 13th Cong., 3rd sess., 689–91, 1518–1738; Arnold, "Congressional Government," 109–12; Pitch, *The Burning of Washington*, 235; Alan Taylor, *The Civil War of 1812: American Citizens, British Subjects, Irish Rebels, & Indian Allies* (New York: Knopf, 2010), 418–21; *National Intelligencer*, Feb. 15, 1815; Senate Journal, 13th Cong., 3rd sess., Feb. 16, 1815, 620.

24. Di Giacomantonio, "All the President's Men," 69; Hamlin, *Benjamin Henry Latrobe*, 434–38; Latrobe to Madison, Feb. 25, 1815, in John C. Van Horne, ed., *The Correspondence and Miscellaneous Papers of Benjamin Henry Latrobe*, vol. 3, 1811–20, Correspondence and Miscellaneous Papers, vol. 4, 630–31; Mar. 13 and 15, 1815, *Proceedings of the Commissioners Appointed to Supervise the Repair or Rebuilding of the Public Buildings in Washington, 1815–1816*, 1–3, Proceedings and Letters Sent, 1815–1816 (National Archives Microfilm Publication M371, roll 2, vol. 7), Records of the Office of Public Buildings and Public Parks of the National Capital, Record Group 42, National Archives Building, Washington, D.C. (hereafter *Repair Proceedings*); Latrobe to Commissioners, Mar. 25 and Apr. 1, 1815, *Letters Received and Drafts of Letters Sent by the Superintendent of the City of Washington and Letters Received by the Commissioners Appointed to Supervise the Repair and Rebuilding of the Public Buildings, Volume 22: March 14–June 7, 1815*, Letters Received, Correspondence (National Archives Microfilm Publication M371, roll 18), General Records, 1790–1931, Records of the Office of Public Buildings and Public Parks of the National Capital, Record Group 42, National Archives Building, Washington, D.C. (hereafter *Repair Letters Received*).

25. "An Act Making an Appropriation for Enclosing and Improving the Public Square Near the Capitol; and to Abolish the Office of Commissioners of the Public Buildings, and of Superintendent, and for the Appointment of One Commissioner for the Public Buildings" Apr. 29, 1816, in Peters, *Statutes at Large*, vol. 3, 324–25; Hamlin, *Benjamin Henry Latrobe*, 442; Latrobe to Madison, Apr. 24, 1816, in Van Horne, *Papers of Latrobe*, 3, 1811–20:765–67; *U.S. Senate Executive Journal*, Apr. 29 and 30, 1816, 14th Cong., 1st sess., 52–53; Monroe to Lane, Apr. 4, 1817, *President's Letters Sent*.

26. Van Horne, *Papers of Latrobe*, 3, 1811–20: 904–6. On Democratic-Republican divisions, see Larson, *Internal Improvement*, 50–67; Rebuilding the Capitol, President's House, and Other Public Buildings in the City of Washington, Nov. 21, 1814, in Walter Lowrie et al., eds., *American State Papers: Miscellaneous* 2: 252–53.

7 / Striving to Be a National City

1. *Federal Republican*, Oct. 17, 1814.

2. "An Act to Pave the Footway on South Side of D Street North, between Eleventh and Twelfth Streets West, and for Other Purposes, An Act Making an Addition

Appropriation for the Improvement of Maryland Avenue, North East of the Capitol," July 1, 1815, and Dec. 8, 1815, in *Acts of the Corporation of the City of Washington Passed by the Thirteenth Council* (Washington: Daniel Rapine, 1816), 4–5, 42–43.

3. "An Act for the Preservation of Trees on the Public Squares, Streets and Avenues, within the First and Second Wards, and An Act for the Preservation of Trees on the Streets and Avenues in the City and Appropriating a Certain Sum for Replacing Trees in the Second Ward," June 24, 1815, Aug. 3, 1815, and May 10, 1816, in *Acts of the Thirteenth Council*, 28–29, 54–55; Bryan, *A History of the National Capital*, vol. 2, 13; Henry W. Lawrence, *City Trees: A Historical Geography from the Renaissance through the Nineteenth Century* (Charlottesville: University of Virginia Press, 2008), 87, 159–71.

4. "An Act Making an Appropriation for the Support of the Poor, Aged and Infirm of the City of Washington," "An Act to Prevent Geese from Going at Large in the City of Washington," and "An Act Making an Appropriation for Defraying the Expense Incurred in Removing a Nuisance on the East Side of Twelfth Street West, between Pennsylvania Avenue and E Street North," July 26, 1815, and May 30, 1816, in *Acts of the Thirteenth Council*, 3, 21–22, and 58.

5. "Problems" quotation in Teaford, *The Municipal Revolution*, 92–110; Paul A. Gilje, *The Road to Mobocracy: Popular Disorder in New York City, 1763–1834* (Chapel Hill: Published for the Institute of Early American History and Culture by the University of North Carolina Press, 1987), 205, 220–32; *Federal Republican*, Sept. 15, 1815.

6. Bryan, *A History of the National Capital*, vol. 2, 98; "An Act to Authorize a Loan for the Use of the City of Washington, and for Funding the Debt Due by the Corporation and An Act Making Provision for the Redemption of the Debt Due by the Corporation of the City of Washington, and for the Payment of the Interest thereof," July 11, 1818, in *Laws Passed by the Sixteenth Council of the City of Washington*, 1819, 3–7.

7. "An Act Authorizing a Lottery or Lotteries in the City of Washington for the Purposes therein Mentioned," and "A Resolution to Raise, by Lottery, the Sum of Ten Thousand Dollars, for the Purposes therein Mentioned," July 24, 1815, and Apr. 20, 1816, in *Acts of the Thirteenth Council*, 14–15 and 60; "An Act to Carry into Effect Certain Resolutions Authorizing the Raising of Money by Lottery," Nov. 17, 1818, in *Laws of the Sixteenth Council*, 28–29; Bryan, *A History of the National Capital*, vol. 2, 81; Green, *Washington: Village and Capital*, 90; *Washington Gazette*, Dec. 7, 1821; *Salem Gazette*, Jan. 15, 1822. A summary of the city's lottery system and the legal case lost by the city can be found in Clark v. Corporation of Washington, 25 U.S. 40–63.

8. *City of Washington Gazette*, Apr. 7, 1820; Bryan, *A History of the National Capital*, vol. 2, 79; George S. Hunsberger, "The Architectural Career of George Hadfield," *Records of the Columbia Historical Society, Washington, D.C.* 51–52 (1951): 46–59; Julia King, *George Hadfield: Architect of the Federal City* (Burlington, VT: Ashgate, 2014), 113–27; Scott and Lee, *Buildings of the District*, 24.

9. Bryan, *A History of the National Capital*, vol. 2, 79–80; Hunsberger, "The Architectural Career of George Hadfield," 56–65; King, *George Hadfield*, 135–49; Scott and Lee, *Buildings of the District*, 183; Green, *Village and Capital*, 89–90.

10. Quotation from Dell Upton, "Architectural History or Landscape History?," *Journal of Architectural Education* 44, no. 4 (1991): 198. On structures as responses rather than mere reflections, see Upton, *Another City*, 7. On the fusion of the physical and the imagined as well as the meaning of civic structures, see Mary P. Ryan,

"'A Laudable Pride in the Whole of Us': City Halls and Civic Materialism," *American Historical Review* 105, no. 4 (Oct. 1, 2000): 1132–34. On the efforts to reinforce and represent authority through architecture, see McInnis, *The Politics of Taste*, 6–7.

11. Bryan, *A History of the National Capital*, vol. 2, 80–81.

12. Bryan, *A History of the National Capital*, vol. 2, 39–40; *Annals of Congress*, 16th Cong., 1st sess., 781–86.

13. Clay, quoted in *Annals of Congress*, 16th Cong., 1st sess., 781–86; *National Intelligencer*, January 4, 1820; Bryan, *A History of the National Capital*, vol. 2, 39–40, 81–82; King, *George Hadfield*, 150–51; "An Act Providing for the Accommodation of the Circuit Court of the United States for Washington county, in the District of Columbia, and for the Preservation f the Records of Said Court," Mar. 3, 1823, in Peters, *Public Statutes*, vol. 3, 785; Scott and Lee, *Buildings of the District*, 183.

14. "An Act to Incorporate the Inhabitants of the City of Washington, and to Repeal all Acts heretofore Passed for That Purpose," May 15, 1820, in Peters, *Statutes at Large*, vol. 3, 583–92; Curry, *The Corporate City*, 5–11; Bryan, *A History of the National Capital*, vol. 2, 25–26; "An Act to Direct Curb Stone to be Set, and the Footway to Be Paved on the North Side of Square Numbered One Hundred and Twenty Seven," June 11, 1820, in *Laws Passed by the Eighteenth Council of the City of Washington, 1821*, 17–18. Lot sales data and calculations are based on three reports compiled by the War Department at the request of the Senate in 1899 and 1900; see chapter 2, n. 40. Estimate of the perimeter of the Capitol grounds taken from *Nicholas King Plats, Washington 1803*, Map IV, Records of the Government of the District of Columbia, Record Group 351, Cartographic and Architectural Section, National Archives at College Park, College Park, MD.

15. "An Act Making Appropriation for the Support of Government for the Year One Thousand Eight Hundred and Twenty Three," Mar. 3, 1823, in Peters, *Statutes at Large*, vol. 3, 758–63.

16. Green, *Village and Capital*, 70; Susan L. Klaus, "'Some of the Smartest Folks Here': The Van Nesses and Community Building in Early Washington," *Washington History* 3, no. 2 (Oct. 1, 1991): 33–34; Clark, *Life and Letters of Dolly Madison*, 191–92; Suzanne Lebsock, *The Free Women of Petersburg: Status and Culture in a Southern Town, 1784–1860* (New York: W. W. Norton, 1985), 201–5; Cynthia A. Kierner, *Beyond the Household: Women's Place in the Early South, 1700–1835* (Ithaca: Cornell University Press, 1998), 191; *National Intelligencer*, Oct. 10, 1815.

17. Green, *Village and Capital*, 70–71; Klaus, "'Some of the Smartest Folks Here,'" 34; Huntington, "The Heiress of Washington City," 97; Anne Newport Royall, *Sketches of History, Life, and Manners, in the United States* (New Haven, 1826), 144.

18. Van Ness, quoted in Klaus, "'Some of the Smartest Folks Here,'" 34; Sarah Harvey Porter, "The Life and Times of Ann Royall, 1769–1854," *Records of the Columbia Historical Society, Washington, D.C.* 10 (Jan. 1, 1907): 1–4; Royall, quoted from *Sketches of History, Life, and Manners, in the United States*, 144–45.

19. Green, *Village and Capital*, 70–71; "An Act to Incorporate the Trustees of the Female Orphan Asylum in Georgetown, and the Washington City Orphan Asylum, in the District of Columbia," May 24, 1828, in Peters, *Public Statutes*, vol. 4, 381–82; Lebsock, *The Free Women of Petersburg*, 200–201; Kierner, *Beyond the Household*, 140, 180–213.

20. On the blurred distinctions between gendered public and private spheres, see Carol Lasser, "Beyond Separate Spheres: The Power of Public Opinion," *Journal of*

the *Early Republic* 21, no. 1 (Apr. 1, 2001): 116–23, doi:10.2307/3125099; and; Kierner, *Beyond the Household*, 2; Catherine Allgor, *Parlor Politics*, 239–42; Teute, "Roman Matron on the Banks of Tiber Creek," 113–16; quote in Lewis, "Politics and the Ambivalence," 146–51.

21. Metropolitan Society quotations in Richard Rathbun, *The Columbian Institute for the Promotion of Arts and Sciences*, Bulletin of the United States National Museum 101 (Washington: U.S. Government Printing Office, 1917), 10–11; Harold T. Pinkett, "Early Agricultural Societies in the District of Columbia," *Records of the Columbia Historical Society, Washington, D.C.* 51–52 (Jan. 1, 1951): 32–39.

22. Sally Kohlstedt, "A Step toward Scientific Self-Identity in the United States: The Failure of the National Institute, 1844," *Isis* 62, no. 3 (Oct. 1971): 340–41. The full text of the Columbian Institute's constitution appears in the appendix of Rathbun, *The Columbian Institute*, 11, 67–70.

23. On the influence of European scientific societies on the formation of American institutions, see W. H. G. Armytage, "The Triple Graft: European Influence on American Science—1727–1861," *Bulletin British Association for American Studies*, n.s., no. 4 (1962): 4–9. On American scientific societies in general, see Alexandra Oleson and Sanborn C. Brown, eds., *The Pursuit of Knowledge in the Early American Republic: American Scientific and Learned Societies from Colonial Times to the Civil War* (Baltimore: Johns Hopkins University Press, 1977). For the Laws and Regulations of the American Philosophical Society, see *Transactions of the American Philosophical Society Held at Philadelphia for Promoting Useful Knowledge*, 2nd ed. corr. (Philadelphia: R. Aitken & Son, 1789), v–ix. On the origin of the APS, see Carl van Doren, "The Beginnings of the American Philosophical Society," *Proceedings of the American Philosophical Society* 87, no. 3 (July 1943): 277–89; Rathbun, *The Columbian Institute*, 67–74.

24. Cutbush's speech is quoted at length in Rathbun, *The Columbian Institute*, 11–16.

25. Rathbun, *The Columbian Institute*, 11–16.

26. "An Act to Incorporate the Columbian Institute, for the Promotion of Arts and Sciences," Apr. 20, 1818, in Peters, *Statutes at Large*, vol. 6, 214–15; Pinkett, "Early Agricultural Societies," 41; Rathbun, *The Columbian Institute*, 6, 23–24.

27. Rathbun, *The Columbian Institute*, 18–37, 67–74; Kohlstedt, "Scientific Self-Identity," 340–41; Therese O'Malley, "Art and Science in American Landscape Architecture: The National Mall, Washington, D.C., 1791–1852" (PhD diss., University of Pennsylvania, 1989), 140–42.

28. "An Act for the Benefit of the Columbian Institute, Established for the Promotion of the Arts and Sciences in the City of Washington," May 8, 1820, and "An Act for the Benefit of [the] Columbian Institute," May 26, 1824, in Peters, *Statutes at Large*, vol. 4, 247–48, 316; draft petition to Congress quoted in Rathbun, *The Columbian Institute*, 37–43; O'Malley, "Art and Science," 123–31.

29. "An Act to Authorize and Empower the Corporation of the City of Washington in the District of Columbia, to Drain the Low Grounds on and near the Public Reservations, and to Improve and Ornament Certain Parts of Such Reservations," May 7, 1822, in Peters, *Statutes at Large*, vol. 3, 691; visitor comment as quoted in Rathbun, *The Columbian Institute*, 42–46.

30. Rathbun, *The Columbian Institute*, 44–51.

31. Rathbun, *The Columbian Institute*, 32–34, 54–62; and on Peale's Museum, see Sidney Hart and David C. Ward, "The Waning of an Enlightenment Ideal: Charles Willson Peale's Philadelphia Museum, 1790–1820," *Journal of the Early Republic* 8, no. 4 (Dec. 1, 1988): 389–418, doi:10.2307/3123178.

32. "George Washington's Uniform," Smithsonian's History Explorer, https://historyexplorer.si.edu/resource/george-washingtons-uniform; Kenneth Hafertepe, *America's Castle: The Evolution of the Smithsonian Building and Its Institution, 1840–1878* (Washington: Smithsonian Institution Press, 1984), 6–7; Smithson's will quoted in George Brown Goode, ed., *The Smithsonian Institution 1846–1896: The History of Its First Half-Century* (Washington, 1897), 19–28; George Brown Goode, "The Genesis of the National Museum," in *Annual Report—United States National Museum* (Washington: U.S. Government Printing Office, 1892), 272–81.

33. Bryan, *A History of the National Capital*, vol. 2, 13; *National Intelligencer*, May 13, 1819.

Part IV: The Seat of a Continental Empire

1. John Quincy Adams, *Memoirs of John Quincy Adams: Comprising Portions of His Diary from 1795 to 1848*, vol. 8 (Philadelphia: J. B. Lippincott & Co., 1876), 49; *Republican Star and General Advertiser*, July 15, 1828.

2. Adams, *Memoirs of J. Q. Adams*, vol. 8, 49–50; Walter S. Sanderlin, *The Great National Project: A History of the Chesapeake and Ohio Canal* (Baltimore: Johns Hopkins University Press, 1946), 19, 51–60; Littlefield, "The Potomac Company," 576–85.

3. Sanderlin, *The Great National Project*, 56–57; Bryan, *A History of the National Capital*, vol. 2, 106–14.

4. Adams, *Memoirs of J. Q. Adams*, vol. 8, 49–50. Reporting of the event by the *National Intelligencer* was republished by a number of papers nationwide, including the July 11, 1828, *Salem Gazette*.

5. *Baltimore Patriot and Mercantile Advertiser*, July 8 and 9, 1828.

6. John F. Stover, *History of the Baltimore and Ohio Railroad* (West Lafayette, IN: Purdue University Press, 1995), 25–27, 41–45; Nancy Goyne Evans, "History on a Bandbox: A Pictorial Record of the Founding of the Baltimore and Ohio Railroad," *Winterthur Portfolio* 5 (Jan. 1, 1969): 123.

7. Green, *Washington: Village and Capital*, 128.

8 / A Symbolic National Capital

1. Gibson and Jung, *Historical Census Statistics*; Campbell Gibson, *Population of the 100 Largest Cities*.

2. "Total Number of Dwelling Houses and other Buildings in the City of Washington on the 31st of December, 1830, from the Actual Count, by John Sessford," in *Laws of the Corporation of the City of Washington Passed by the Twenty-Eighth Council* (Washington: Way & Gideon, 1831), 79; "Sessford's Statistical Table of Improvements Made in the City of Washington during the Year 1827, also a Tabular Statement of the Number of Deaths during the Same Period, &c.," in *Laws of the Corporation of the City of Washington Passed by the Twenty-Fifth Council* (Washington: Way & Gideon, 1827), vii.

3. For city population data, see Gibson and Jung, *Historical Census Statistics*; U.S. population data drawn from "Annual Population Estimates for the United States: 1790

to 1970," in U.S. Bureau of the Census, *Historical Statistics of the United States: Colonial Times to 1970: Bicentennial Edition, Part 2* (Washington: U.S. Government Printing Office, 1975), 8; H. Paul Caemmerer, *A Manual on the Origin and Development of Washington*, 49; Mark David Richards, "The Debates over the Retrocession of the District of Columbia, 1801–2004," *Washington History* 16, no. 1 (Apr. 1, 2004): 61–72; Alexandria Retrocession Petition, undated, Committee on the District of Columbia, Petitions and Memorials Referred to Committees (HR18A-F4.1), 18th Congress, Records of the U.S. House of Representatives, Record Group 233, National Archives, Washington, D.C.

4. Stover, *History of the Baltimore and Ohio Railroad*, 1–4. A similar regional breakdown appears in Douglass North, *The Economic Growth of the United States, 1790–1860* (Englewood Cliffs, NJ: Prentice-Hall, 1961), 257.

5. Daniel Feller, *The Public Lands in Jacksonian Politics* (Madison: University of Wisconsin Press, 1984), xi–xvi.; Howe, *What Hath God Wrought*, 136–38, 411–23, 563–65.

6. For the purposes of the above calculations, I included Vermont among the states along the eastern seaboard and considered all states to the west of those states as those in the interior. Apportionment statistics taken from Table 3, "Apportionment of Membership of the House of Representatives: 1789 to 1990," in U.S. Bureau of the Census, *1990 Census of Population and Housing: Population and Housing Unit Counts* (Washington: U.S. Government Printing Office, 1993), 3–4; Larson, *Internal Improvement*, 181–82.

7. Howe, *What Hath God Wrought*, 489–91; M. J. Heale, "The Role of the Frontier in Jacksonian Politics: David Crockett and the Myth of the Self-Made Man," *Western Historical Quarterly* 4, no. 4 (Oct. 1973): 406–9; David Crockett, *A Narrative of the Life of David Crockett, Written by Himself* (Philadelphia: E. L. Cary and A. Hart, 1834), 109–13.

8. Howe, *What Hath God Wrought*, 116–17, 563–65; Adam Rothman, *Slave Country: American Expansion and the Origins of the Deep South* (Cambridge, MA: Harvard University Press, 2007), 45–57, 165–83; North, *Economic Growth*, 189–97.

9. *Baltimore Patriot and Mercantile Advertiser*, July 8, 1828.

10. Pamela Scott, *Capital Engineers: The U.S. Army Corps of Engineers in the Development of Washington, D.C., 1790–2000* (Alexandria, VA: Office of History, U.S. Army Corps of Engineers, 2012), 2–3, 23–25; Forest G. Hill, *Roads, Rails & Waterways: The Army Engineers and Early Transportation* (Norman: University of Oklahoma Press, 1957), 3–95; Robert P. Wettemann Jr., *Privilege vs. Equality: Civil-Military Relations in the Jacksonian Era, 1815–1845* (Santa Barbara, CA: ABC-CLIO, 2009), 74–91.

11. Andrés Reséndez, *Changing National Identities at the Frontier: Texas and New Mexico, 1800–1850* (New York: Cambridge University Press, 2004), 93–96; William Lee Miller, *Arguing about Slavery: The Great Battle in the United States Congress* (New York: Knopf, 1996), 181, 207–8.

12. Richard S. Newman, *The Transformation of American Abolitionism: Fighting Slavery in the Early Republic* (Chapel Hill: University of North Carolina Press, 2002), 1–8, 107–23.

13. William W. Freehling, *The Road to Disunion*, vol. 1: *Secessionists at Bay, 1776–1854* (New York: Oxford University Press, 1990), 290–95. On the influence of slave rebellions on Southern fears of abolitionism, see Edward B. Rugemer, "Caribbean

Slave Revolts and the Origins of the Gag Rule: A Contest between Abolitionism and Democracy, 1797–1835," in *Contesting Slavery: The Politics of Bondage and Freedom in the New American Nation*, ed. John Craig Hammond and Matthew Mason (Charlottesville: University of Virginia Press, 2011), 94–97.

14. Rugemer, "Caribbean Slave Revolts," 94; Howe, *What Hath God Wrought*, 512–15.

15. Pamela L. Baker, "The Washington National Road Bill and the Struggle to Adopt a Federal System of Internal Improvement," *Journal of the Early Republic* 22, no. 3 (Autumn 2002): 455–63, doi:10.2307/3124811. For discussion of the gag rule's place in antebellum politics, see Howe, *What Hath God Wrought*, 512–15; and Freehling, *The Road to Disunion*, 308–52.

16. Susan Zaeske, *Signatures of Citizenship: Petitioning, Antislavery, & Women's Political Identity* (Chapel Hill: University of North Carolina Press, 2003), 53; Miller, *Arguing about Slavery*, 27–62; *Register of Debates in Congress*, 24th Cong., 1st sess., 2066–77.

17. *Register of Debates in Congress*, 24th Cong., 1st sess., 2066–77.

18. An extensive discussion of race relations in early republic and antebellum Washington can be found in Gillette, *Between Justice and Beauty*, 27–43 Detail of the petition from District residents appears in Zaeske, *Signatures of Citizenship*, 33, 189 n. 9. A list of the signatories to the ACS Constitution appears in Henry Noble Sherwood, "The Formation of the American Colonization Society," *Journal of Negro History* 2, no. 3 (July 1, 1917): 227, doi:10.2307/2713765. Signatories compared to *Fourth Census of the United States, 1820* (NARA microfilm publication M33, reel 5), Records of the Bureau of the Census, Record Group 29. National Archives, Washington, DC, accessed via http://www.ancestry.com.

19. Green, *Washington: Village and Capital*, 140–45; Bryan, *A History of the National Capital*, vol. 2, 144–45; Gibson and Jung, "Population Totals by Race."

20. On the impact of the gag rule on abolitionist petitions, see Zaeske, *Signatures of Citizenship*, 72–104. On John Quincy Adams's activity in the House, see Howe, *What Hath God Wrought*, 514–15; and Miller, *Arguing about Slavery*, 153–514. The estimate of signatures from the Twenty-Fifth Congress appears in Gerda Lerner, *The Grimké Sisters from South Carolina: Pioneers for Women's Rights and Abolition* (New York: Oxford University Press, 1998), 206. The estimate of pre–gag rule signatures appears in Richard A. Primus, *The American Language of Rights* (New York: Cambridge University Press, 1999), 139.

9 / Federal Intervention

1. Constance McLaughlin Green, "The Jacksonian 'Revolution' in the District of Columbia," *Mississippi Valley Historical Review* 45, no. 4 (Mar. 1959): 592–93; Sanderlin, *The Great National Project*, 85–101.

2. Green, *Village and Capital*, 122; Green, "The Jacksonian 'Revolution,'" 594–95.

3. Sanderlin, *The Great National Project*, 52–55.

4. Larson, *Internal Improvement*, 50–77. For details on Jefferson and Madison, see Baker, "The Washington National Road Bill," 440–42; and Joseph H. Harrison, "'Sic Et Non': Thomas Jefferson and Internal Improvement," *Journal of the Early Republic* 7, no. 4 (Winter 1987): 341–44.

5. For a detailed examination of the battle between the friends and foes of internal improvements, see Larson, *Internal Improvement*, 109–93; and for detail on the

Democratic-Republican split and Jackson's political calculations, see Howe, *What Hath God Wrought*, 275–76, 357–61.

6. U.S. Bureau of the Census, *Historical Statistics of the United States*, 1115.

7. Sanderlin, *The Great National Project*, 55–57; "Resolution Authorizing Accommodation for the Sittings of the Canal Convention, and Making an Appropriation Therefore," Dec. 12, 1806, in *Laws of the Corporation of the City of Washington Passed by the Twenty-Fourth Council* (Washington: Way & Gideon, 1827), 88; "An Act to Authorize a Subscription to the Capital Stock of the Chesapeake and Ohio Canal Company," Sept. 13, 1827, in *Laws of the Twenty-Fifth Council*, 20; "An Act Authorizing a Subscription to the Stock of the Chesapeake and Ohio Canal Company," May 24, 1828, and "An Act to Enlarge the Powers of the Several Corporations of the District of Columbia, and for Other Purposes," May 24, 1828 in Peters, *Public Statutes*, vol. 4, 293–97.

8. Sanderlin, *The Great National Project*, 175–82; Bryan, *A History of the National Capital*, vol. 2, 109–13; "An Act Authorizing the Purchase of the Washington Canal, and for the Completion Thereof," May 5, 1831, in Andrew Rothwell, *Laws of the Corporation of the City of Washington, to the End of the Thirtieth Council—June 1833* (Washington: F. W. De Krafft, 1833), 242–44.

9. *Federal Payment to the District of Columbia 1790–1980: A Reference Compendium of Documents, Studies, Reports, and Proposals—Staff Study for the Committee on the District of Columbia House of Representatives, Ninety-Sixth Congress, First Session* (Washington: U.S. Government Printing Office, 1979), 7–9; *Journal of the Senate of the United States of America: Being the Second Session of the Nineteenth Congress: Begun and Held at the City of Washington December 4, 1826, and in the Fifty-First Year of the Independence of the Said United States* (Washington: Gales and Seaton, 1826), 252; S. 97, 19th Cong. (1827).

10. *Street, Capitol to Executive Offices: To Accompany Bill H.R. No. 224*, Report No. 184, Feb. 10, 1830, *Transcribed Reports of the Committee on the District of Columbia*.

11. "An Act for Improving Pennsylvania Avenue, Supplying the Public Buildings with Water, and for Paving the Walk from the Western Gate to the Capitol with Flagging," May 25, 1832, in Peters, *Public Statutes*, vol. 4, 518; Green, "The Jacksonian 'Revolution' in the District of Columbia," 599–601; Fred A. Emery, "Washington's Historic Bridges," 58–59; Bryan, *A History of the National Capital*, vol. 2, 117–19.

12. Green, "The Jacksonian 'Revolution,'" 601–2.

13. Bryan, *A History of the National Capital*, vol. 2, 110–11; Green, *Village and Capital*, 127–29; "Abstract of Appropriations by the Corporation 1819–1833" and "An Act to Authorize the Collection of a Portion of the Tax Assessed and Laid on the Real and Personal Estate, within the City of Washington, by an Act of Congress, Entitled 'An Act to Enlarge the Powers of the Several Corporations within the District of Columbia, and for Other Purposes,'" Approved May Twenty-Fourth, Eighteen Hundred and Twenty-Eight, Dec. 26, 1832, in Rothwell, *Laws of the Corporation of Washington . . . to 1833*, 291–315; appropriations for fiscal year 1833–34 found in *Laws of the Corporation of the City of Washington Passed by the Thirty-First Council* (Washington: Way & Gideon, 1833), 37–39; tax rates and financial information for Washington and other cities can be found in Leonard P. Curry, *The Corporate City*, 31–72.

14. Senate Report No. 97, 23rd Cong., 2nd sess., Feb. 2, 1835, in *Federal Payment*, 160–78; Michael J. Birkner, *Samuel L. Southard: Jeffersonian Whig* (Rutherford, VA:

Fairleigh Dickinson University Press and Associated University Presses, 1984), 175–76; Andrew Cunningham McLaughlin and Albert Bushnell Hart, *Cyclopedia of American Government*, vol. 1 (New York: D. Appleton and Company, 1914), 390.

15. Senate Report No. 97, 23rd Cong., 2nd sess., Feb. 2, 1835, in *Federal Payment*, 160–78; Miller, *Arguing about Slavery*, 51–62.

16. *Register of Debates in Congress*, 23rd Cong., 1st sess., 4393–402.

17. *Journal of the House of Representatives of the United States: Being the First Session of the Twenty-Fourth Congress: Begun and Held at the City of Washington December 7, 1835* (Washington: Blair and Rives, 1835), 783–89.

18. On nullification, see Harry L. Watson, *Liberty and Power: The Politics of Jacksonian America* (New York: Hill and Wang, 2006), 117–31; Matthew S. Brogdon, "Defending the Union: Andrew Jackson's Nullification Proclamation and American Federalism," *Review of Politics* 73, no. 2 (Spring 2011): 245–73.

19. Mills's quote in Pamela Scott, *Fortress of Finance: The United States Treasury Building* (Washington: Treasury Historical Association, 2010), 55; John Morrill Bryan, *Robert Mills: America's First Architect* (New York: Princeton Architectural Press, 2001), 257–58.

20. Scott, *Fortress of Finance*, 33–34, 41–49. For the connection between the New York fire and the desire for fireproof buildings, see Bryan, *Robert Mills*, 257; Goode, *Capital Losses*, 190–91; "An Act in Addition to the Act Entitled 'An Act Making Appropriations, in Part, for the Support of Government, for the Year Eighteen Hundred and Thirty-Six, and for Other Purposes,'" in Peters, *Public Statutes*, vol. 5, 112–16.

21. Scott, *Fortress of Finance*, 55–89; Scott and Lee, *Buildings of the District*, 154–57.

22. Yell quoted in Blair and Rives, ed., *The Congressional Globe: Containing Sketches of the Debates and Proceedings of the Twenty-Fifth Congress: Second Session Volume VI* (Washington, 1838), app. 275. The Yell quote is reproduced and a full rundown of the congressional row over the Treasury Building is provided in Scott, *Fortress of Finance*, 67–85.

23. Scott, *Fortress of Finance*, 72–82.

24. For a description of the boom and bust experienced during the 1830s, see Charles Sellers, *The Market Revolution: Jacksonian America, 1815–1846* (New York: Oxford University Press, 1994), 332–63. For the full comments of Pratt and Yell, see Blair and Rives, *The Congressional Globe: Containing Sketches of the Debates and Proceedings of the Twenty-Fifth Congress: Second Session Volume VI*, app. 274–75, 410–12; Scott, *Fortress of Finance*, 67–85.

25. Scott, *Fortress of Finance*, 84–85; Douglas E. Evelyn, "The Washington Years: The U.S. Patent Office," in *Robert Mills, Architect*, ed. John M. Bryan (Washington: American Institute of Architects Press, 1989), 120; R. W. Liscombe, *Altogether American: Robert Mills, Architect and Engineer, 1781–1855* (New York: Oxford University Press, 1994), 209–13.

26. Upton, *Another City*, 180–202.

27. Blair and Rives, *The Congressional Globe: Containing Sketches of the Debates and Proceedings of the Twenty-Fifth Congress: Second Session Volume VI*, app. 336–41.

28. Scott and Lee, *Buildings of the District of Columbia*, 189–91; Scott, *Fortress of Finance*, 63–64; Charles F. Robertson, *Temple of Invention: History of a National Landmark* (London: Scala Publishers, 2006), 23–31, 60.

29. Scott and Lee, *Buildings of the District*, 191–93.

30. Bryan, *Robert Mills*, 276–79; Bryan, *A History of the National Capital*, vol. 2, 247–48; congressional discussion of marble and the "palaces" quote by Congressman John Taliaferro appears in Blair and Rives, ed., *The Congressional Globe: Containing Sketches of the Debates and Proceedings of the Twenty-Fifth Congress: Third Session Volume VII, nos. 12 and 15* (Washington, 1839), 185–86, 228–29; *Public Buildings: Marble or Granite*, Committee Report No. 305, Feb. 25, 1839, *Transcribed Reports of the Committee on the District of Columbia*.

31. *New Executive Office Buildings*, Report No. 90, Feb. 5, 1835, *Building Committee Reports*, 225–26; Lois A. Craig, *The Federal Presence: Architecture, Politics, and National Design* (Cambridge, MA: MIT Press, 1984), 48–69.

Epilogue

1. Richards, "The Debates over the Retrocession," 73–74; Green, *Washington: Village and Capital*, 155–57; *Seventh Census of the United States, 1850* (National Archives Microfilm Publication M432, reel 56), Records of the Bureau of the Census, Record Group 29. National Archives Building, Washington, D.C.

2. On Seaton and the Smithsonian, see Goode, *The Smithsonian Institution*, 62–70; Green, *Village and Capital*, 169–72.

3. *Report of the Committee of Arrangements of the First National Fair for the Exhibition of American Manufactures: Held at the City of Washington, in May 1846* (Washington, D.C., 1846), 3–31; Green, *Village and Capital*, 157.

4. Morgan, "Robert Brent, First Mayor of Washington City," 247; Allen C. Clark, "Doctor and Mrs. William Thornton," *Records of the Columbia Historical Society, Washington, D.C.* 18 (1915): 197; George Alfred Townsend, "Thomas Law, Washington's First Rich Man," *Records of the Columbia Historical Society, Washington, D.C.* 4 (1901): 242–43; Frances Carpenter Huntington, "The Heiress of Washington City," 100; Margaret Bayard Smith, *The First Forty Years of Washington Society* (New York: C. Scribner's Sons, 1906), viii; Carne, "Life and Times of William Cranch," 296–307.

5. On generational change in elite Washington, see Brown, *Free Negroes*, 8; and Green, *Village and Capital*, 153–55.

6. Kate Masur, *An Example for All the Land: Emancipation and the Struggle over Equality in Washington, D.C.* (Chapel Hill: University of North Carolina Press, 2010), 13–31; Green, *Village and Capital*, 21.

7. Lessoff, *The Nation and Its City*, 7–8; Barber, *Marching on Washington*, 3–9.

REFERENCES

Manuscripts Cited

Anna Maria Brodeau Thornton Papers, 1793–1861. Library of Congress, Washington, D.C.

Christopher P. Cranch Papers. Massachusetts Historical Society, Boston, MA.

Committee on the District of Columbia. Petitions and Memorials Referred to Committees (HR18A-F4.1). Eighteenth Congress. Records of the U.S. House of Representatives, Record Group 233. National Archives Building, Washington, D.C.

Cranch Family Papers. Massachusetts Historical Society, Boston, MA.

District of Columbia Board of Education Trustees' Minutes Aug. 5, 1805–July 11, 1818. Library of Congress, Manuscript Division, Washington, D.C.

Dwight-Howard Papers. Massachusetts Historical Society, Boston, MA.

Journals of the Commissioners for the District of Columbia. Financial Records 1791–1924. Records of the Commissioners for the District of Columbia 1791–1925. Records of the Office of Public Buildings and Public Parks of the National Capital. Record Group 42. National Archives Building, Washington, D.C.

Letters Received and Draft Letters Sent by the Superintendent of the City of Washington (National Archives Microfilm Publication M371, reel 18). Correspondence, 1791–1931. General Records, 1790–1931. Records of the Office of Public Buildings and Public Parks of the National Capital. Record Group 42. National Archives Building, Washington, D.C.

Letters Received and Drafts of Letters Sent by the Superintendent of the City of Washington and Letters Received by the Commissioners Appointed to Supervise the Repair and Rebuilding of the Public Buildings, Volume 22:

March 14–June 7, 1815 (National Archives Microfilm Publication M371, roll 18). General Records, 1790–1931. Records of the Office of Public Buildings and Public Parks of the National Capital. Record Group 42. National Archives Building, Washington, D.C.

Letters Received by the Commissioners for the District of Columbia (National Archives Microfilm Publication M371, reels 8–27). Correspondence, 1791–1931. General Records, 1790–1931. Records of the Office of Public Buildings and Public Parks of the National Capital. Record Group 42. National Archives Building, Washington, D.C.

Letters Sent by the Commissioners for the District of Columbia (National Archives Microfilm Publication M371, reels 3–4). Proceedings and Letters Sent, 1791–1802. Records of the Commissioners for the District of Columbia, 1791–1925. Records of the Office of Public Buildings and Public Parks of the National Capital. Record Group 42. National Archives Building, Washington, D.C.

Nicholas King Plats, Washington 1803. Records of the Government of the District of Columbia. Record Group 351. Cartographic and Architectural Section. National Archives at College Park, College Park, MD.

Papers of William Cranch. Library of Congress, Manuscript Division, Washington, D.C.

Photostatic Copies of Letters from Presidents of the United States to the Commissioners for the District of Columbia and Their Successors, 1791–1869. Correspondence, 1791–1931. General Records, 1790–1931. Records of the Office of Public Buildings and Public Parks of the National Capital, Record Group 42. National Archives Building, Washington, D.C.

Proceedings of the Commissioners Appointed to Supervise the Repair or Rebuilding of the Public Buildings in Washington, 1815–1816 (National Archives Microfilm Publication M371, roll 2). Records of the Office of Public Buildings and Public Parks of the National Capital. Record Group 42. National Archives Building, Washington, D.C.

Proceedings of the Commissioners for the District of Columbia, 1791–1802 (National Archives Microfilm Publication M371, reel 1). Proceedings and Letters Sent, 1791–1802. Records of the Commissioners for the District of Columbia, 1791–1925. Records of the Office of Public Buildings and Public Parks of the National Capital. Record Group 42. National Archives Building, Washington, D.C.

Record of Squares. Cartographic Files, vol. 3. Records of the Government of the District of Columbia. Record Group 351. Cartographic and Architectural Section. National Archives at College Park, College Park, MD.

Sequestered John Nicholson Papers. General Correspondence, 1772–1819 (series #96m1). Manuscript Group 96. Pennsylvania State Archives, Harrisburg, PA (as viewed on National Historical Publications Commission microfilm of the John Nicholson Papers, roll 9).

Transcribed Reports of the Committees of the U.S. House of Representatives, 1789–1841. (National Archives Microfilm Publication M1267). Records of the U.S. House of Representatives at the National Archives, 1789–1989. Record Group 233. National Archives Building, Washington, D.C.

U.S. Bureau of the Census. *Second Census of the United States, 1800* (NARA microfilm publication M32, 32 reels). Records of the Bureau of the Census. Record Group 29. National Archives, Washington, D.C.

——. *Fourth Census of the United States, 1820* (National Archives Microfilm Publication M33, reel 5). Records of the Bureau of the Census. Record Group 29. National Archives Building, Washington, D.C.

——. *Seventh Census of the United States, 1850* (National Archives Microfilm Publication M432, reel 56), Records of the Bureau of the Census. Record Group 29. National Archives Building, Washington, D.C.

William Thornton Papers, 1741–1865 (7 microfilm reels). Library of Congress, Manuscript Division, Washington, D.C.

Newspapers and Periodicals

Baltimore Patriot and Mercantile Advertiser. Baltimore, MD.

City of Washington Gazette. Washington, D.C.

Federal Republican. Georgetown, D.C.

National Intelligencer. Washington, D.C.

Republican Star and General Advertiser. Easton, MD.

Salem Gazette. Salem, MA.

Washington Federalist. Washington, D.C.

(Each of the above accessed via Readex: America's Historical Newspapers.)

Published Primary Source Collections

Abbott, W. W., ed. *The Papers of George Washington, Confederation Series, vol. 2, 18 July 1784–18 May 1785.* Charlottesville: University Press of Virginia, 1992.

Acts of the Corporation of the City of Washington Passed by the First Council to Which Is Prefixed the Act of Incorporation. Washington: A. and G. Way, 1803.

Acts of the Corporation of the City of Washington Passed by the Second Council to Which Is Prefixed a Supplement to the Act of Incorporation. Washington: A. and G. Way, 1804.

Acts of the Corporation of the City of Washington Passed by the Third Council. Washington: A. and G. Way, 1805.

Acts of the Corporation of the City of Washington Passed by the Fourth Council. Washington: A. and G. Way, 1806.

Acts of the Corporation of the City of Washington Passed by the Fifth Council. Washington: A. and G. Way, 1807.

Acts of the Corporation of the City of Washington Passed by the Sixth Council. Washington: A. and G. Way, 1808.

Acts of the Corporation of the City of Washington Passed by the Seventh Council. Washington: A. and G. Way, 1809.

Acts of the Corporation of the City of Washington Passed by the Eighth Council. Washington: A. and G. Way, 1810.

Acts of the Corporation of the City of Washington Passed by the Ninth Council. Washington: A. and G. Way, 1811.

Acts of the Corporation of the City of Washington Passed by the Tenth Council. Washington: A. and G. Way, 1813.

Acts of the Corporation of the City of Washington Passed by the Thirteenth Council. Washington: Daniel Rapine, 1816.

Adams, Abigail, and John Quincy Adams. *Letters of Mrs. Adams, the Wife of John Adams.* 4th ed. Boston: Wilkins, Carter, and Co., 1848.

Adams, John Quincy. *Memoirs of John Quincy Adams: Comprising Portions of His Diary from 1795 to 1848.* Vol. 8. Philadelphia: J. B. Lippincott & Co., 1876.

American State Papers: Documents Legislative and Executive of the Congress of the United States, 1789–183. 38 vols. Washington: Gales and Seaton, 1832–61.

Annals of the Congress of the United States. Washington: Gales and Seaton, 1854.

Blair and Rives, eds. *The Congressional Globe: Containing Sketches of the Debates and Proceedings of the Twenty-Fifth Congress: Second Session Volume VI.* Washington, 1838.

———. *The Congressional Globe: Containing Sketches of the Debates and Proceedings of the Twenty-Fifth Congress: Third Session Volume VII.* Washington, 1839.

Carter II, Edward C., John C. Van Horne, and Lee W. Formwalt, eds. *The Journals of Benjamin Henry Latrobe 1799–1820 from Philadelphia to New Orleans.* Vol. 3. Journals I. New Haven: Published for the Maryland Historical Society by Yale University Press, 1984.

Clark v. Corporation of Washington. 25 U.S. 40–63.

Crockett, David. *A Narrative of the Life of David Crockett, Written by Himself.* Philadelphia: E. L. Cary and A. Hart, 1834.

Federal Payment to the District of Columbia 1790–1980: A Reference Compendium of Documents, Studies, Reports, and Proposals—Staff Study for the Committee on the District of Columbia House of Representatives, Ninety-Sixth Congress, First Session. Vol. Serial No. S-1. Washington: U.S. Government Printing Office, 1979.

Gibson, Campbell. *Population of the 100 Largest Cities and Other Urban Places in the United States: 1790 to 1990.* Washington: U.S. Bureau of the Census, Population Division, June 1998. http://www.census.gov/population/www/documentation/twps0027/twps0027.htm.

Gibson, Campbell, and Kay Jung. *Historical Census Statistics on Population Totals by Race, 1790 to 1990, and by Hispanic Origin, 1970 to 1990, for Large*

Cities and Other Urban Places in the United States. Washington: U.S. Census Bureau, Population Division, February 2005. http://www.census.gov/population/www/documentation/twps0076/twps0076.htm.

Jefferson, Thomas. *Notes on the State of Virginia.* Boston: Lilly and Wait, 1832.

———. *The Papers of Thomas Jefferson.* Edited by Julian P. Boyd and Ruth W. Lester. Princeton: Princeton University Press, 1982.

———. *The Writings of Thomas Jefferson: Volume VII, 1795–1801.* Edited by Paul Leicester Ford. New York: G. P. Putnam's Sons, 1896.

Journal of the House of Representatives of the United States: Being the First Session of the Twenty-Fourth Congress: Begun and Held at the City of Washington December 7, 1835. Washington: Blair and Rives, 1835.

Journal of the Senate of the United States of America: Being the Second Session of the Nineteenth Congress: Begun and Held at the City of Washington December 4, 1826, and in the Fifty-First Year of the Independence of the Said United States. Washington: Gales and Seaton, 1826.

Laws of the Corporation of the City of Washington Passed by the Twenty-Fourth Council. Washington: Way & Gideon, 1827.

Laws of the Corporation of the City of Washington Passed by the Twenty-Fifth Council. Washington: Way & Gideon, 1827.

Laws of the Corporation of the City of Washington Passed by the Twenty-Eighth Council. Washington: Way & Gideon, 1831.

Laws of the Corporation of the City of Washington Passed by the Thirty-First Council. Washington, DC: Way & Gideon, 1833.

Laws Passed by the Sixteenth Council of the City of Washington. Publication information unknown.

L'Enfant, Peter Charles. "L'Enfant's Reports to President Washington, Bearing Dates of March 26, June 22, and August 19, 1791." *Records of the Columbia Historical Society, Washington, D.C.* 2 (1899): 26–48.

Lowrie, Walter, et al., eds. *American State Papers.* Washington: Gales and Seaton, 1832–61.

Madison, James. *The Writings of James Madison: Volume VIII, 1808–1819.* Edited by Gaillard Hunt. New York: G. P. Putnam's Sons, 1908.

Padover, Saul K., ed. *Thomas Jefferson and the National Capital.* Washington: U.S. Government Printing Office, 1946.

Peters, Richard, ed. *The Public Statutes at Large of the United States of America Vols. I–V.* Boston: Charles C. Little and James Brown, 1850.

Report of the Committee of Arrangements of the First National Fair for the Exhibition of American Manufactures: Held at the City of Washington, in May 1846. Washington: 1846.

Rothwell, Andrew. *Laws of the Corporation of the City of Washington, to the End of the Thirtieth Council—June 1833.* Washington: F. W. De Krafft, 1833.

Royall, Anne Newport. *Sketches of History, Life, and Manners, in the United States.* New Haven, 1826.

Sharp, John G., ed. *The Diary of Michael Shiner Relating to the History of the Washington Navy Yard, 1813–1869*. Department of the Navy, Naval History & Heritage Command. Navy Department Library, October 2007. https://www.history.navy.mil/research/library/online-reading-room/title-list-alphabetically/d/diary-of-michael-shiner.html.

Smith, John Cotton. *The Correspondence and Miscellanies of the Hon. John Cotton Smith, LL.D., Formerly Governor of Connecticut*. New York: Harper & Brothers, 1847.

Smith, Margaret Bayard. *The First Forty Years of Washington Society*. New York: C. Scribner's Sons, 1906.

Thornton, Anna Maria Brodeau. "Diary of Mrs. William Thornton: Capture of Washington by the British." Edited by W. B. Bryan. *Records of the Columbia Historical Society, Washington, D.C.* 19 (1916): 172–82.

Transactions of the American Philosophical Society Held at Philadelphia for Promoting Useful Knowledge. 2nd ed. corrected. Philadelphia: R. Aitken & Son, 1789.

Treasures of American History Exhibition. Smithsonian Institution. National Museum of American History, Kenneth E. Behring Center. Accessible online at http://americanhistory.si.edu/collections/search/object/nmah_434863.

U.S. Bureau of the Census. *Historical Statistics of the United States: Colonial Times to 1970: Bicentennial Edition, Part 2*. Washington: U.S. Government Printing Office, 1975.

———. *1990 Census of Population and Housing: Population and Housing Unit Counts*. Washington: U.S. Bureau of the Census, 1993.

U.S. Congress. *Annals of Congress*. Washington: Gales and Seaton, 1834–56.

———. *Senate Executive Journal*. Washington: Duff Green, 1828.

U.S. Congress. Senate. 1878. *Statement of Appropriations and Expenditures from the National Treasury for Public and Private Purposes in the District of Columbia from July 16, 1790 to June 30, 1876: 45th Cong., 2nd sess. Ex. Doc. No. 84*.

———. 1899. *Partial List of Lots in the District of Columbia Sold by the United States*. 55th Cong., 3rd sess., S. Doc. No. 47.

———. 1899. *Partial List of Lots in the District of Columbia Sold by the United States*. 56th Cong., 1st sess., S. Doc. No. 47.

———. 1900. *Additional and Final, List of Lots in the District of Columbia Sold by the United States*. 56th Cong., 2nd sess., S. Doc. No. 32.

———. 1901. *List of Squares and Lots Assigned to Original Proprietors of Land in Washington, D.C.* 57th Cong., 1st sess., S. Doc. No. 18.

Van Horne, John C., ed. *The Correspondence and Miscellaneous Papers of Benjamin Henry Latrobe*. Vol. 3, 1811–20. Correspondence and Miscellaneous Papers IV. New Haven: Published for the Maryland Historical Society by Yale University Press, 1988.

———. *The Papers of Benjamin Henry Latrobe*. Vol. 2, 1805–10. Correspondence

and Miscellaneous Papers IV. New Haven: Published for the Maryland Historical Society by Yale University Press, 1986.

Van Horne, John C., and Lee W. Formwalt, eds. *The Papers of Benjamin Henry
Latrobe*. Vol. 1, 1784–1804. Correspondence and Miscellaneous Papers IV.
New Haven: Published for the Maryland Historical Society by Yale Univer-
sity Press, 1984.

Washington, George. "The Writings of George Washington Relating to the
National Capital." *Records of the Columbia Historical Society Washington,
D.C.* 17 (1914): 3–232.

Secondary Works

Abbott, Carl. *Political Terrain: Washington, D.C., from Tidewater Town to
Global Metropolis*. Chapel Hill: University of North Carolina Press, 1999.

Achenbach, Joel. *The Grand Idea: George Washington's Potomac and the Race to
the West*. New York: Simon and Schuster, 2004.

Allgor, Catherine. *Parlor Politics: In Which the Ladies of Washington Help Build
a City and a Government*. Jeffersonian America. Charlottesville: University
Press of Virginia, 2000.

American Academy of Arts and Sciences. "The Early History of the American
Academy of Arts and Sciences." *Bulletin of the American Academy of Arts
and Sciences* 24, no. 4 (January 1, 1971): 3–23.

Arbuckle, Robert D. *Pennsylvania Speculator and Patriot: The Entrepreneurial
John Nicholson, 1757–1800*. University Park: Pennsylvania State University
Press, 1975.

Armytage, W. H. G. "The Triple Graft: European Influence on American
Science—1727–1861." *Bulletin British Association for American Studies*, n.s.,
no. 4 (1962): 4–16.

Arnebeck, Bob. *Slave Labor in the Capital: Building Washington's Iconic Federal
Landmarks*. Charleston, SC: History Press, 2014.

———. *Through a Fiery Trial: Building Washington, 1790–1800*. New York: Madison Books, 1994.

———. "Tracking the Speculators: Greenleaf and Nicholson in the Federal City."
Washington History 3, no. 1 (Spring–Summer 1991): 112–25.

Arnold, Linda. "Congressional Government of the District of Columbia, 1800–
1846." PhD diss., Georgetown University, 1975.

Baker, Abby Gunn. "The Erection of the White House." *Records of the Columbia
Historical Society, Washington, D.C.* 16 (1913): 120–49.

Baker, Pamela L. "The Washington National Road Bill and the Struggle to Adopt
a Federal System of Internal Improvement." *Journal of the Early Republic* 22,
no. 3 (Autumn 2002): 437–64.

Barber, Lucy G. *Marching on Washington: The Forging of an American Political
Tradition*. Berkeley: University of California Press, 2003.

Bedini, Silvio A. "The Survey of the Federal Territory: Andrew Ellicott and Benjamin Banneker." *Washington History* 3, no. 1 (Spring–Summer 1991): 76–95.

Bednar, Michael. *L'Enfant's Legacy: Public Open Spaces in Washington, D.C.* Baltimore: Johns Hopkins University Press, 2006.

Benedetto, Robert, Jane Donovan, and Kathleen DuVall. *Historical Dictionary of Washington, D.C.* Lanham, MD: Scarecrow Press, 2003.

Birkner, Michael J. *Samuel L. Southard: Jeffersonian Whig.* Rutherford, VA: Fairleigh Dickinson University Press and Associated University Presses, 1984.

Bowling, Kenneth R. *Creating the Federal City, 1774–1800: Potomac Fever.* Washington: American Institute of Architects Press, 1988.

———. *The Creation of Washington, D.C.* Fairfax, VA: George Mason University Press, 1991.

———. "Dinner at Jefferson's: A Note on Jacob E. Cooke's 'The Compromise of 1790'." *William and Mary Quarterly*, 3rd ser., 28, no. 4 (October 1, 1971): 629–48.

———. "The Other G. W.: George Walker and the Creation of the National Capital." *Washington History* 3, no. 2 (Fall–Winter 1991–92): 4–21.

———. *Peter Charles L'Enfant: Vision, Honor and Male Friendship in the Early American Republic.* Washington: Friends of the George Washington University Libraries, 2002.

Brogdon, Matthew S. "Defending the Union: Andrew Jackson's Nullification Proclamation and American Federalism." *Review of Politics* 73, no. 2 (Spring 2011): 245–73.

Brown, Gordon. *Incidental Architect: William Thornton and the Cultural Life of Early Washington, D.C., 1794–1828.* Athens: Published for the U.S. Capitol Historical Society by Ohio University Press, 2009.

Brown, Letitia Woods. *Free Negroes in the District of Columbia, 1790–1846.* Urban Life in America. New York: Oxford University Press, 1972.

Bryan, Alfred Cookman. *History of State Banking in Maryland.* Baltimore: Johns Hopkins University Press, 1899.

Bryan, John Morrill. *Robert Mills: America's First Architect.* New York: Princeton Architectural Press, 2001.

———, ed. *Robert Mills, Architect.* Washington: American Institute of Architects Press, 1989.

Bryan, W. B. "The Beginnings of Government in the District." *Records of the Columbia Historical Society, Washington, D.C.* 6 (January 1, 1903): 65–96.

———. "Correspondence: The Name White House." *Records of the Columbia Historical Society, Washington, D.C.* 33–34 (January 1, 1932): 306–8.

———. *A History of the National Capital from Its Foundation through the Period of the Adoption of the Organic Act.* Vols. I and II. New York: Macmillan, 1914 and 1916.

Caemmerer, H. Paul. "The Life of Pierre Charles L'Enfant." *Records of the Columbia Historical Society, Washington, D.C.* 50 (1948): 323–40.

——. *A Manual on the Origin and Development of Washington.* Washington: U.S. Government Printing Office, 1939.

Carne, William F. "Life and Times of William Cranch, Judge of the District Circuit Court, 1801–1855." *Records of the Columbia Historical Society, Washington, D.C.* 5 (1902): 294–310.

Clark, Allen C. "Doctor and Mrs. William Thornton." *Records of the Columbia Historical Society, Washington, D.C.* 18 (1915): 144–208.

——. *Greenleaf and Law in the Federal City.* Washington: W. F. Roberts Co., 1901.

——. *Life and Letters of Dolly Madison.* Washington: Press of W. F. Roberts Co, 1914.

——. "The Mayoralty of Robert Brent." *Records of the Columbia Historical Society, Washington, D.C.* 33–34 (1932): 267–305.

Cooke, Jacob E. "The Compromise of 1790." *William and Mary Quarterly,* 3rd ser., 27, no. 4 (October 1, 1970): 524–45.

Craig, Lois A. *The Federal Presence: Architecture, Politics, and National Design.* Cambridge, MA: MIT Press, 1984.

Cranch, Christopher Pearse. "William Cranch." In *Memorial Biographies of the New England Historic Genealogical Society: Volume II, 1853–1855,* 446–69. Boston: New England Historic Genealogical Society, 1882.

Curry, Leonard P. *The Corporate City: The American City as a Political Entity, 1800–1850.* Westport, CT: Greenwood Publishing Group, 1997.

di Giacomantonio, William C. "All the President's Men: George Washington's Federal City Commissioners." *Washington History* 3, no. 1 (Spring–Summer 1991): 52–75.

Dougherty, J. P. "Baroque and Picturesque Motifs in L'Enfant's Design for the Federal Capital." *American Quarterly* 26, no. 1 (March 1974): 23–36.

Ely, James W. "'There Are Few Subjects in Political Economy of Greater Difficulty': The Poor Laws of the Antebellum South." *American Bar Foundation Research Journal* 10, no. 4 (October 1, 1985): 849–79.

Emery, Fred A. "Washington's Historic Bridges." *Records of the Columbia Historical Society, Washington, D.C.* 39 (1938): 49–70.

Evans, Nancy Goyne. "History on a Bandbox: A Pictorial Record of the Founding of the Baltimore and Ohio Railroad." *Winterthur Portfolio* 5 (January 1, 1969): 123–28.

Everly, Elaine C., and Howard H. Wehmann. "'Then Let Us to the Woods Repair': Moving the Federal Government and Its Records to Washington in 1800." In *Establishing Congress: The Removal to Washington, D.C., and the Election of 1800,* edited by Kenneth R. Bowling and Donald R. Kennon, 56–71. Athens: Published for the United States Capitol Historical Society by Ohio University Press, 2005.

Farrar, Margaret E. *Building the Body Politic: Power and Urban Space in Washington, D.C.* Urbana: University of Illinois Press, 2008.

Feller, Daniel. *The Public Lands in Jacksonian Politics.* Madison: University of Wisconsin Press, 1984.

Ferling, John, and Lewis E. Braverman. "John Adams's Health Reconsidered." *William and Mary Quarterly* 55, no. 1 (1998): 83–104.

Fleming, E. McClung. "From Indian Princess to Greek Goddess: The American Image, 1783–1815." *Winterthur Portfolio* 3 (January 1, 1967): 37–66.

Fortenbaugh, Robert. *The Nine Capitals of the United States.* York, PA: Maple Press, 1948.

Freehling, William W. *The Road to Disunion.* Vol. 1: *Secessionists at Bay, 1776–1854.* New York: Oxford University Press, 1990.

French, H. R. "Urban Agriculture, Commons and Commoners in the Seventeenth and Eighteenth Centuries: The Case of Sudbury, Suffolk." *Agricultural History Review* 48, no. 2 (January 1, 2000): 171–99.

Gilfoyle, Timothy J. "White Cities, Linguistic Turns, and Disneylands: The New Paradigms of Urban History." *Reviews in American History* 26, no. 1 (1998): 175–204.

Gilje, Paul A. *The Road to Mobocracy: Popular Disorder in New York City, 1763–1834.* Chapel Hill: Published for the Institute of Early American History and Culture by the University of North Carolina Press, 1987.

Gillette, Howard, Jr. *Between Justice and Beauty: Race, Planning, and the Failure of Urban Policy in Washington, D.C.* Baltimore: Johns Hopkins University Press, 1995.

Goldin, Claudia. *Urban Slavery in the American South, 1820–1860: A Quantitative History.* Chicago: University of Chicago Press, 1976.

Goode, George Brown, ed. *The Smithsonian Institution 1846–1896: The History of Its First Half-Century.* Washington, 1897.

Goode, James M. *Capital Losses: A Cultural History of Washington's Destroyed Buildings.* Washington: Smithsonian Books, 2003.

———. With photography by Bruce White. *Capital Houses: Historic Residences of Washington, D.C. and Its Environs, 1735–1965.* New York: Acanthus Press, 2015.

Grant III, U. S. "The L'Enfant Plan and Its Evolution." *Records of the Columbia Historical Society, Washington, D.C.* 33–34 (1932): 1–23.

Green, Constance McLaughlin. "The Jacksonian 'Revolution' in the District of Columbia." *Mississippi Valley Historical Review* 45, no. 4 (March 1959): 591–605.

———. *Washington, Capital City, 1879–1950.* Princeton: Princeton University Press, 1963.

———. *Washington: Village and Capital, 1800–1878.* Princeton: Princeton University Press, 1962.

Hamilton, Alexander, James Madison, and John Jay. *The Federalist Papers*. New York: Penguin Books, 1961.

Hamlin, Talbot. *Benjamin Henry Latrobe*. New York: Oxford University Press, 1955.

Harrison, Joseph H. "'Sic et Non': Thomas Jefferson and Internal Improvement." *Journal of the Early Republic* 7, no. 4 (Winter 1987): 335–49.

Hartigan-O'Connor, Ellen. *The Ties That Buy: Women and Commerce in Revolutionary America*. Philadelphia: University of Pennsylvania Press, 2009.

Hartog, Hendrik. *Public Property and Private Power: The Corporation of the City of New York in American Law, 1730–1870*. Chapel Hill: University of North Carolina Press, 1983.

Hawkins, Don Alexander. "The Landscape of the Federal City: A 1792 Walking Tour." *Washington History* 3, no. 1 (Spring–Summer, 1991): 10–33.

Heale, M. J. "Humanitarianism in the Early Republic: The Moral Reformers of New York, 1776–1825." *Journal of American Studies* 2, no. 2 (October 1, 1968): 161–75.

———. "The Role of the Frontier in Jacksonian Politics: David Crockett and the Myth of the Self-Made Man." *Western Historical Quarterly* 4, no. 4 (October 1973): 405–23.

Herman, Bernard L. "Southern City, National Ambition: Washington's Early Town Houses." In *Southern City, National Ambition: The Growth of Early Washington, D.C., 1800–1860*, edited by Howard Gillette, 21–46. Washington: Published by George Washington University Center for Washington Area Studies in conjunction with the American Architectural Foundation, 1995.

———. *Town House: Architecture and Material Life in the Early American City, 1780–1830*. Chapel Hill: University of North Carolina Press, 2005.

Hibben, Henry B. *Navy-Yard, Washington: History from Organization, 1799, to Present Date*. Washington: U.S. Government Printing Office, 1890.

Hill, Forest G. *Roads, Rails & Waterways: The Army Engineers and Early Transportation*. Norman: University of Oklahoma Press, 1957.

Hixon, Ada Hope. "George Washington Land Speculator." *Journal of the Illinois State Historical Society (1908–1984)* 11, no. 4 (1919): 566–75.

Hofstra, Warren R. *George Washington and the Virginia Backcountry*. Madison, WI: Madison House, 1998.

Holton, Woody. *Forced Founders: Indians, Debtors, Slaves, and the Making of the American Revolution in Virginia*. Chapel Hill: University of North Carolina Press, 1999.

Howe, Daniel Walker. *What Hath God Wrought: The Transformation of America, 1815–1848*. New York: Oxford University Press, 2007.

Hunsberger, George S. "The Architectural Career of George Hadfield." *Records of the Columbia Historical Society, Washington, D.C.* 51–52 (1951): 46–65.

Huntington, Frances Carpenter. "The Heiress of Washington City: Marcia

Burnes Van Ness, 1782–1832." *Records of the Columbia Historical Society, Washington, D.C.* 69–70 (January 1, 1969): 80–101.

Kierner, Cynthia A. *Beyond the Household: Women's Place in the Early South, 1700–1835.* Ithaca, NY: Cornell University Press, 1998.

King, Julia. *George Hadfield: Architect of the Federal City.* Burlington, VT: Ashgate, 2014.

Kite, Elizabeth. *L'Enfant and Washington, 1791–1792: Published and Unpublished Documents Now Brought Together for the First Time.* Baltimore: Johns Hopkins University Press, 1929.

Klaus, Susan L. "'Some of the Smartest Folks Here': The Van Nesses and Community Building in Early Washington." *Washington History* 3, no. 2 (October 1, 1991): 22–45.

Kohlstedt, Sally. "A Step toward Scientific Self-Identity in the United States: The Failure of the National Institute, 1844." *Isis* 62, no. 3 (October 1971): 339–62.

Larson, John Lauritz. *Internal Improvement: National Public Works and the Promise of Popular Government in the Early United States.* Chapel Hill: University of North Carolina Press, 2001.

Lasser, Carol. "Beyond Separate Spheres: The Power of Public Opinion." *Journal of the Early Republic* 21, no. 1 (April 1, 2001): 115–23.

Lebsock, Suzanne. *The Free Women of Petersburg: Status and Culture in a Southern Town, 1784–1860.* New York: W. W. Norton, 1985.

Lerner, Gerda. *The Grimké Sisters from South Carolina: Pioneers for Women's Rights and Abolition.* New York: Oxford University Press, 1998.

Lessoff, Alan. *The Nation and Its City: Politics, Corruption, and Progress in Washington, D.C., 1861–1902.* Baltimore: Johns Hopkins University Press, 1994.

Lewis, Jan. "Politics and the Ambivalence of the Private Sphere: Women in Early Washington, D.C." In *A Republic for the Ages: The United States Capitol and the Political Culture of the Early Republic,* edited by Donald R. Kennon, 122–54. Charlottesville: Published for the United States Capitol Historical Society by the University Press of Virginia, 1999.

Liscombe, R. W. *Altogether American: Robert Mills, Architect and Engineer, 1781–1855.* New York: Oxford University Press, 1994.

Littlefield, Douglas R. "The Potomac Company: A Misadventure in Financing an Early American Internal Improvement Project." *Business History Review* 58, no. 4 (Winter 1984): 562–85.

Mann, Bruce H. *Republic of Debtors: Bankruptcy in the Age of American Independence.* Cambridge, MA: Harvard University Press, 2002.

Masur, Kate. *An Example for All the Land: Emancipation and the Struggle over Equality in Washington, D.C.* Chapel Hill: University of North Carolina Press, 2010.

McAlester, Virginia, and Arcie Lee McAlester. *A Field Guide to American Houses.* New York: Knopf, 1984.

McCoy, Drew R. *The Elusive Republic: Political Economy in Jeffersonian America*. Chapel Hill: Published for the Institute of Early American History and Culture, Williamsburg, Va., by the University of North Carolina Press, 1980.

McInnis, Maurie Dee. *The Politics of Taste in Antebellum Charleston*. Chapel Hill: University of North Carolina Press, 2005.

McLaughlin, Andrew Cunningham, and Albert Bushnell Hart. *Cyclopedia of American Government*. Vol. 1. New York: D. Appleton and Company, 1914.

McNeil, Priscilla W. "Rock Creek Hundred: Land Conveyed for the Federal City." *Washington History* 3, no. 1 (Spring–Summer 1991): 34–51.

Miller, William Lee. *Arguing about Slavery: The Great Battle in the United States Congress*. New York: Knopf, 1996.

Morgan, James Dudley. "Robert Brent, First Mayor of Washington City." *Records of the Columbia Historical Society, Washington, D.C.* 2 (1899): 236–51.

Morris, Richard B. "Labor Controls in Maryland in the Nineteenth Century." *Journal of Southern History* 14, no. 3 (1948): 385–400.

Nash, Gary B. *Urban Crucible: Social Change, Political Consciousness, and the Origins of the American Revolution*. Cambridge, MA: Harvard University Press, 1979.

———. "Urban Wealth and Poverty in Pre-Revolutionary America." *Journal of Interdisciplinary History* 6, no. 4 (April 1, 1976): 545–84.

———. "Work in the Cities of Colonial British North America." *Journal of Urban History* 33, no. 6 (September 2007): 1021–32.

Nelson, John. *Liberty and Property: Political Economy and Policymaking in the New Nation, 1789–1812*. Baltimore: Johns Hopkins University Press, 1987.

Newman, Richard S. *The Transformation of American Abolitionism: Fighting Slavery in the Early Republic*. Chapel Hill: University of North Carolina Press, 2002.

Nichols, Frederick. *Thomas Jefferson, Landscape Architect*. Charlottesville: University Press of Virginia, 1978.

North, Douglass. *The Economic Growth of the United States, 1790–1860*. Englewood Cliffs, NJ: Prentice-Hall, 1961.

Oleson, Alexandra, and Sanborn C. Brown, eds. *The Pursuit of Knowledge in the Early American Republic: American Scientific and Learned Societies from Colonial Times to the Civil War*. Baltimore: Johns Hopkins University Press, 1977.

O'Malley, Therese. "Art and Science in American Landscape Architecture: The National Mall, Washington, D.C., 1791–1852." PhD diss., University of Pennsylvania, 1989.

Pinkett, Harold T. "Early Agricultural Societies in the District of Columbia." *Records of the Columbia Historical Society, Washington, D.C.* 51–52 (January 1, 1951): 32–45.

Pitch, Anthony S. *The Burning of Washington: The British Invasion of 1814*. Annapolis, MD: Naval Institute Press, 1998.

Porter, Sarah Harvey. "The Life and Times of Ann Royall, 1769–1854." *Records of the Columbia Historical Society, Washington, D.C.* 10 (January 1, 1907): 1–37.

Preston, Emmett D. "The Development of Negro Education in the District of Columbia, 1800–1860." *Journal of Negro Education* 12, no. 2 (April 1, 1943): 189–98.

Primus, Richard A. *The American Language of Rights.* New York: Cambridge University Press, 1999.

Rathbun, Richard. *The Columbian Institute for the Promotion of Arts and Sciences.* Bulletin of the United States National Museum 101. Washington: U.S. Government Printing Office, 1917.

Reiff, Daniel. *Washington Architecture, 1791–1861: Problems in Development.* Washington: U.S. Commission of Fine Arts, 1971.

Reps, John W. *The Making of Urban America: A History of City Planning in the United States.* Princeton: Princeton University Press, 1992.

———. *Monumental Washington: The Planning and Development of the Capital Center.* Princeton: Princeton University Press, 1967.

———. *Washington on View: The Nation's Capital since 1790.* Chapel Hill: University of North Carolina Press, 1991.

Reséndez, Andrés. *Changing National Identities at the Frontier: Texas and New Mexico, 1800–1850.* New York: Cambridge University Press, 2004.

Richard, Carl J. *The Founders and the Classics: Greece, Rome, and the American Enlightenment.* Cambridge, MA: Harvard University Press, 1995.

Richards, Mark David. "The Debates over the Retrocession of the District of Columbia, 1801–2004." *Washington History* 16, no. 1 (April 1, 2004): 54–82.

Ridout V, Orlando. *Building the Octagon.* Octagon Research Series. Washington: American Institute of Architects Press, 1989.

Robertson, Charles F. *Temple of Invention: History of a National Landmark.* London: Scala Publishers, 2006.

Rockman, Seth. *Scraping By: Wage Labor, Slavery, and Survival in Early Baltimore.* Baltimore: Johns Hopkins University Press, 2008.

———. *Welfare Reform in the Early Republic: A Brief History with Documents.* Boston: Bedford/St. Martin's Press, 2003.

Rohrbough, Malcolm J. *The Land Office Business: The Settlement and Administration of American Public Lands, 1789–1837.* New York: Oxford University Press, 1968.

Rohrs, Richard C. "Sectionalism, Political Parties, and the Attempt to Relocate the National Capital in 1814." *Historian* 62, no. 3 (2000): 535–55.

Rothman, Adam. *Slave Country: American Expansion and the Origins of the Deep South.* Cambridge, MA: Harvard University Press, 2007.

Rourke, Francis E. "Urbanism and American Democracy." *Ethics* 74, no. 4 (July 1, 1964): 255–68.

Rugemer, Edward B. "Caribbean Slave Revolts and the Origins of the Gag Rule:

A Contest between Abolitionism and Democracy, 1797–1835." In *Contesting Slavery: The Politics of Bondage and Freedom in the New American Nation*, edited by John Craig Hammond and Matthew Mason, 94–116. Charlottesville: University of Virginia Press, 2011.

Ryan, Mary P. "'A Laudable Pride in the Whole of Us': City Halls and Civic Materialism." *American Historical Review* 105, no. 4 (October 1, 2000): 1131–70.

Sakolski, A. M. *The Great American Land Bubble: The Amazing Story of Land-Grabbing, Speculations, and Booms from Colonial Days to the Present Time*. New York: Harper & Brothers, 1932.

Sanderlin, Walter S. *The Great National Project: A History of the Chesapeake and Ohio Canal*. Baltimore: Johns Hopkins University Press, 1946.

Savage, Kirk. *Monument Wars: Washington, D.C., the National Mall, and the Transformation of the Memorial Landscape*. Berkeley: University of California Press, 2011.

Schmeckebier, Laurence. *The District of Columbia, Its Government and Administration*. Baltimore: Johns Hopkins University Press, 1928.

Schuyler, David. *The New Urban Landscape: The Redefinition of City Form in Nineteenth-Century America*. Baltimore: Johns Hopkins University Press, 1986.

Scott, Pamela. *Capital Engineers: The U.S. Army Corps of Engineers in the Development of Washington, D.C., 1790–2000*. Alexandria: Office of History, U.S. Army Corps of Engineers, 2012.

———. "'The City of Living Green': An Introduction to Washington's Street Trees." *Washington History* 18, no. 1–2 (2006): 20–45.

———. *Fortress of Finance: The United States Treasury Building*. Washington: Treasury Historical Association, 2010.

———. "L'Enfant's Washington Described: The City in the Public Press, 1791–1795." *Washington History* 3, no. 1 (Spring–Summer 1991): 96–111.

Scott, Pamela, and Antoinette J. Lee. *Buildings of the District of Columbia*. 1st ed. New York: Oxford University Press, 1993.

Searcy, James K., and Luther C. Davis Jr. *Time of Travel of Water in the Potomac River Cumberland to Washington*. Geological Survey Circular 438. Washington: United States Department of the Interior, United States Geological Survey, 1961.

Sellers, Charles. *The Market Revolution: Jacksonian America, 1815–1846*. New York: Oxford University Press, 1994.

Shammas, Carole. "The Space Problem in Early United States Cities." *William and Mary Quarterly*, 3rd ser., 57, no. 3 (July 1, 2000): 505–42.

Shaw, Diane. *City Building on the Eastern Frontier: Sorting the New Nineteenth-Century City*. Baltimore: Johns Hopkins University Press, 2004.

Sherwood, Henry Noble. "The Formation of the American Colonization Society." *Journal of Negro History* 2, no. 3 (July 1, 1917): 209–28.

Smith, Merritt Roe. "George Washington and the Establishment of the Harper's

Ferry Armory." *Virginia Magazine of History and Biography* 81, no. 4 (1973): 415–36.

Starobin, Robert S. "The Economics of Industrial Slavery in the Old South." *Business History Review* 44, no. 2 (Summer 1970): 131–74.

Stover, John F. *History of the Baltimore and Ohio Railroad.* West Lafayette, IN: Purdue University Press, 1995.

Sutcliffe, Anthony. Foreword to *Planning Twentieth Century Capital Cities,* edited by David L. A. Gordon. New York: Routledge, 2006.

Taylor, Alan. *The Civil War of 1812: American Citizens, British Subjects, Irish Rebels, & Indian Allies.* New York: Knopf, 2010.

———. "The Late Loyalists: Northern Reflections of the Early American Republic." *Journal of the Early Republic* 27, no. 1 (2007): 1–34.

Teaford, Jon. *The Municipal Revolution in America: Origins of Modern Urban Government, 1650–1825.* Chicago: University of Chicago Press, 1975.

Tehranian, Katharine. *Modernity, Space, and Power: The American City in Discourse and Practice.* Cresskill, NY: Hampton Press, 1995.

Teute, Fredrika J. "Roman Matron on the Banks of Tiber Creek: Margaret Bayard Smith and the Politicization of Spheres in the Nation's Capital." In *A Republic for the Ages: The United States Capitol and the Political Culture of the Early Republic,* edited by Donald R. Kennon, 89–121. Charlottesville: Published for the United States Capitol Historical Society by the University Press of Virginia, 1999.

Tindall, William. *Origin and Government of the District of Columbia.* Washington: U.S. Government Printing Office, 1908.

Townsend, George Alfred. "Thomas Law, Washington's First Rich Man." *Records of the Columbia Historical Society, Washington, D.C.* 4 (1901): 222–45.

Upton, Dell. *Another City: Urban Life and Urban Spaces in the New American Republic.* New Haven: Yale University Press, 2008.

———. "Architectural History or Landscape History?" *Journal of Architectural Education* 44, no. 4 (1991): 195–99.

———. "Vernacular Domestic Architecture in Eighteenth-Century Virginia." *Winterthur Portfolio* 17, no. 2–3 (July 1, 1982): 95–119.

———. "White and Black Landscapes in Eighteenth-Century Virginia." In *Material Life in America, 1600–1860,* edited by Robert Blair St George, 357–69. Boston: Northeastern University Press, 1988.

van Doren, Carl. "The Beginnings of the American Philosophical Society." *Proceedings of the American Philosophical Society* 87, no. 3 (July 1943): 277–89.

Verheyen, Egon. "On Meaning in Architecture." In *The Emblem and Architecture: Studies in Applied Emblematics from the Sixteenth to the Eighteenth Centuries,* edited by Hans J. Böker and Peter M. Daly, 17–41. Imago Figurata. Turnhout: Brepols, 1999.

———. "'Unenlightened by a Single Ray from Antiquity': John Quincy Adams and the Design of the Pediment for the United States Capitol." *International Journal of the Classical Tradition* 3, no. 2 (October 1, 1996): 208–31.

Walsh, John Joseph. *Early Banks in the District of Columbia, 1792–1818*. Washington: Catholic University of America Press, 1940.

Watson, Harry L. *Liberty and Power: The Politics of Jacksonian America*. New York: Hill and Wang, 2006.

Watts, Steven. *The Republic Reborn: War and the Making of Liberal America, 1790–1820*. Baltimore: Johns Hopkins University Press, 1989.

Wenger, Mark R. "Thomas Jefferson and the Virginia State Capitol." *Virginia Magazine of History and Biography* 101, no. 1 (January 1, 1993): 77–102.

Wettemann, Robert P., Jr. *Privilege vs. Equality: Civil-Military Relations in the Jacksonian Era, 1815–1845*. Santa Barbara, CA: ABC-CLIO, 2009.

White, Richard. *The Middle Ground: Indians, Empires, and Republics in the Great Lakes Region, 1650–1815*. New York: Cambridge University Press, 1991.

Wilson, J. Ormond. "Eighty Years of the Public Schools of Washington: 1805 to 1885." *Records of the Columbia Historical Society, Washington, D.C.* 1 (January 1, 1897): 119–70.

Winterer, Caroline. "From Royal to Republican: The Classical Image in Early America." *Journal of American History* 91, no. 4 (March 1, 2005): 1264–90.

———. *The Culture of Classicism: Ancient Greece and Rome in American Intellectual Life, 1780–1910*. Baltimore: Johns Hopkins University Press, 2002.

Wordie, J. R. "The Chronology of English Enclosure, 1500–1914." *Economic History Review*, n.s., 36, no. 4 (November 1, 1983): 483–505.

Wright, Carroll Davidson. "The Economic Development of the District of Columbia." *Proceedings of the Washington Academy of Sciences* 1 (December 29, 1899): 161–87.

Yazawa, Melvin. "Republican Expectations: Revolutionary Ideology and the Compromise of 1790." In *A Republic for the Ages: The United States Capitol and the Political Culture of the Early Republic*, edited by Donald R. Kennon, 3–35. Charlottesville: Published for the United States Capitol Historical Society by the University Press of Virginia, 1999.

Zaeske, Susan. *Signatures of Citizenship: Petitioning, Antislavery, & Women's Political Identity*. Chapel Hill: University of North Carolina Press, 2003.

Index

EARLY AMERICAN PLACES

Slavery on the Periphery: The Kansas-Missouri Border in the Antebellum and Civil War Eras
by Kristen Epps

In the Shadow of Dred Scott: *St. Louis Freedom Suits and the Legal Culture of Slavery in Antebellum America*
by Kelly M. Kennington

Brothers and Friends: Kinship in Early America
by Natalie R. Inman

George Washington's Washington: Visions for the National Capital in the Early American Republic
by Adam Costanzo

CPSIA information can be obtained
at www.ICGtesting.com
Printed in the USA
LVOW12*2201070318
569002LV00006BA/153/P